THE School AS A Home FOR THE Mind

SECOND
EDITION

ARTHUR L. COSTA

THE School AS A Home FOR THE Mind

Creating Mindful Curriculum,
Instruction, and Dialogue

FOREWORD
BY
**ROBIN
FOGARTY**

SECOND
EDITION

CORWIN PRESS
A SAGE Publications Company
Thousand Oaks, CA 91320

For information:

Corwin Press
A Sage Publications Company
2455 Teller Road
Thousand Oaks, California 91320
www.corwinpress.com

Sage Publications Ltd.
1 Oliver's Yard
55 City Road
London EC1Y 1SP
United Kingdom

Sage Publications India Pvt. Ltd.
B 1/I 1 Mohan Cooperative Industrial Area
Mathura Road, New Delhi 110 044
India

Sage Publications Asia-Pacific Pte. Ltd.
33 Pekin Street #02-01
Far East Square
Singapore 048763

Printed in the United States of America

Library of Congress Cataloging-in-Publication Data

Costa, Arthur L.
The school as a home for the mind: creating mindful curriculum, instruction, and dialogue/Arthur L. Costa.—2nd ed.
    p. cm.
Includes bibliographical references and index.
ISBN 978-1-4129-5073-2 (cloth)
ISBN 978-1-4129-5074-9 (pbk.)
    1. Thought and thinking—Study and teaching—United States.
2. Cognition in children—United States. I. Title.

LB1590.3.C68 2008
372.13—dc22   2007017361

This book is printed on acid-free paper.

07   08   09   10   11   10 9 8 7 6 5 4 3 2 1

Acquisitions Editor:	Rachel Livsey
Managing Editor:	Dan Alpert
Editorial Assistants:	Phyllis Cappello, Tatiana Richards
Project Editor:	Astrid Virding
Copy Editor:	Pam Suwinsky
Typesetter:	C&M Digitals (P) Ltd.
Proofreader:	Tracy Marcynzsyn
Indexer:	Sheila Bodell
Cover Designer:	Rose Storey
Graphic Designer:	Karine Hovsepian

Contents

Foreword

Robin Fogarty, PhD

There is no perfect metaphor. Yet, "school as a home for the mind," the self-conceived metaphor of Costa's classic collection, is about as perfect a metaphor as one can find. Much like the home, school provides the comfort and care of a safe environment for thinking. It affords thoughtful lessons as catalysts for growth and development. School provides the time for learning through the toil of trial and error. And, in the end, school as a home for the mind fosters the reflective moments that anchor learning for a lifetime. School as a home for the mind is an elegant and enduring concept that manifests itself in this collection of timely and timeless essays.

For as long as I can remember, in my academic career and in my interactions with Art Costa and his work, he has unequivocally advocated a stunning and profound idea. With his usual graciousness and understated genius, he would say, "What if process was the content? What if the processes of higher-order thinking, intelligent behavior, and habits of mind were to become the targeted content of our schools? Wouldn't that guarantee the desired results of the educated mind that, we, as custodial caretakers, covet for our young students?"

In this masterful collection of essays by Arthur L. Costa, Professor Emeritus, are the underpinnings of this profound vision: school as a home for the mind. School as a home for mindfulness and thoughtfulness as productive problem solvers and sound decision makers; for originators of unique ideas and viable solutions; and for keepers of societal values that ensure a safe and fulfilling future for the generations to come.

The foundation is laid with five pieces that manifest this vision for mindfulness. From the original metaphor of school as a home for the mind, and creating a culture for mindfulness, to the lasting concepts of "habits of mind" and the launching of self-directed learners, the vision become real. Following this presentation of the vision, a "mindful curriculum" sets the scene for teaching for, of, and about thinking through curriculum-mapping efforts, a changed curriculum, and an advocacy of maturing outcomes.

In turn, as this profound vision of school as a home for the mind con-tinues to unfold, explicit discussions about mindful instruction, specific teaching behaviors, and metacognitive mediations that bridge immediate lessons into lifelong learnings represent some of the finest thinking of this author (a.k.a., architect of the intellect), Art Costa. In addition, attention is given to mindful reflections through the discussion about critical friends, cognitive coaching, collaborations, and habits of reflection.

In closing, Costa's dream of the school as a home for the mind rallies the forces of his readership in a farewell piece titled, "Mind Workers Unite!" How fitting a finale for this magnificent metaphor. To read the myriad ideas in this robust collection, *The School as a Home for the Mind*, the reader is soon privy to a noble and notable vision of schooling in which mindfulness permeates the metaphorical walls of the school and all of its structural components: the curriculum, the instruction, and the reflective practices of those immersed in the vision.

Acknowledgments

B ack in 1991, I couldn't believe that anyone would be interested in reading a collection of my writings. However, Robin Fogarty collected many of my articles and organized them into a coherent assemblage for the first edition of *The School as a Home for the Mind*. For that I am extremely grateful.

Now, 17 years later, Robin and others still have faith that there is something to be learned from my ramblings. I am even more grateful, not only to Robin but also to the editors at Corwin Press: Rachel Livsey, who persisted with gentle reminders and conversational cajoling to organize this new and revised edition; to Phyllis Cappello for her editorial guidance; and to Pam Suwinsky of Thalia Publishing Services for her scrutiny and attention to detail.

Some of the chapters are holdovers from the first edition. Some are new. My mind has not been on pause for the past decade. And times are different than they were in 1991. We are beset with new economic, social, global, and environmental problems that tax our resources and ingenuity; we have new educational legislation with accountability that pressures us to conform to standards; and we have new understandings of how the brain demands a more engaged form of learning. Furthermore, our youth has changed. Today's indulged post–9/11 children expect more services than the previous decade's more tractable generation. An educational renaissance is needed.

I cannot take full credit for all the writings contained here. I must also acknowledge my colleagues from whom I have learned, prospered, and grown: my mentors and coauthors Bob Garmston, Bena Kallick, Bill Baker, and Stan Shalit (deceased). Furthermore, the learnings reflected in these pages have their roots in my interactions with many others over the years: Reuven Feuerstein, Howardine Hoffman, Chuck Lavaroni, Laura Lipton, Larry Lowery, David Perkins, J. Richard Suchman (deceased), Bob Swartz, Bob Watanabe, Bruce Wellman, and Diane Zimmerman. These are the giants on whose shoulders I stand and whose teachings have influenced me so greatly.

Over the past decade I have also worked with numerous schools throughout the world assisting in their desire to make themselves and their schools more mind-full. I have drawn examples and artifacts from several of them to illustrate their progress and to celebrate their achievements. To all of them I shall be indebted.

Organizing this volume took time. And that was time away from my loved ones: my wife, Nancy; three daughters, Shelley, Gina, and Maria; and six granddaughters, Shaun, Sarah, Catherine, Elena, Gabriella, and Danielle. However, they are the reasons why all this matters.

The contributions of the following reviewers are gratefully acknowledged:

Charles Adamchik
Corporate Director of Curriculum
Learning Sciences International
Blairsville, PA

Mark Bower
Director of Elementary Education and
    Staff Development
Hilton CSD
Hilton, NY

David Hyerle
Director
Thinking Foundation
Lyme, NH

Gloria L. Kumagai
Coordinator of Licensure & Leadership
Development, Educational Policy & Administration
University of Minnesota
Minneapolis, MN

Marti Richardson
Executive Director
Tennessee Staff Development Council
Knoxville, TN

About the Author

Arthur L. Costa, EdD, is Emeritus Professor of Education at California State University, Sacramento, and cofounder of the Institute for Intelligent Behavior in El Dorado Hills, California. He has served as a classroom teacher, a curriculum consultant, an assistant superintendent for instruction, and as the director of educational programs for the National Aeronautics and Space Administration. He has made presentations and conducted workshops in all fifty states as well as Mexico, Central and South America, Canada, Australia, New Zealand, Africa, Europe, Asia, and the islands of the South Pacific. Dr. Costa has written numerous books, including *Techniques for Teaching Thinking* (with Lawrence F. Lowery), *The School as a Home for the Mind* (First Edition), and *Cognitive Coaching: A Foundation for Renaissance Schools* (with Robert J. Garmston). He is editor of *Developing Minds: A Resource Book for Teaching Thinking*, coeditor (with Rosemarie Liebmann) of the *Process as Content Trilogy: Envisioning Process as Content, Supporting the Spirit of Learning*, and *The Process-Centered School*. He is coeditor (with Bena Kallick) of the four-book developmental series, *Habits of Mind*, and coauthor (with Bena Kallick) of *Assessment Strategies for Self-Directed Learning*. He is coauthor (with Bob Swartz, Barry Beyer, Rebecca Reagan, and Bena Kallick) of *Thinking-Based Learning*. Active in many professional organizations, he served as president of the California Association for Supervision and Curriculum Development and was the National President of the Association for Supervision and Curriculum Development, 1988 to 1989.

PART I

The School as a Home for the Mind: A Vision of Mindfulness

In a school that is a home for the mind, there is an inherent faith that all people can continue to improve their intellectual capacities throughout life; that learning to think is as valid a goal for the "at-risk," the handicapped, the disadvantaged, and the foreign-speaking as it is for the "gifted and talented"; and that all of us have the potential for even greater creativity and intellectual power.

Arthur L. Costa

CHAPTER ONE

The School as a Home for the Mind

Teachers are more likely to teach for thinking in an intellectually stimulating environment. When the conditions in which teachers work signal, promote, and facilitate their intellectual growth, they will gradually align their classrooms and instruction to promote students' intellectual growth as well. As teachers teach students to think, become more aware of conditions that promote student thinking, and become more powerful thinkers themselves, they will demand and create school climate conditions than are intellectually growth producing as well. Thus, respect for intelligent behavior grows to pervade all levels of the institution.

Three climate conditions in particular facilitate intellectual growth: (1) all participants share a common vision of the school as a home for the mind, (2) the process of thinking is the content of curriculum and instruction, and (3) schools and classrooms are interdependent communities. These conditions provide a sharper image of a climate for thinking in schools and classrooms that are dedicated to becoming homes for the mind. (See Figure 1.1.)

A COMMON VISION

Effective organizations are characterized by a deep sense of purposefulness and a vision of the future. Members at all levels share a commitment

SOURCE: Reprinted by permission. Costa, A. L. (1991). The School as a Home for the Mind in *Developing minds: A resource book for teaching thinking* (2nd ed., pp. 47–54). Alexandria, VA: Association for Supervision and Curriculum Development.

3

Figure 1.1   Effects of School and Classroom Climates

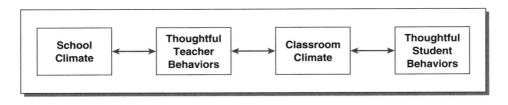

to that vision, a sense of ownership, and an internal responsibility for performance. This shared vision is evident in several ways.

Faith in Human Intellectual Potential

In a school that is a home for the mind, there is an inherent faith that all people can continue to improve their intellectual capacities throughout life; that learning to think is as valid a goal for the "at-risk," the handicapped, the disadvantaged, and the foreign-speaking as it is for the "gifted and talented"; and that all of us have the potential for even greater creativity and intellectual power. Students, teachers, and administrators realize that learning to use and continually refine their intelligent behavior is the purpose of their lifelong education. Such a belief is expressed in many ways.

Thinking is valued not only for all students and certificated staff but for the classified staff as well. A principal of a "thinking school" in Davis, California, reported that a newly hired custodian constantly asked her to check on how well he was cleaning the classrooms and to tell him whether he was doing an adequate job. She decided to help him develop a clear mental image of what a clean classroom looked like and then worked to enhance his ability to evaluate for himself how well the room he cleaned fit that image.

School staff members continue to define and clarify thinking as a goal and seek ways to gain assistance in achieving it. Their commitment is reinforced when they are able to report and share progress toward installing thinking in their schools and classrooms. A school superintendent reviews with site administrators their long-range goals and progress toward including the development of skillful thinking in the school's mission. In classrooms, students keep journals and periodically report new insights about their own creative problem-solving and decision-making strategies.

Philosophy, Policies, and Practices

The vision is also expressed in the school board's policies. In Edmonton, Canada, for example, the superintendent promotes self-directedness and uniqueness in each school, and in Glenora School self-directed learning is its cornerstone (see Figure 1.2).

Figure 1.2   Glenora School Model for Metacognition

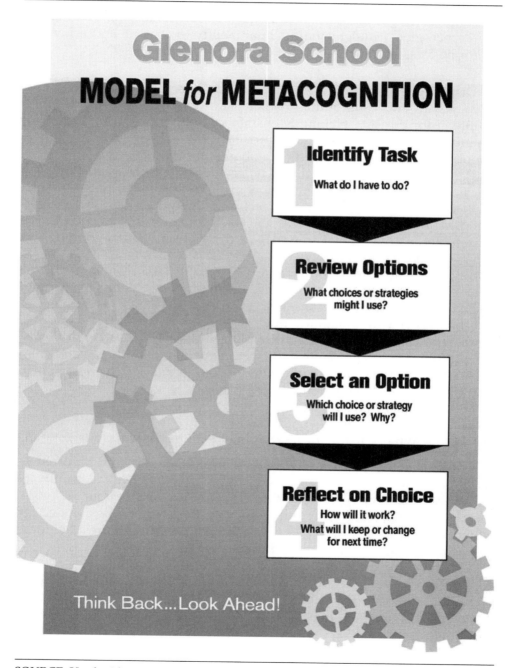

SOURCE: Used with permission.

The school's adopted motto, "Think Back . . . Look Ahead!" reflects mindfulness. Encinal High School in the Acalanes School District in Alameda, California, developed and adopted the following mission statement:

> Encinal High School is a home for the active mind—a cooperative community promoting knowledge, self-understanding, mutual respect, global understanding, adaptability to change, and a love for lifelong learning.

District policies and practices are constantly scrutinized for their consistency with and contribution to that philosophy. Evidence of their use as criteria for decision making is examined. Furthermore, procedures for continuing to study, refine, and improve districtwide practices encourage schools to keep growing toward more thoughtful practice.

Personnel practices, for example, reflect the desire to infuse thinking. Job specifications for hiring new personnel include skills in teaching thinking. Teachers are empowered to make decisions that affect their jobs. Supervision, mentoring, evaluation, and staff development practices enhance the perceptions and intellectual growth of certificated staff and honor their role as professional decision makers.[1]

Selection criteria for texts, tests, instructional materials, and other media include their contribution to thinking. Counseling, discipline,[2] library, and psychological services are constantly evaluated for their enhancement of and consistency with thoughtful practice.

In schools and classrooms, discipline practices appeal to students' thoughtful behavior. Students participate in generating rational and compassionate classroom and school rules and continually strive to evaluate their own behavior in relation to those criteria.

Protecting What's Important—Saying "No" to Distractions

Sometimes our vision of the desired school is temporarily blurred or obscured. We are distracted from our intellectual focus by fads, bandwagons, other educational "panaceas," and by pressures from public and vocal special-interest groups. Our purposes may be temporarily clouded by politically and financially expedient decisions. We must ignore all of these distractions as irrelevant to our central issue.

On the other hand, we need to encourage philosophical discussion because it gives voice to alternative views. Considering other perspectives, discussing educational, political, and social issues creates tensions, honors divergent thinking, and expands and refines our vision. Such discussion encourages staff members to include modes of thinking and inquiring in their definition of literacy. Discussion strengthens the staff's commitment to the principle that to learn anything—to gain cultural literacy or basic skills—requires an engagement of the mind. Each of these practices helps to build a thoughtful—sensitive and caring and thought-full—environment that supports the importance of skillful thinking.

Some mindful schools have initiated book study. The staff studies a book one chapter at a time. They delve into its meaning. They use the same close study of text that they would expect students to use in their classrooms.

Highly successful educators discuss student progress with their colleagues and share ideas with each other. They believe that collegial discussions centered on teaching, learning, and student work have more impact on their practices than formal administrative observations and evaluations.

Knowing that thinking is the important goal, all inhabitants of the school believe that their right to think will be protected. District leaders keep this primary goal in focus as they make day-to-day decisions. Teachers' rights to be involved in the decisions affecting them are protected, as are the rights of those who choose not to be involved in decision making. Since change and growth are viewed as intellectual processes, not events, we value the time invested in ownership, commitment, and learning.

Communications

Embedded in an organization's communications are expressions of what it prizes. Pick up any newspaper and you see a reflection of society's values in its major sections: sports, business and finance, and entertainment.

As a school becomes a home for the mind, the vision increasingly pervades all of its communications. In the Tahoma School District in Maple Valley, Washington, report cards, parent conferences, and other progress reports include indicators of the growth of students' intelligent behaviors: questioning, metacognition, flexibility of thinking, persistence, listening to others' points of view, and creativity.

Growth in student's thinking abilities is assessed and reported in numerous ways, including teacher-made tests, structured observations, rubrics, journals, exhibitions, electronic portfolios, interviews, and so on. Following are some examples:

Journals

Students maintain journals to record their own thinking and metacognition; they share, compare, and evaluate their own growth of insight, creativity, and problem-solving strategies over time.

This fourth grader from Crow Island Elementary School in Winnetka, Illinois, wrote:

Self-Modification—Persisting

"I have used my perseverance. When I was doing long division. It was very long and hard but I did it. I still want to improve for the future when I'm in high school."

And from high school students at Sir Francis Drake High School in Mill Valley, California:

Listening With Understanding and Empathy

"If you don't listen to others' ideas and problems you could overlook a great idea or a giant problem that you had been unaware of before."

"Listening before prejudging someone's contribution makes sense. Being patient helps. I was surprised at the great ideas and how much everyone added."

Thinking Interdependently

"At first I was not a good group worker because I felt controlling and perfectionist. I had to step back and examine my thinking and adjust to be cooperative and open. I changed the way I thought about my role in the group process."

Drawing on Past Knowledge

"Every time I finished a project, I was able to enter the next one with more knowledge of the group process. Also, with each project I became more technologically advanced, which helped me add value to the group."

Rubrics

Sixth graders at the Tamalpais Elementary School in Marin County, California, developed the scoring rubric shown in Figure 1.3.

Parents, too, look for ways in which their children are transferring intellectual growth from the classroom to family and home situations. In Waikiki School, Honolulu, Hawaii, parents of kindergartners observe for indicators of caring behaviors at home and report such incidents to the teacher.

Figure 1.3   Group Cooperation: A Scoring Rubric

4	Demonstrates interdependence. All members contribute. Shows indicators of cooperation and working together, compromising, and staying on task. Disagreements are welcomed as learning opportunities. Completes task with accuracy and within time limits. Members listen to others' points of view. Paraphrasing, clarifying, and empathizing are in evidence.
3	Members disagree but reach agreements through arguing and debate. Some paraphrasing and clarifying is in evidence. Group sometimes strays from task. Some members remain silent or refrain from participating.
2	Some members are off task. Group rushes to complete task in the most expedient way due to the pressure of time. Evidence of arguing or encouraging others to get it over with.
1	Few on task. Evidence of arguing and disinterest. Some members occupied with other work.
0	Chaos. Task not completed. Many put-downs. Some members leave before task is complete. Complaints about having to participate in task.

Portfolios and Artwork

Portfolios of students' work show how their organizational abilities, conceptual development, and creativity are growing. Test scores report such critical thinking skills as vocabulary growth, syllogistic thinking, reasoning by analogy, problem solving, and fluency.

Student artwork provides a unique opportunity for students to disclose their understanding of the Habits of Mind and their thinking abilities, as demonstrated by the sculpture shown in Figure 1.5 and the poster in Figure 1.6.

Parents and community members of the Wolftrap School in Vienna, Virginia, receive newspaper articles, calendars, and newsletters informing them of the school's intent and ways they can engage children's intellects. *The Rational Enquirer* is the name given to the Auburn, Washington, School District's Thinking Skills network newsletter.

Mottoes, slogans, and mission statements are visible everywhere. "LINCOLN SCHOOLS ARE THOUGHT-FULL SCHOOLS" is painted on one district's delivery trucks for all to see. In the Plymouth-Canton, Michigan, Public Schools, the superintendent distributes bookmarks, reminding the community that thinking is the schools' goal; "THOUGHT IS TAUGHT AT HUNTINGTON BEACH HIGH" is emblazoned on that school's note pads. "PANTHERS 'PAWS' TO THINK" is the motto of the Patti Welder Middle School in Galveston, Texas. "THINKING SPOKEN

Figure 1.4 Parent Recognition Form

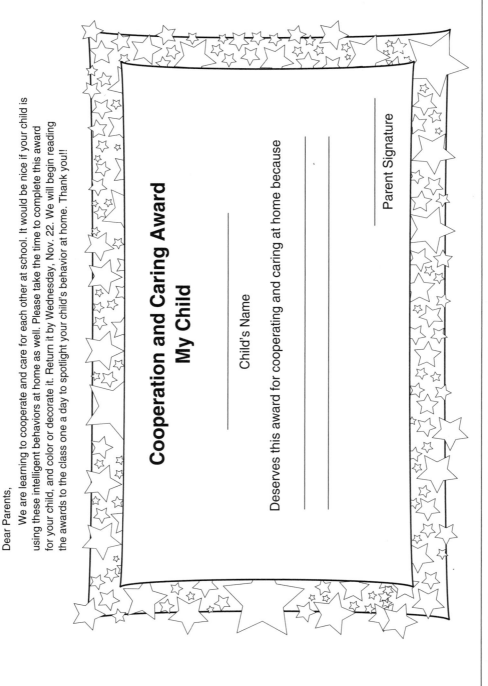

Dear Parents,

We are learning to cooperate and care for each other at school. It would be nice if your child is using these intelligent behaviors at home as well. Please take the time to complete this award for your child, and color or decorate it. Return it by Wednesday, Nov. 22. We will begin reading the awards to the class one a day to spotlight your child's behavior at home. Thank you!!

Cooperation and Caring Award
My Child

_____
Child's Name

Deserves this award for cooperating and caring at home because

_____

_____
Parent Signature

SOURCE: Printed with permission from Waikiki School, Honolulu, Hawaii.

Figure 1.5   Bull Sculpture

Juan said when he was doing this work, he was thinking about how hard the kids at Furr had to work and what they had to overcome in order to succeed. The body is the body of a student and the head represents our mascot, the bull. The uplifted hand stands for persistence.

SOURCE: Furr High School, Houston, Texas. Reprinted by permission.

HERE" is a constant classroom reminder of Stockton, California, history teacher Dan Theile's explicit goals for students.

Student-made posters, such as the one from Midland School in New Jersey shown in Figure 1.7, adorn the classrooms and corridors as reminders of the attitudes and habits that the school promotes.

"WE'RE TRAINING OUR BRAINS" is the motto on buttons proudly produced, sold, and worn by the special education students at Jamestown Elementary School, Pennsylvania. The staff of the Bleyl Junior High

Figure 1.6   Don't Call Out in Assembly

SOURCE: School District 54, Smithers, British Columbia.

School in the Cypress Fairbanks School District in Houston, Texas, refer to themselves as "The United Mind Workers."

At Furr High School in Houston, Texas (Figure 1.8), and in the Waikiki Elementary School in Honolulu, Hawaii (Figure 1.9), the Habits of Mind are plainly exhibited on the walls, corridors, and stairways.

At St. Paul's Convent School in Hong Kong posters are displayed in both English (Figure 1.10) and Chinese (Figure 1.11).

At the Fernridge School in Masterton, New Zealand, a row of trees was planted adjacent to the driveway leading up to the school. Each tree was dedicated to one of the Habits of Mind (see Figure 1.12).

Figure 1.7   Perseverance

SOURCE: Poster design and photograph by Robert Marion, Midland School, Paramus, NJ.

Tangible Support

How teachers, school administrators, and other leadership personnel expend their valuable and limited resources—time, energy, and money—signals the organization's value system. In several school districts, the school board provides a profound example of this point. The board requires elementary school principals to spend 50 percent of their

Figure 1.8   Remain Open

Figure 1.9   Practice Metacognition

Figure 1.10   Questioning in English   **Figure 1.11**   Questioning in Chinese

SOURCE: Reprinted with permission from Lawrence Law, assistant principal, St. Paul's Convent School, Hong Kong.

time in curriculum and instructionally related activities. To ensure that this happens, administrative assistants were hired to provide support for principals.

The school that is becoming a home for the mind allocates financial resources to promote thinking. Substitutes are hired so that teachers can be released to visit and coach each other, attend staff development programs, and to plan together. Staff members and parents are sent to workshops, courses, conferences, and inservice sessions to learn more about effective thinking and the teaching of thinking.

Figure 1.12   Fernridge Trees

SOURCE: Photographed and printed with permission of Daniel Melville.

Instructional materials and programs related to thinking are purchased, and time is provided to plan for and to train teachers in the use of these materials and to gather evidence of their effectiveness. Consultants discuss and report new learnings about intellectual development and implications for program improvement. Vignettes and "critical incidents" are recorded, described, and analyzed as indicators of students' application of critical and creative thinking skills and dispositions.

Administrators use their time and energy to visit classrooms to learn more about and to coach instruction in thinking. Teachers spend time planning lessons and observing each other teach for thinking. Time in classrooms, as well, is allocated to thinking skills and talking about thinking.

Thus, we see that the whole school community—students, teachers, administrators, classified personnel, board members, and parents—share a common vision of the school as a home for the mind. They continually work to sharpen that image, to clarify their goals, and to align daily practices with that vision of the future.

PROCESS AS CONTENT

In the school that is becoming a home for the mind, development of the intellect, learning to learn, knowledge production, metacognition, decision making, creativity, and problem solving are the subject matter of instruction. Content is selected because of its contribution to process and thus becomes a vehicle for thinking processes.

Problem Solving, Decision Making, and Open Communication

Being committed to the improvement of intellectual growth, everyone in the school is willing to discuss their strategies for improving school climate, interpersonal relationships, and the quality of their interactions and problem solving. Students and school personnel practice, evaluate, and improve their listening skills of paraphrasing, empathizing, and clarifying and understanding.

At school board, administrative, and faculty meetings, decision-making processes are discussed, explained, and adopted. Process observers are invited to give feedback about the group's effectiveness and growth in decision-making, consensus-seeking, and communication skills.

Each group member's opinions and questions are respected. Disagreements are stated without fear of damaging relationships. Debates and critical assessment of alternate points of view are encouraged. Responsibility for "errors, omissions, and inadequacies" is accepted without blaming others. Responses are given and justified, and new ideas are advanced without fear of criticism or judgment. Group members' differing priorities, values, logic, and philosophical beliefs become the topics of analysis, dialogue, understanding, and further questions.

Continuing to Learn—Expanding the Knowledge Base

Knowledge about thinking and the teaching of thinking is vast, complex, uncertain, and incomplete. We will never know it all, nor would we wish to reduce teaching thinking to a simplistic, step-by-step lesson plan. In a school that is a home for the mind, the inhabitants continually expand their knowledge base: gaining more content, learning more about learning, and thinking more about thinking. They add to their repertoire of instructional skills and strategies, seeking greater diversity rather than conformity.

Knowing that the school's mission is to develop the intellect, teachers increasingly strive to invest thoughtful learning, craftsmanship, metacognition, and rigor into curriculum and instruction. They expand their repertoire of instructional skills and strategies to develop a wide range of reasoning, creative, and cooperative abilities in students.

Teachers increase their knowledge of the sciences, math, and humanities because it helps them ask more provocative questions that invite inquiry and critical thinking. A wider knowledge base supports the transfer of concepts across several subject areas and encourages appreciation for the disciplined methodologies of great thinkers throughout history.

Teachers draw from their growing repertoire of knowledge about instructional techniques and strategies to make decisions based on goals, students' characteristics, and the context in which they are working. They vary their lesson designs according to students' developmental levels, cognitive styles, and modality preferences.

While their students expand their range of intelligent behaviors, teachers and administrators improve their own thinking skills and strategies by pursuing course work in philosophy, logic, and critical thinking. Thinking skills include not only knowing how to perform specific thought processes[3] but also knowing what to do when solutions to problems are not immediately known; study skills and learning-to-learn, reasoning, problem-solving, and decision-making strategies are important. Teachers and administrators learn about their own cognitive styles and how to cooperate with and value others who have differing styles. They learn how to cause their own "creative juices" to flow through brainstorming, inventing metaphor, synectics, and concept mapping.

Modeling

Thinking is probably best learned through imitation and emulation of good thinkers. Adults in the school that is becoming a home for the mind try to model the same qualities and behaviors they want students to develop. Teachers and administrators share their metacognitive strategies in the presence of students and others as they teach, plan, and solve problems.

Staff members restrain their impulsiveness during emotional crises. They listen to students, parents, and each other with skillfulness, understanding, and empathy. They reflect on and evaluate their own behaviors to make them more consistent with the core value that thoughtful behavior is a valid goal of education.[4]

THE SCHOOL AS A COMMUNITY

Humans, as social beings, mature intellectually in reciprocal relationships with other people. Vygotsky points out that the higher functions actually originate in interactions with others.

> Every function in . . . cultural development appears twice: first, on the social level, and later on the individual level; first between people (interpsychological), and then inside (intrapsychological). This applies equally to voluntary attention, to logical memory, and

to the formation concepts. All the higher functions originate as actual relationships between individuals.[5]

Together, individuals generate and discuss ideas, eliciting thinking that surpasses individual effort. Together and privately, they express different perspectives, agree and disagree, point out and resolve discrepancies, and weigh alternatives. Because people grow by this process, collegiality is a crucial climate factor.

Collegiality

The essence of collegiality is that people in the school community are working together to better understand the nature of intelligent behavior. Professional collegiality at the district level is evident when administrators form support groups to assist each other; when teachers and administrators from different schools, subject areas, and grade levels form networks to coordinate efforts to enhance intelligent behavior across all content areas and in district policies and practices. Committees and advisory groups assess staff needs, identify and locate talent, and participate in district-level prioritizing and decision making. They support and provide liaison with school site efforts, plan districtwide inservice and articulation to enhance teachers' skills, and develop an aligned, coordinated, and developmentally appropriate curriculum for students.

Selection committees for instructional materials review and recommend adoption of materials and programs to enhance students' thinking. Through districtwide networks, teachers share information and materials and teach each other about skills, techniques, and strategies they have found to be effective. The staff at Tigard, Oregon, calls this "Think Link."

In schools, teachers plan, prepare, and evaluate teaching materials. In St. Paul, Minnesota, teachers visit each other's classrooms frequently to coach and give feedback about the relationship between their instructional decisions and student behaviors. In Chugiak, Alaska, high school teachers are members of "instructional skills teams." Together they prepare, develop, remodel, and rehearse lessons. They then observe, coach, and give feedback to each other about their lessons.

Teachers and administrators continue to discuss and refine their vision of the school as a home for the mind. Definitions of thinking and the teaching and evaluation of students' intellectual progress are continually clarified. Child-study teams keep portfolios of students' work and discuss each student's developmental thought processes and learning styles. Teams explore instructional problems and generate experimental solutions. Faculty meetings are held in classrooms where the host teacher shares instructional practices, materials, and videotaped lessons with the rest of the faculty. Teacher teams sequence, articulate, and plan for continuity, reinforcement, and assessment of thinking skills across grade levels and subject areas.

An Environment of Trust

People are more likely to engage and grow in higher-level, creative, and experimental thought when they are in a trusting, risk-taking climate.[6] MacLean's[7] concept of the triune brain illuminates the need for operating in an environment of trust. For the neomammalian brain (the neocortex) to become fully engaged in its functions of problem solving, hypotheses formation, experimentation, and creativity, the reptilian brain (R-Complex) and the paleomammalian brain (Limbic System) need to be in harmony. Under stress or trauma, the more basic survival needs demanded by the reptilian brain and the emotional security and personal identity required by the paleomammalian brain can override and disrupt the more complex neocortical functioning.

Because higher-order thinking is valued as a goal for everyone in the school, the school's climate is monitored continually for signs of stress that might close down complex and creative thinking. Risk taking requires a nonjudgmental atmosphere where information can be shared without fear that it will be used to evaluate success or failure.

A climate of trust is evident when experiments are conducted with lesson designs, instructional sequences, and teaching materials to determine their effects on small groups of students (or with colleagues before they're used with a group). Various published programs and curriculums are pilot tested, and evidence is gathered over time of the effects on students' growth in thinking skills. Teachers become researchers when alternate classroom arrangements and instructional strategies are tested and colleagues observe student interactions.

Appreciation and Recognition

Whether a work of art, athletic prowess, acts of heroism, or precious jewels, what is valued in society is given public recognition. Core values are communicated when people see what is appreciated. If thinking is valued, it, too, is recognized by appreciation expressed to students and to teachers and administrators as well.

Students are recognized for persevering, striving for precision and accuracy, cooperating, considering another person's point of view, planning ahead, and expressing empathy. Students applaud each other for acts of ingenuity, compassion, and persistence. The products of their creativity, cooperation, and thoughtful investigation are displayed throughout the school.

Teachers at Wasatch Elementary School in Salt Lake City award blue ribbons to students who display intelligent behaviors. Similarly, teachers in East Orange, New Jersey, give certificates for "good thinking."

One form of appreciation is to invite teachers to describe their successes and unique ways of organizing for teaching thinking. In faculty meetings, teachers share videotaped lessons and showcase the positive results of their lesson planning, strategic teaching, and experimentation.

Schools within the district receive banners, flags, trophies, or certificates of excellence for their persistence, thoughtful actions, creativity, cooperative efforts, or meritorious service to the community. Some schools have even established a "Thinkers Hall of Fame."

Sharing, Caring, and Celebrating

Thinking skills are pervasive in schools that value thinking. They are visible in the traditions, celebrations, and everyday events of school life.

Staff members are often overheard sharing humorous anecdotes of students who display their thought processes. ("I saw two seventh grade boys on the athletic field yesterday ready to start duking it out. Before I could get to them, another boy intervened and said, 'Hey, you guys, restrain your impulsivity.'")

Teachers and administrators share personal, humorous, and sometimes embarrassing anecdotes of their own problems with thinking (tactics for remembering people's names, finding their cars in the parking lot, or solving the dilemma of locking the keys in the car).

At career days, local business and industry leaders describe what reasoning, creative problem solving, and cooperative skills are needed in various jobs. At school assemblies, students and teachers are honored for acts of creativity, cooperation, thoughtfulness, innovation, and scholarly accomplishments. Academic decathlons, thinking and science fairs, problem-solving tournaments, dialogical debates, invention conventions, art exhibits, and musical programs all celebrate the benefits of strategic planning, careful research, insightfulness, sustained practice, and cooperative efforts.

THE ULTIMATE PURPOSE: ENHANCING STUDENT THINKING

A common vision, process as content, and the school as a community are not ends in themselves. We must constantly remind ourselves that the reason we construct our schools is to serve our youth.

As the cornerstones and building blocks of school climate are gradually cemented into a sturdy foundation, teachers will in turn create classrooms with corresponding climate factors that recognize and support growth in students' intelligent behaviors.

The vision of education as the development of critical thinking abilities is evident as students deliberate and persevere in their problem solving, as they work to make their oral and written work more precise and accurate, as they consider others' points of view, as they generate questions, and as they explore the alternatives and consequences of their actions. Students engage in increasingly rigorous learning activities that challenge the intellect and imagination. Such scholarly pursuits require the acquisition, comprehension, and application of new knowledge and activate the need for perseverance, research, and increasingly complex forms of problem solving.

Since such processes of thinking as problem solving, strategic reasoning, and decision making are explicitly stated as the content of lessons, they become the "tasks that students are on." The metacognitive processes engaged in while learning and applying the knowledge are discussed. Thus students' thinking becomes more conscious, more reflective, more efficient, more flexible, and more transferable.

Collegiality is evident as students work together cooperatively with their "study buddies," in learning groups, and in peer problem solving. In class meetings, students are observed learning to set goals, establish plans, and set priorities. They generate, hold, and apply criteria for assessing the growth of their own thoughtful behavior. They take risks, experiment with ideas, share thinking strategies (metacognition), and venture forth with creative thoughts without fear of being judged. Accepting, listening, empathizing with, and clarifying each other's ideas replace value judgments and criticisms.[8]

The Greeks had a word for it: *padeia*. The term, popularized by Adler's Padaiea Proposal,[9] is an ideal concept we share: a school in which learning, fulfillment, and becoming more humane are the primary goals for all students, faculty, and support staff. It is the Athenian concept of a learning society in which self-development, intellectual empowerment, and lifelong learning are esteemed core values and all institutions within the culture are constructed to contribute to those goals.

NOTES

1. Costa, A., & Garmston, R. (2002). *Cognitive Coaching: A foundation for Renaissance schools.* Norwood, MA: Christopher-Gordon.

2. Kevin Reimer, Vice Principal of the Courtenay Middle School, Courtenay, British Columbia, Canada, provides students with a reflective paper to complete when they are sent to him for disciplining. A copy of this form is presented as Appendix 1.1.

3. Beyer, B. K. (1997). *Improving student thinking.* Boston: Allyn and Bacon.

4. Swartz, R., Costa, A., Beyer, B. K., Reagan, R., & Kallick, B. (2007). *Thinking-Based Learning.* Norwood, MA: Christopher-Gordon.

5. Vygotsky, L. (1978). *Society of mind.* Cambridge, MA: Harvard University Press.

6. Bryk, A., & Schneider, B. (2001). *Trust in schools: A core resource for improvement.* New York: Russell Sage.

7. MacLean, P. (1987). A Mind of Three Minds: Educating the Triune Brain. In J. Chall & A. Mirsky (Eds.), *Education and the Brain*. Chicago: University of Chicago Press.

8. Costa, A. (2001). Teacher Behaviors That Enable Student Thinking. In A. Costa (Ed.), *Developing Minds: A Resource Book for Teaching Thinking*. Alexandria, VA: Association for Supervision and Curriculum Development.

9. Adler, M. J. (1983). *The Paideia Proposal: An Educational Manifesto*. New York: Macmillan.

Appendix 1.1   Behavior Improvement Plan

Habits of Mind Think Paper

You have been referred to the office because your behaviour has been inappropriate. At Courtenay Middle we have adopted a Habits of Mind approach to encourage students to improve their critical thinking skills. By completing this behaviour improvement plan you have been given the opportunity to review why your behaviour was inappropriate and use your problem-solving skills to create a plan to ensure that this behaviour or similar behaviours do not occur again. Take a moment to answer the questions thoroughly and completely. The Courtenay Middle School Code of Conduct sidebar outlines the behaviour expectations for our learning community.

COURTENAY MIDDLE SCHOOL CODE OF CONDUCT

Learning and Productivity
Everyone at Courtenay Middle School . . .
- has the right and responsibility to teach and learn without disruption.
- chooses behaviours that are considerate of the learning environment.
- attends each class on time, with the proper materials, prepared to work and learn to the best of their ability.
- takes pride in putting forth their best effort.

Safety
Everyone at Courtenay Middle School . . .
- recognizes that their personal safety is their own responsibility and takes the appropriate measures to always remain safe.
- refrains from using unsafe behaviour. Horseplay, running in the halls, etc. are not tolerated.
- raises their voices in emergency situations only.
- alerts adults regarding potential safety hazards.

Respect
Everyone at Courtenay Middle School . . .
- uses positive language and behaviours to demonstrate respect for themselves and others. Inappropriate language, intimidating, and bullying behaviour are not tolerated.
- dresses appropriately for the learning environment. Clothing which is overly revealing, offensive, or promotes alcohol or drug use is not acceptable.

Responsibility
Everyone at Courtenay Middle School . . .
- accepts responsibility for his or her actions.
- takes positive action when someone or something is at risk.
- is expected to contribute to the good of the Courtenay Middle Community. We all positively represent Courtenay Middle School as ambassadors for our community.

Health and Environment
Everyone at Courtenay Middle School . . .
- has the right to work and learn in a safe environment that is free from tobacco, alcohol, and drugs.
- keeps the school grounds free from litter.

Skateboards, hats, and Discmans are
not allowed at Courtenay Middle School.
Teachers may choose to collect these items from
students if students choose to bring them to school.

_____   _____
Student Name   *Date*

1. Managing Impulsivity
Without blaming others explain how **your behaviour** was inappropriate?
(be honest)
_____
_____
_____
_____
_____
_____

2. Think about Thinking (Metacognition)
What caused you to behave this way?
_____
_____
_____
_____
_____
_____

3. Be Empathetic
How might others be affected by your behaviour?
_____
_____
_____
_____
_____

4. Problem Solving
How could you solve the issue in a positive manner if it happened again?
_____
_____
_____
_____
_____
_____

5. Think and Communicate With Clarity and Precision

What have you learned from the situation?

_____

_____

_____

6. Flexibility in Thinking

Restitution means seeking to correct an error or make amends to another person. How might you fix the problem?

_____

_____

_____

7. Striving for Accuracy and Precision

Consequences are the result of inappropriate behaviour. What is an appropriate consequence for your behaviour?

_____

_____

_____

_____

Parent signature

❒ Meeting requested by parent. Please call _____ to arrange a time.
❒ Meeting requested by school. Please call 334-4089 to arrange a time.

FOLLOW-UP MEETING	Date _____	In attendance _____

The Habits of Mind Think Paper must be signed and returned to the office the following day.
Failure to return it on time and signed may result in additional consequences.

SOURCE: Used with permission from Kevin Reimer, Courtenay Middle School, British Columbia.

CHAPTER TWO

Aesthetics

Where Thinking Originates

All information gets to the brain through our sensory channels—our tactile, gustatory, olfactory, visual, kinesthetic, and auditory senses. Those whose sensory pathways are open, alert, and acute absorb more information from the environment than those whose pathways are withered, immune, and oblivious to sensory stimuli. It is proposed, therefore, that *aesthetics* is an essential element of thinking skills programs. Cognitive education should include the development of sensory acumen.

Permeating the spirit of inquiry, inherent in creativity, and prerequisite to discovery, the aesthetic dimensions of thought have received little concern or attention as a part of cognitive instruction. The addition of aesthetics implies that learners become not only cognitively involved, but also enraptured with the phenomena, principles, and discrepancies they encounter in their environment. In order for the brain to comprehend, the heart must first listen.

Aesthetics, as used here, means sensitivity to the artistic features of the environment and the qualities of experience that evoke feelings in individuals. Such feelings include enjoyment, exhilaration, awe, and satisfaction. Thus, aesthetics is the sensitive beginning of rational thought, which leads to enlightenment about the complexities of our environment. It may be that from within the aesthetic realm the skills of observing, investigating, and questioning germinate. These are bases for further scientific inquiry. Aesthetics may be the key to sustaining motivation, interest, and enthusiasm in young children; since they must become aware of their environment

SOURCE: Reprinted by permission. Costa, A. L. (1985). Aesthetics: Where Thinking Originates in *Developing minds: A resource book for teaching thinking* (pp. 118–119). Alexandria, VA: Association for Supervision and Curriculum Development.

before they can explain it, use it wisely, and adjust to it. With the addition of aesthetics, cognition shifts from a mere passive comprehension to a tenacious quest.

Children need many opportunities to commune with the world around them. Time needs to be allotted for children to reflect on the changing formations of a cloud, to be charmed by the opening of a bud, and to sense the logical simplicity of mathematical order. They must find beauty in a sunset, intrigue in the geometrics of a spider web, and exhilaration in the iridescence of a hummingbird's wings. They must see the congruity and intricacies in the derivation of a mathematical formula, recognize the orderliness and adroitness of a chemical change, and commune with the serenity of a distant constellation.

We need to observe and nurture these aesthetic qualities in children. Students who respond to the aesthetic aspects of their world will demonstrate behaviors manifesting such intangible values. They will derive more pleasure from thinking as they advance to higher grade levels. Their curiosity will become stronger as the problems they encounter become more complex. Their environment will attract their inquiry as their senses capture the rhythm, patterns, shapes, colors, and harmonies of the universe. They will display cognizant and compassionate behavior toward other life forms as they are able to understand the need for protecting their environment, respecting the roles and values of other human beings, and perceiving the delicate worth, uniqueness, and relationships of everything and everyone they encounter. After the period of inspiration comes the phase of execution; as children explore, investigate, and observe, their natural curiosity leads them to ask "What?" "How?" "Why?" and "What if?"

Children need help in developing this feeling for, awareness of, and intuitiveness about the forces affecting the universe—the vastness of space, the magnitude of time, and the dynamics of change. But can this attitude be taught in specific lesson plans and instructional models? Are steps for its development written in method books? Can we construct instructional theory for cognitive education that includes aesthetics as a basis for learning? Or do children derive this attitude from their associations and interactions with significant other adults who exhibit it?

Perhaps we need to identify teachers who approach thinking with an aesthetic sense. It may be teachers who generate awareness of the outside world in children. They are often the underlying inspiration for children to become ardent observers and insatiable questioners. Teachers may be the ones who develop in others a compassionate attitude toward the environment and a curiosity with which they go wondering through life—a prerequisite for higher-level thought.

CHAPTER THREE

Habits of Mind

Learnings That Last

> When we no longer know what to do we have come to our real work and when we no longer know which way to go we have begun our real journey. The mind that is not baffled is not employed. The impeded stream is the one that sings.
>
> Wendell Berry

A critical distinction of *intelligent* human beings is that they not only have information, they also know how to act on it. They know how to perform effectively under those challenging conditions that demand strategic reasoning, insightfulness, perseverance, creativity, and craftsmanship to resolve a complex problem. While they may be deemed "smart" because they possess many answers, they also know how to behave intelligently when they *don't* know answers. As educators, therefore, we should focus on teaching students how to *produce* knowledge rather than merely how to *reproduce* knowledge.

By definition, a problem is any stimulus, question, task, phenomenon, or discrepancy the explanation for which is not immediately known. What behaviors are indicative of the efficient, effective problem solver? What do human beings do when they approach and resolve problems intelligently? Considerable research by Ames (1997); Briggs (1999); Ennis (2001); Feuerstein, Rand, Hoffman, and Miller (1980); Glatthorn and Baron (1985);

SOURCE: Reprinted by permission. Costa, A. L. (1991). The Search for Intelligent Life in *Developing minds: A resource book for teaching thinking* (2nd ed., pp. 100–106). Alexandria, VA: Association for Supervision and Curriculum Development.

Goleman (1995); Perkins (1985, 1995); and Sternberg (1984), indicates that there are some identifiable characteristics of effective thinkers. These are not necessarily "geniuses" or the wealthy who demonstrate these attributes. These characteristics have been identified in successful artists, physicians, engineers, auto mechanics, teachers, entrepreneurs, salespeople, and parents—people in all walks of life.

We call these characteristics "Habits of Mind" (Resnick, 2001). They are patterns of thinking and behaving in intelligent ways and are displayed when confronted with life's complexities and ambiguities.

DESCRIBING HABITS OF MIND

> To learn new habits is everything, for it is to reach the substance of life. Life is but a tissue of habits.
>
> Henri Fredric Amiel

A Habit of Mind means having a disposition toward behaving intelligently when confronted with problems. When humans experience dichotomies, are confused by dilemmas, or come face to face with uncertainties, our most effective actions require drawing forth certain patterns of intellectual behavior. When we draw upon these intellectual resources, the results that are produced are more powerful, of higher quality, and of greater significance than if we fail to employ them.

Employing Habits of Mind requires a composite of many skills, attitudes, cues, past experiences, and proclivities. Being in the habit of using one or more of these patterns means

- *Valuing it:* Choosing to employ a pattern of intellectual behaviors rather than other, less productive patterns. It means that we value one pattern of thinking over another, and therefore it implies conscious choice making about which pattern should be employed at this time.

- *Being inclined to use it:* Feeling the tendency or proclivity toward employing a pattern of intellectual behaviors. Greater satisfaction and feelings of efficacy, power, and control are enjoyed when the behaviors are employed.

- *Remaining alert to situations:* Being sensitive to, perceiving opportunities for, and appropriateness of employing the pattern of behavior. There is an alertness to the contextual cues that signal this as an appropriate time and circumstance in which the employment of this pattern would be useful.

• *Applying capabilities:* Possessing the basic skills and capacities to carry through with the behaviors. A level of skillfulness is required to employ and execute the behaviors effectively over time.

• *Making a commitment:* Constantly striving to reflect on and improve performance of the pattern of intellectual behavior. As a result of each experience in which these behaviors were employed, the effects of their use are reflected upon, evaluated, modified, and carried forth to future applications.

Sixteen Habits of Mind

Following are descriptions and an elaboration of 16 attributes of what human beings do when they behave intelligently. We refer to them here as Habits of Mind. These habits are seldom performed in isolation. Rather, clusters of such habits are drawn forth and employed in various situations. When listening intently, for example, one employs flexibility, metacognition, precise language, and perhaps questioning.

Do not think that there are only 16 ways in which humans display their intelligence. This list is not meant to be complete. It should serve to initiate the collection of additional attributes. Although 16 Habits of Mind are described here, you, your colleagues, and your students will want to continue the search for additional Habits of Mind by adding to and elaborating on this list and the descriptions.

1. Persisting

> If I had to select one quality, one personal characteristic that I regard as being most highly correlated with success whatever the field, I would pick the trait of persistence. Determination. The will to endure to the end, to get knocked down 70 times and get up off the floor saying, "Here comes number 71!"
>
> Richard M. Devos, businessman

Efficacious people stick to a task until it is completed. They don't give up easily. They are able to analyze a problem, to develop a system, structure, or strategy to attack a problem. They employ a range and have a repertoire of alternative strategies for problem solving. They collect evidence to indicate their problem-solving strategy is working, and if one strategy doesn't work, they know how to back up and try another. They recognize when a theory or idea must be rejected and another employed. They have systematic methods of analyzing a problem, which include knowing how to begin, knowing what steps must be performed, and what data need to be generated or collected. Because they are able to sustain a problem-solving process over time, they are comfortable with ambiguous situations.

Students often give up in despair when the answer to a problem is not immediately known. They sometimes crumple their papers and throw them away saying, "I can't do this," "It's too hard," or they write down any answer to get the task over with as quickly as possible. Some have attention deficits; they have difficulty staying focused for any length of time, they are easily distracted, they lack the ability to analyze a problem, to develop a system, structure, or strategy of problem attack. They may give up because they have a limited repertoire of problem-solving strategies. If their strategy doesn't work, they give up because they have no alternatives.

2. Managing Impulsivity

> Goal-directed self-imposed delay of gratification is perhaps the essence of emotional self-regulation: the ability to deny impulse in the service of a goal, whether it be building a business, solving an algebraic equation, or pursuing the Stanley cup.
>
> Daniel Goleman, *Emotional Intelligence*

Effective problem solvers have a sense of deliberativeness: They think before they act. They intentionally form a vision of a product, plan of action, goal, or destination before they begin. They strive to clarify and understand directions, develop a strategy for approaching a problem and withhold immediate value judgments before fully understanding an idea. Reflective individuals consider alternatives and consequences of several possible directions prior to taking action. They decrease their need for trial and error by gathering information, taking time to reflect on an answer before giving it, making sure they understand directions, and listening to alternative points of view.

Often students blur out the first answer that comes to mind. Sometimes they shout out an answer, start to work without fully understanding the directions, or lack an organized plan or strategy for approaching a problem. They may take the first suggestion given or operate on the most obvious and simple idea that comes to mind rather than considering more complex alternatives and consequences of several possible directions.

3. Listening to Others—With Understanding and Empathy

> Listening is the beginning of understanding. . . .
> Wisdom is the reward for a lifetime of listening.
> Let the wise listen and add to their learning and let the discerning get guidance. . . .
>
> Proverbs 1:5

Highly effective people spend an inordinate amount of time and energy listening (Covey, 1989). Some psychologists believe that the ability to listen to another person, to empathize with, and to understand their point of view is one of the highest forms of intelligent behavior. Being able to paraphrase another person's ideas, detecting indicators (cues) of their feelings or emotional states in their oral and body language (empathy), accurately expressing another person's concepts, emotions, and problems— all are indications of listening behavior (Piaget called it "overcoming egocentrism"). They are able to see through the diverse perspectives of others. They gently attend to another person, demonstrating their understanding of and empathy for an idea or feeling by paraphrasing it accurately, building upon it, clarifying it, or giving an example of it.

Senge, Ross, Smith, Roberts, and Kleiner (1994) suggest that to listen fully means to pay close attention to what is being said beneath the words. You listen not only to the "music," but also to the essence of the person speaking. You listen not only for what someone knows, but also for what he or she is trying to represent. Ears operate at the speed of sound, which is far slower than the speed of light the eyes take in. Generative listening is the art of developing deeper silences in yourself, so you can slow your mind's hearing to your ears' natural speed and hear beneath the words to their meaning.

We spend 55 percent of our lives listening, yet it is one of the least taught skills in schools. We often say we are listening, but in actuality we are rehearsing in our head what we are going to say next when our partner is finished. Some students ridicule, laugh at, or put down other students' ideas. They interrupt, are unable to build upon, consider the merits of, or operate on another person's ideas. We want our students to learn to devote their mental energies to another person and invest themselves in their partner's ideas.

We wish students to learn to hold in abeyance their own values, judgments, opinions, and prejudices in order to listen to and entertain another person's thoughts. This is a very complex skill requiring the ability to monitor one's own thoughts while, at the same time, attending to one's partner's words. This does not mean that we can't disagree with someone. A good listener tries to understand what the other person is saying. In the end he may disagree sharply, but because he disagrees, he wants to know exactly what it is he is disagreeing with.

4. Thinking Flexibly

> If you never change your mind, why have one?
>
> Edward deBono

An amazing discovery about the human brain is its plasticity—its ability to "rewire," change, and even repair itself to become smarter. Flexible people are the ones with the most control. They have the capacity to change their minds as they receive additional data. They engage in multiple and simultaneous outcomes and activities, draw upon a repertoire of problem-solving strategies, and can practice style flexibility, knowing when it is appropriate to be broad and global in their thinking and when a situation requires detailed precision. They create and seek novel approaches and have a well-developed sense of humor. They envision a range of consequences.

Flexible people can approach a problem from a new angle using a novel approach (deBono [1991] refers to this as "lateral thinking"). They consider alternative points of view or deal with several sources of information simultaneously. Their minds are open to change based on additional information and data or reasoning that contradicts their beliefs. Flexible people know that they have and can develop options and alternatives to consider. They understand means-ends relationships, are able to work within rules, criteria, and regulations, and they can predict the consequences of ignoring them. They understand not only the immediate reactions but are also able to perceive the bigger purposes that such constraints serve. Thus, flexibility of mind is essential for working with social diversity, enabling an individual to recognize the wholeness and distinctness of other people's ways of experiencing and making meaning.

Flexible thinkers are able to shift, at will, through multiple perceptual positions. One perceptual orientation is what Jean Piaget called *egocentrism*—perceiving from our own point of view. By contrast, *allocentrism* is the position in which we perceive through another person's orientation. We operate from this second position when we empathize with other's feelings, predict how others are thinking, and anticipate potential misunderstandings.

Another perceptual position is "macro-centric." It is similar to looking down from a balcony at ourselves and our interactions with others. This bird's-eye view is useful for discerning themes and patterns from assortments of information. It is intuitive, holistic, and conceptual. Since we often need to solve problems with incomplete information, we need the capacity to perceive general patterns and jump across gaps of incomplete knowledge when some of the pieces are missing.

Yet another perceptual orientation is micro-centric—examining the individual and sometimes minute parts that make up the whole. This "worm's-eye view," without which science, technology, and any complex enterprise could not function, involves logical analytical computation and searching for causality in methodical steps. It requires attention to detail, precision, and orderly progressions.

Flexible thinkers display confidence in their intuition. They tolerate confusion and ambiguity up to a point, and they are willing to let go of a problem, trusting their subconscious to continue creative and productive work on it. Flexibility is the cradle of humor, creativity, and repertoire. While there are many possible perceptual positions—past, present, future, egocentric, allocentric, macro-centric, visual, auditory, kinesthetic—the flexible mind is activated by knowing when to shift perceptual positions.

Some students have difficulty in considering alternative points of view or dealing with more than one classification system simultaneously. *Their* way to solve a problem seems to be the *only* way. They perceive situations from a very ego-centered point of view: "My way or the highway!" Their mind is made up: "Don't confuse me with facts, that's it."

5. Thinking About Our Thinking (Metacognition)

> When the mind is thinking it is talking to itself.
>
> Plato

Occurring in the neocortex, metacognition is our ability to know what we know and what we don't know. It is our ability to plan a strategy for producing what information is needed, to be conscious of our own steps and strategies during the act of problem solving, and to reflect on and evaluate the productiveness of our own thinking. While "inner language," thought to be a prerequisite, begins in most children around age 5, metacognition is a key attribute of formal thought, flowering about age 11.

Probably the major components of metacognition are developing a plan of action, maintaining that plan in mind over a period of time, then reflecting back on and evaluating the plan upon its completion. Planning a strategy before embarking on a course of action assists us in keeping track of the steps in the sequence of planned behavior at the conscious awareness level for the duration of the activity. It facilitates making temporal and comparative judgments, assessing the readiness for more or different activities, and monitoring our interpretations, perceptions, decisions, and behaviors. An example of this would be what superior teachers do daily: developing a teaching strategy for a lesson, keeping that strategy in mind throughout the instruction, then reflecting back upon the strategy to evaluate its effectiveness in producing the desired student outcomes.

Intelligent people plan for, reflect on, and evaluate the quality of their own thinking skills and strategies. Metacognition means becoming increasingly aware of one's actions and the effect of those actions on others and on the environment, forming internal questions as one searches for information and meaning, developing mental maps or plans of action, mentally rehearsing prior to performance, monitoring those plans as they are employed—being conscious of the need for midcourse correction if the plan is not meeting expectations, reflecting on the plan upon completion of the implementation for the purpose of self-evaluation, and editing mental pictures for improved performance.

Interestingly, not all humans achieve the level of formal operations (Chiabetta, 1976). And as Alexander Luria, the Russian psychologist, found, not all adults metacogitate (Whimbey & Whimbey, 1975). The most likely reason is that we do not take the time to reflect on our experiences. Students often do not take the time to wonder why we are doing what we are doing. They seldom question themselves about their own learning strategies or evaluate the efficiency of their own performance. Some children virtually have no idea of what they should do when they confront a problem and are often unable to explain their strategies of decision making (Sternberg, 1984). When teachers ask, "How did you solve that problem; what strategies did you have in mind?" or, "Tell us what went on in your head to come up with that conclusion," students often respond by saying, "I don't know, I just did it."

We want our students to perform well on complex cognitive tasks. A simple example of this might be drawn from a reading task. It is a common experience while reading a passage to have our minds "wander" from the pages. We "see" the words but no meaning is being produced. Suddenly we realize that we are not concentrating and that we've lost contact with the meaning of the text. We "recover" by returning to the passage to find our place, matching it with the last thought we can remember, and, once having found it, reading on with connectedness. This inner awareness and the strategy of recovery are components of metacognition.

6. Striving for Accuracy and Precision

> A man who has committed a mistake and doesn't correct it is committing another mistake.
>
> Confucius

Embodied in the stamina, grace, and elegance of a ballerina or a shoemaker is the desire for craftsmanship, mastery, flawlessness, and economy of energy to produce exceptional results. People who value accuracy, precision, and craftsmanship take time to check over their products. They review the rules by which they are to abide, they review the models and visions they are to follow, and they review the criteria they are to employ and confirm that their finished product matches the criteria exactly. To be craftsman-like means knowing that one can continually perfect one's craft by working to attain the highest possible standards and pursue ongoing learning in order to bring a laser-like focus of energies to task accomplishment. These people take pride in their work and have a desire for accuracy as they take time to check over their work. Craftsmanship includes exactness, precision, accuracy, correctness, faithfulness, and fidelity. For some people, craftsmanship requires continuous reworking. Mario Cuomo, a great speechwriter and politician, once said that his speeches were never done—it was only a deadline that made him stop working on them!

Some students may turn in sloppy, incomplete, or uncorrected work. They are more anxious to get rid of the assignment than to check it over for accuracy and precision. They are willing to suffice with minimum effort rather than investing their maximum. They may be more interested in expedience rather than excellence.

7. Questioning and Posing Problems

> The formulation of a problem is often more essential than its solution, which may be merely a matter of mathematical or experimental skill. To raise new questions, a new possibility, to regard old problems from a new angle, requires creative imagination and marks real advances.
>
> Albert Einstein

One of the distinguishing characteristics between humans and other forms of life is our inclination and ability to *find* problems to solve. Effective problem solvers know how to ask questions to fill in the gaps between what they know and what they don't know. Effective questioners are inclined to ask a range of questions. For example, they pose questions that

- Request data to support others' conclusions and assumptions. For example,

  "What evidence do you have . . . ?"

  "How do you know that's true?"

  "How reliable is this data source?"

- Seek alternative points of view. For example,

  "From whose viewpoint are we seeing, reading, or hearing?"

  "From what angle, what perspective are we viewing this situation?"

- Search for causal connections and relationships. For example,

  "How are these people (events) (situations) related to each other?"

  "What produced this connection?"

- Suggest hypothetical problems ("iffy"-type questions). For example,

  "What do you think would happen *if* . . . ?"

  "*If* that is true, then what might happen if . . . ?"

Inquirers recognize discrepancies and phenomena in their environment and probe into their causes: "Why do cats purr?" "How high can birds fly?" "Why does the hair on my head grow so fast, while the hair on my arms and legs grows so slowly?" "What would happen if we put the saltwater fish in a freshwater aquarium?" "What are some alternative solutions to international conflicts other than wars?"

Some students may be unaware of the functions, classes, syntax, or intentions in questions. They may not realize that questions vary in complexity, structure, and purpose. They may pose simple questions intending to derive maximal results. When confronted with a discrepancy, they may lack an overall strategy of search and solution finding.

8. Applying Past Knowledge to New Situations

> I've never made a mistake. I've only learned from experience.
>
> Thomas A. Edison

Intelligent human beings learn from experience. When confronted with a new and perplexing problem, they will often draw forth experience from their past. They can often be heard to say, "This reminds me of . . . " or "This is just like the time when I. . . ." They explain what they are doing now in terms of analogies with or references to previous experiences. They call upon their store of knowledge and experience as sources of data to support theories to explain or processes to solve each new challenge. Furthermore, they are able to abstract meaning from one experience, carry it forth, and apply it in a new and novel situation.

Too often students begin each new task as if it were being approached for the very first time. Teachers are often dismayed when they invite students to recall how they solved a similar problem previously and students don't remember. It's as if they never heard of it before, even though they had the same type of problem just recently. It is as if each experience is encapsulated and has no relationship to what has come before or what comes afterward. Their thinking is what psychologists refer to as an "episodic grasp of reality" (Feuerstein et al., 1980). That is, each event in life is a separate and discrete event with no connections to what may have come before or with no relation to what follows. Furthermore, their learning is so encapsulated that they seem unable to draw forth from one event and apply it in another context.

9. Thinking and Communicating With Clarity and Precision

> I do not so easily think in words. . . . After being hard at work having arrived at results that are perfectly clear . . . I have to translate my thoughts in a language that does not run evenly with them.
>
> Francis Galton, geneticist

Language refinement plays a critical role in enhancing a person's cognitive maps and their ability to think critically, which is the knowledge base for efficacious action. Enriching the complexity and specificity of language simultaneously produces effective thinking.

Language and thinking are closely entwined. Like two sides of a coin, they are inseparable. When you hear fuzzy language, it is a reflection of fuzzy thinking. Intelligent people strive to communicate accurately in both written and oral form, taking care to use precise language, defining terms, using correct names and universal labels and analogies. They strive to avoid overgeneralizations, deletions, and distortions. Instead they support their statements with explanations, comparisons, quantification, and evidence.

We sometimes hear students and other adults using vague and imprecise language. They describe objects or events with words like *weird, nice,* or *okay.* They call specific objects using such nondescriptive words as *stuff, junk,* and *things.* They punctuate sentences with meaningless interjections like *ya know, er,* and *uh.* They use vague or general nouns and pronouns: "*They* told me to do it." "*Everybody* has one." "*Teachers* don't understand me." They use nonspecific verbs: "Let's *do* it," and unqualified comparatives: "This soda is *better;* I like it *more.*"

10. Gathering Data Through All Senses

> Observe perpetually.
>
> Henry James

The brain is the ultimate reductionist. It reduces the world to its elementary parts: photons of light, molecules of smell, sound waves, vibrations of touch—which send electrochemical signals to individual brain cells that store information about lines, movements, colors, smells, and other sensory inputs.

Intelligent people know that all information gets into the brain through the sensory pathways: gustatory, olfactory, tactile, kinesthetic, auditory, visual. Most linguistic, cultural, and physical learning is derived from the environment by observing or taking in through the senses. To know a wine it must be drunk, to know a role it must be acted, to know a game it must be played, to know a dance it must be moved, to know a goal it must be envisioned. Those whose sensory pathways are open, alert, and acute absorb more information from the environment than those whose pathways are withered, immune, and oblivious to sensory stimuli do. Furthermore, we are learning more about the impact of arts and music on improved mental functioning. Forming mental images is important in mathematics and engineering; listening to classical music seems to improve spatial reasoning.

Social scientists solve problems through scenarios and role-playing, scientists build models, engineers use CAD-CAM, mechanics learn through hands-on experimentation, and artists experiment with colors and textures.

Musicians experiment by producing combinations of instrumental and vocal music.

Some students, however, go through school and life oblivious to the textures, rhythms, patterns, sounds, and colors around them. Sometimes children are afraid to touch, get their hands "dirty," or feel some object that might be "slimy" or "icky." They operate within a narrow range of sensory problem-solving strategies, wanting only to "describe it but not illustrate or act it," or "listen but not participate."

11. Creating, Imagining, and Innovating

> The future is not some place we are going to but one we are creating. The paths are not to be found, but made, and the activity of making them changes both the maker and the destination.
>
> John Schaar, political scientist, Santa Clara University,
> author, *Loyalty in America*

All human beings have the capacity to generate novel, original, clever, or ingenious products, solutions, and techniques—if that capacity is developed. Creative human beings try to conceive problem solutions differently, examining alternative possibilities from many angles. They tend to project themselves into different roles using analogies, starting with a vision and working backward, imagining they are the objects being considered. Creative people take risks and frequently push the boundaries of their perceived limits (Perkins, 1985). They are intrinsically rather than extrinsically motivated, working on the task because of the aesthetic challenge rather than the material rewards. Creative people are open to criticism. They hold up their products for others to judge and seek feedback in an ever-increasing effort to refine their technique. They are uneasy with the status quo. They constantly strive for greater fluency, elaboration, novelty, parsimony, simplicity, craftsmanship, perfection, beauty, harmony, and balance.

Students, however, are often heard saying, "I can't draw," "I was never very good at art," "I can't sing a note," or "I'm not creative." Some people believe creative humans are just born that way; it's in their genes and chromosomes.

12. Responding With Wonderment and Awe

> The most beautiful experience in the world is the experience of the mysterious.
>
> Albert Einstein

Describing the 200 best and brightest of the All USA College Academic Team identified by *USA Today*, Tracey Wong Briggs (1999) states, "They are creative thinkers who have a passion for what they do." Efficacious people have not only an "I can" attitude, but also an "I enjoy" feeling. They seek problems to solve for themselves and to submit to others. They delight in making up problems to solve on their own and request enigmas from others. They enjoy figuring things out by themselves and continue to learn throughout their lifetimes.

Some children and adults avoid problems and are "turned off" to learning. They make such comments as, "I was never good at these brain teasers," or "Go ask your father; he's the brain in this family." "It's boring." "When am I ever going to use this stuff?" "Who cares?" "Lighten up, teacher, thinking is hard work," or "I don't do thinking!" Many people never enrolled in another math class or other "hard" academic subjects after they didn't have to in high school or college. Many people perceive thinking as hard work and therefore recoil from situations that demand "too much" of it.

We want our students, however, to be curious; to commune with the world around them, to reflect on the changing formations of a cloud, feel charmed by the opening of a bud, and sense the logical simplicity of mathematical order. Students can find beauty in a sunset, intrigue in the geometrics of a spider web, and exhilaration at the iridescence of a hummingbird's wings. They see the congruity and intricacies in the derivation of a mathematical formula, recognize the orderliness and adroitness of a chemical change, and commune with the serenity of a distant constellation. We want them to feel compelled, enthusiastic, and passionate about learning, inquiring, and mastering.

13. Taking Responsible Risks

> There has been a calculated risk in every stage of American development—the pioneers who were not afraid of the wilderness, businessmen who were not afraid of failure, dreamers who were not afraid of action.
>
> Brooks Atkinson

Flexible people seem to have an almost uncontrollable urge to go beyond established limits. They are uneasy about comfort; they "live on the edge of their competence." They seem compelled to place themselves in situations where they do not know what the outcome will be. They accept confusion, uncertainty, and the higher risks of failure as part of the normal process and they learn to view setbacks as interesting, challenging, and growth producing. However, they are not behaving impulsively.

Their risks are educated. They draw on past knowledge, are thoughtful about consequences, and have a well-trained sense of what is appropriate. They know that all risks are not worth taking!

How individuals see risk taking can be considered in two categories: those who see it as a venture and those who see it as adventure. The venture part of risk taking might be described by the venture capitalist. When a person is approached to take the risk of investing in a new business, she will look at the markets, see how well organized the ideas are, and study the economic projections. If she finally decides to take the risk, it is a well-considered one.

The adventure part of risk taking might be described by the experiences from "Project Adventure." In this situation, there is spontaneity, a willingness to take a chance in the moment. Once again, a person will only take the chance if they know that there is either past history that suggests that what they are doing is not going to be life threatening or if they believe that there is enough support in the group to protect them from harm. Ultimately, the learning from such high-risk experiences is that people are far more able to take actions than they previously believed.

It is only through repeated experiences that risk taking becomes educated. It often is a cross between intuition, drawing on past knowledge, and a sense of meeting new challenges.

Bobby Jindal, executive director of the National Bipartisan Commission on the Future of Medicare states, "The only way to succeed is to be brave enough to risk failure" (quoted in Briggs, 1999, p. 2A).

When someone holds back from taking risks, he is confronted constantly with missed opportunities. Some students seem reluctant to take risks. Some students hold back games, new learning, and new friendships because their fear of failure is far greater than their experience of venture or adventure. They are reinforced by the mental voice that says, "If you don't try it, you won't be wrong," or "If you try it and you are wrong, you will look stupid." The other voice that might say, "If you don't try it, you will never know" is trapped in fear and mistrust. They are more interested in knowing whether their answer is correct or not than in being challenged by the process of finding the answer. They are unable to sustain a process of problem solving and finding the answer over time, and therefore they avoid ambiguous situations. They have a need for certainty rather than an inclination for doubt.

We hope that students will learn how to take intellectual as well as physical risks. Students who are capable of being different, going against the grain of the common, thinking of new ideas, and testing them with peers as well as teachers are more likely to be successful in an era of innovation and uncertainty.

14. Finding Humor

> You can increase your brain power three- to fivefold simply by laughing and having fun before working on a problem.
>
> Doug Hall

Another unique attribute of human beings is our sense of humor. Laughter transcends all human beings. Its positive effects on psychological functions include a drop in the pulse rate, the secretion of endorphins, and increased oxygen in the blood. It has been found to liberate creativity and provoke such higher-level thinking skills as anticipation, finding novel relationships, creating visual imagery, and making analogies. People who engage in the mystery of humor have the ability to perceive situations from original and often interesting vantage points. They tend to initiate humor more often, to place greater value on having a sense of humor, to appreciate and understand others' humor, and to be verbally playful when interacting with others. Having a whimsical frame of mind, they thrive on finding incongruity and perceiving absurdities, ironies, and satire, finding discontinuities and being able to laugh at situations and themselves. Some students find humor in all the "wrong places"—human differences, ineptitude, injurious behavior, vulgarity, violence, and profanity. They laugh at others yet are unable to laugh at themselves.

We want our students to acquire the characteristics of creative problem solvers: they can distinguish between situations of human frailty and fallibility that require compassion and those that are truly funny (Dyer, 1997).

15. Thinking Interdependently

> Take care of each other. Share your energies with the group. No one must feel alone, cut off, for that is when you do not make it.
>
> Willie Unsoeld, renowned mountain climber

Human beings are social beings. We congregate in groups, find it therapeutic to be listened to, draw energy from one another, and seek reciprocity. In groups we contribute our time and energy to tasks that we would quickly tire of when working alone. In fact, we have learned that one of the cruelest forms of punishment that can be inflicted on an individual is solitary confinement.

Cooperative humans realize that all of us together are more powerful, intellectually and/or physically, than any one individual. Probably the foremost disposition in the postindustrial society is the heightened ability to think in concert with others; to find ourselves increasingly more interdependent and sensitive to the needs of others. Problem solving has become so complex that no one person can go it alone. No one has access to all the data needed to make critical decisions; no one person can consider as many alternatives as several people can.

Some students may not have learned to work in groups; they have underdeveloped social skills. They feel isolated; they prefer their solitude. "Leave me alone—I'll do it by myself." "They just don't like me." "I want to be alone." Some students seem unable to contribute to group work, either by being a "job hog" or, conversely, letting others do all the work.

Working in groups requires the ability to justify ideas and to test the feasibility of solution strategies on others. It also requires the development of a willingness and openness to accept the feedback from a critical friend. Through this interaction the group and the individual continue to grow. Listening, consensus seeking, giving up an idea to work with someone else's, empathy, compassion, group leadership, knowing how to support group efforts, altruism—all are behaviors indicative of cooperative human beings.

16. Learning Continuously

> Whoever ceases to be a student has never been a student.
>
> George Iles

Intelligent people are in a continuous learning mode. Their confidence, in combination with their inquisitiveness, allows them to continually search for new and better ways. People with this Habit of Mind are always striving for improvement, always growing, always learning, always modifying and improving themselves. They seize problems, situations, tensions, conflicts, and circumstances as valuable opportunities to learn.

A great mystery about humans is that we confront learning opportunities with fear rather than mystery and wonder. We seem to feel better when we know rather than when we learn. We defend our biases, beliefs, and storehouses of knowledge rather than inviting the unknown, the creative, and the inspirational. Being certain and closed gives us comfort, while being doubtful and open gives us fear.

From an early age, employing a curriculum of fragmentation, competition, and reactiveness, students are trained to believe that deep learning means figuring out the truth rather than developing capabilities for effective and thoughtful action. They have been taught to value certainty rather than doubt, to give answers rather than to inquire, to know which choice is correct rather than to explore alternatives.

Our wish is for creative students and people who are eager to learn. That includes the humility of knowing that we don't know, which is the highest form of thinking we will ever learn. Paradoxically, unless you start off with humility you will never get anywhere, so as the first step you have to have already what will eventually be the crowning glory of all learning: the humility to know—and admit—that you don't know and are not afraid to find out.

WHY TEACH TOWARD HABITS OF MIND?

Numerous schools throughout the world have adopted the Habits of Mind with beneficial results. School leaders report an increase in student achievement; decreases in discipline problems; greater self-awareness, self-control, and self-confidence; a more unified and coherent approach to curriculum; greater parent involvement; and a more focused school culture. Some of the reasons for these achievements are thought to be as follows.

Shared Vision

Senge et al. (1994) suggests that a culture is people thinking together. As individuals share meaning, they negotiate and build a culture. As groups become more skillful in employing the Habits of Mind, the habits begin to pervade the value system, resulting in the changing of the practices and beliefs of the entire organization. By employing the Habits of Mind, the group mind illuminates issues, solves problems, and accommodates differences. By using the Habits of Mind, the group builds an atmosphere of trust in human relationships, trust in the processes of interaction, and trust throughout the organization. The Habits of Mind facilitate the creation of a shared vision.

Transdisciplinary

> Habit is a cable; we weave a thread of it each day, and at last we cannot break it.
>
> Horace Mann, American educator

A shared vision transcends grade levels and subject areas. The Habits of Mind apply to all grade levels and disciplines. All teachers can agree on these desirable qualities. Persistence is as valued in social sciences as it is in music and physical education. Creative thinking is as basic to science as it is to literature and the arts. Striving for accuracy and precision is as important to vocational education as it is to mathematics. Students are more likely to achieve and habituate because they are reinforced, transferred, and revisited throughout the school, at home, and in the community.

Working together, instructional teams decide, Which Habits of Mind do we wish students would develop and employ? What will we do to assist their development? How might we work collaboratively to determine if students are becoming more habituated over time? What will we see or hear in student behaviors as evidence of their growth? How might we practice and assess our own growth toward these Habits of Mind through our work together?

As Good for Adults as They Are for Children

> If there is anything that we wish to change in the child, we should first examine it and see whether it is not something that could better be changed in ourselves.
>
> Carl Jung

Furthermore, the dispositions are as applicable to developing adult capacities for effective problem solvers and continuous learners as they are to students. All members of the learning organization continue to become more thoughtful. The outcomes for students and the work culture of the school become congruent and synonymous.

No one ever "achieves mastery" of the Habits of Mind. All of us can continue to perfect our performance, to develop our capacities, to be more alert to opportunities for their use, and to more deliberately employ the Habits of Mind throughout our lifetimes. What makes the Habits of Mind "value added" is that they are as suitable for the adults in the school and community as they are for students. All of us can become continual learners.

Long-Range, Essential, and Enduring Learnings

> Excellence is an art won by training and habituation. We do not act rightly because we have virtue or excellence, but we rather have those because we have acted rightly. We are what we repeatedly do. Excellence, then, is not an act but a habit.
>
> Aristotle

Modern society recognizes a growing need for informed, skilled, and compassionate citizens who value truth, openness, creativity, interdependence, balance, and love as well as the search for personal and spiritual freedom in all areas of one's life.

As professional educators, we may be pressured for immediate, measurable results on standardized performances. This assumes that if teachers taught academic subjects and if students were to learn and be evaluated on how well they learn the minute subskills in each content area, they will somehow become the kind of people we want them to be (Seiger-Eherenberg, 1991, p. 6). Our desire is to make learning and instruction more reflective, more complex, and more relevant to society's and students' diverse needs and interests now and in their future. We want our children to develop those habits that lead them to become lifelong learners, effective problem solvers and decision makers, able to communicate with a diverse population and to understand how to live successfully in a rapidly changing, high-tech world.

IN SUMMARY

Drawn from research on human effectiveness, descriptions of virtuoso performers, and analyses of the characteristics of remarkable people, 16 Habits of Mind have been identified. These Habits of Mind may serve as mental disciplines. When confronted with problematic situations, students, parents, and teachers might habitually employ one or more of these Habits of Mind by asking themselves, "What is the most *intelligent thing* I can do right now?"

- How can I learn from this experience? What are my resources? How can I draw on my past successes with problems like this? What do I already know about the problem? What resources do I have available or need to generate?
- How can I approach this problem *flexibly*? How might I look at the situation in another way? How can I draw upon my repertoire of problem-solving strategies? How can I look at this problem from a fresh perspective?
- How can I illuminate this problem to make it clearer and more precise? Do I need to check out my data sources? How might I break this problem down into its component parts and develop a strategy for understanding and accomplishing each step?
- What do I know or not know? What questions do I need to ask? What strategies are in my mind now, what am I aware of in terms of my own beliefs, values, and goals with this problem? What feelings or emotions am I aware of which might be blocking or enhancing my progress?
- To whom might I turn for help? How does this problem affect others? How can we solve it together and what can I learn from others that would help me become a better problem solver?

These Habits of Mind transcend all subject matters commonly taught in school. They are characteristic of peak performers in homes, schools, athletic fields, organizations, the military, governments, churches, or corporations. They are what make marriages successful, learning continual, workplaces productive, and democracies enduring.

The goal of education, therefore, should be to support others and ourselves in liberating, developing, and habituating these Habits of Mind more fully. Taken together, they are a force directing us toward increasingly authentic, congruent, and ethical behavior—the touchstones of integrity. They are the tools of disciplined choice making. They are the primary vehicles in the lifelong journey toward integration. They are the "right stuff" that makes human beings efficacious.

REFERENCES

Ames, J. E. (1997). *Mastery: Interviews with 30 remarkable people.* Portland, OR: Rudra Press.

Briggs, T. W. (1999, February 25). Passion for what they do keeps alumni on first team. *U.S.A. Today,* pp. 1A–2A.

Chiabetta, E. L. A. (1976). Review of Piagetian studies relevant to science instruction at the secondary and college levels. *Science Education, 60,* 253–261.

Covey, S. (1989). *The seven habits of highly effective people.* New York: Simon and Schuster.

deBono, E. (1991). The Cort Thinking Program. In A. Costa (Ed.), *Developing minds: Programs for teaching thinking* (pp. 27–32). Alexandria, VA: Association for Supervision and Curriculum Development.

Dyer, J. (1997). Humor as process. In A. Costa & R. Liebmann (Eds.), *Envisioning process as content: Toward a Renaissance curriculum* (pp. 211–229). Thousand Oaks, CA: Corwin Press.

Ennis, R. (2001). Goals for a critical thinking curriculum and its assessment. In A. L. Costa (Ed.), *Developing minds: A resource book for teaching thinking,* 3rd ed. (pp. 44–46). Alexandria, VA: Association for Supervision and Curriculum Development.

Feuerstein, R., Rand, Y. M., Hoffman, M. B., & Miller, R. (1980). *Instrumental enrichment: An intervention program for cognitive modifiability.* Baltimore: University Park Press.

Glatthorn, A., & Baron, J. (1985). The good thinker. In A. L. Costa (Ed.), *Developing minds: A resource book for teaching thinking* (pp. 49–53). Alexandria, VA: Association for Supervision and Curriculum Development.

Goleman, D. (1995). *Emotional intelligence: Why it can matter more than I.Q.* New York: Bantam Books.

Perkins, D. (1985). What creative thinking is. In A. L. Costa (Ed.), *Developing minds: A resource book for teaching thinking* (pp. 85–88). Alexandria, VA: Association for Supervision and Curriculum Development.

Perkins, D. (1995). *Outsmarting I.Q.: The emerging science of learnable intelligence.* New York: Free Press.

Resnick, L. (2001). Making America smarter: The real goal of school reform. In A. L. Costa (Ed.), *Developing minds: A resource book for teaching thinking* (pp. 3–6). Alexandria, VA: Association for Supervision and Curriculum Development.

Seiger-Eherenberg, S. (1991). Educational outcomes for a K–12 curriculum. In A. Costa, (Ed.), *Developing minds: A resource book for teaching thinking* (pp. 6–9). Alexandria, VA: Association for Supervision and Curriculum Development.

Senge, P., Ross, R., Smith, B., Roberts, C., & Kleiner, A. (1994). *The fifth discipline fieldbook: Strategies and tools for building a learning organization.* New York: Doubleday/Currency.

Sternberg, R. (1983). *How can we teach intelligence?* Philadelphia: Research for Better Schools.

Sternberg, R. (1984). *Beyond I.Q.: A triarchic theory of human intelligence.* New York: Cambridge University Press.

Whimbey, A., & Whimbey, L. S. (1975). *Intelligence can be taught.* New York: Lawrence Erlbaum Associates.

CHAPTER FOUR

Launching Self-Directed Learners

With Bena Kallick

> He who controls others is powerful but he who masters himself is more powerful still.
>
> Lao-tzu

Schooling is much like the launch pad for a spaceship. All the "life support" systems remain attached until that moment of lift-off when, while it is always in communication with the command center, the spaceship is "on its own." So, too, we must prepare students to launch their journey from school to life, internalizing the lessons we have taught to navigate their own spaceship. We need, therefore, to establish feedback systems so that students learn how to guide themselves along the way, monitoring progress toward their destinations, making small maneuvers and midcourse corrections using on-board "mental trim tabs." Education must provide experiences by which students gradually learn to take charge of their own learning, to become increasingly more aware of their behaviors and their effects on others, and to strengthen their fortitude and resilience to self-correct and self-modify. Thus, the school becomes the launch pad for a life of self-directed learning.

SOURCE: Reprinted by permission. Costa, A. L., & Kallick, B. (2004, September). Launching self-directed learners. *Educational Leadership, 62*(1), 51–57. Alexandria, VA: Association for Supervision and Curriculum Development.

Unfortunately, being awash in a sea of too many standards for the number of days in a school year, educators are struggling to find their direction (Marzano & Kendall, 1998). Furthermore, in the current politics of education, the key to school success is higher test scores. Externally administered assessments tied to these standards shift the focus toward the transmission of test-related information, making it difficult to embrace and sustain curriculum and instructional strategies designed for individual meaning-making and personal, self-directed learning. While we may desire to develop students' capacities for self-directedness, we may be contributing to a generation of "other-directed," dependent, externally motivated learners.

The struggle for educators is to develop self-directed learners in an "other-directed" educational era. In our search for balance between external and internal demands, the external context is so imperative that to search for the inner quest for what is meaningful is indeed arduous. We must reclaim our sense of direction, based on what we most value, and provide educational experiences by which students become responsible, self-directed, continuous learners.

DEFINING SELF-DIRECTEDNESS

What does it mean to be self-directed? We believe that when confronted with complex tasks, self-directed people exhibit the behaviors required to be self-managing, self-monitoring, and self-modifying (Costa & Garmston, 2002, pp. 17–18; Costa & Kallick, 2004).

Self-Managing

Self-managing people control their first impulse for action and delay premature conclusions. Rather, they are inclined to approach tasks by clarifying outcomes, formulating questions to gather the data they need to illuminate the problem. They are flexible and are able to create alternative strategies to accomplish their goals. They equip themselves with necessary data and knowledge from past experiences. They anticipate success indicators and create alternatives for accomplishment.

Some of the Habits of Mind that describe a self-managing individual include

- Managing impulsivity
- Thinking flexibly
- Questioning and problem posing
- Drawing forth past knowledge and applying it to new and novel situations
- Gathering data through all senses
- Imagining, creating, innovating (Costa & Kallick, 2000)

Self-Monitoring

Self-monitoring people think about their own thinking, behaviors, biases and beliefs and their effects on others and on the environment. They have sufficient self-knowledge to know what works for them. They establish conscious metacognitive strategies to alert the perceptions for in-the-moment indicators of whether the strategic plan is working or not and to assist in the decision-making processes of altering the plan and choosing the right actions and strategies. They monitor for accuracy and precision, knowing when to self-correct and to modify strategies. They persevere using alternative strategies and know-how and where to turn to resources when confronted with perplexing situations.

Some of the Habits of Mind that describe a self-monitoring individual are

- Thinking about thinking (metacognition)
- Persisting
- Monitoring accuracy and precision
- Listening with understanding and empathy

Self-Modifying

Self-modifying people are able to change themselves. They reflect on, evaluate, analyze, and construct meaning from experience and apply the learning to future activities, tasks, and challenges. They communicate their conclusions with clarity, precision, and caution. They readily admit that they have more to learn and are intrigued, curious, and internally motivated to learn more.

Some of the Habits of Mind that describe a self-modifying individual are

- Thinking and communicating with clarity and precision
- Responding with wonderment and awe
- Remaining open to continuous learning

These dispositions transcend all subject matter commonly taught in school. They are characteristic of peak performers whether they be in homes, schools, athletic fields, organizations, the military, governments, churches, or corporations. They are what make marriages successful, learning continual, workplaces productive, and democracies enduring.

One goal of education, therefore, should be to support others and ourselves in liberating, developing, and habituating these intellectual dispositions more fully.

DEVELOPING STUDENTS' CAPACITIES FOR SELF-DIRECTED LEARNING

The challenge for educators is to move this set of expectations from rhetoric to reality. Following are descriptions of several structured opportunities intended to help students become aware of and practice these dispositions of self-directedness and to assess how well they plan for, monitor, and construct meaning from them in their daily learning interactions. They will need to make a conscious effort to gather evidence of their continued growth toward mastery.

Conferences With Critical Friends

Students meet with an established critical friend. They review the goals that they have set for their work. They follow a protocol so that each partner has time to give and receive feedback. The presenter discusses the goals that he has set for accomplishing the work. He discusses his timeline and pays attention to whether he is on target for the due date.

1. The responder asks clarifying questions and tries to understand the work plan.

2. Both parties discuss any possible modifications the student might need to make so that he can meet or modify his goals.

3. Partners agree on a time to meet again so that they can check for accuracy and quality.

Conferences With Teachers

Students bring their plans to the conference with the teacher. They reflect on where they are in their project at this point in time. Some questions that might be asked are

- What is your work plan?
- What difficulties are you having in accomplishing your plan?
- How realistic are your goals given the time frame that you have for accomplishing the work?
- What are you especially interested in?
- What strategies have you tried? What strategies might you try?
- How will you know when your work is ready to turn in?

A group of elementary teachers developed this set of questions for students in preparation for a conference on goals for the school year:

WHAT ARE MY GOALS FOR THIS YEAR?

My goal concerns myself and my study habits. It is

_____

_____

A reason I selected this goal is

_____

_____

The actions I will take to meet this goal are

_____

_____

Self-Reflection Worksheets

Kathleen Reilly, a teacher formerly in the Scarsdale, New York, School District, used a series of reflections in her advanced senior seminar. In the second quarter of the year, some of the questions she asked were

1. When you look through your essays, what particular areas of writing are you struggling with?

2. How are these individual conferences helpful to you? In what ways can I be more helpful to you?

By the last quarter, some of the questions she asked were

1. Do you have a graphic image of the format of an essay firmly etched in your brain? If so, how does it look? If not, tell me what format you do see.

2. At what specific point within the past 40 weeks did you sense that you were actually changing or changed as a writer and thinker about literature? Did you find that you could analyze and support your ideas, reach for insight? If not, what were your frustrations?

3. Please identify your perception of your own strengths as a writer. And then, please follow with your understanding of weaknesses you still have.

4. What else do you need to learn in this course that was not accomplished? What further information would you like me to know?

Glenora Elementary School in Edmonton, Canada, has a set of questions that can be adjusted for any subject or age group. All teachers have access to these questions and can draw from them to construct metacognitive reflection sheets. They can be the basis of a worksheet or checklist and can be given at various points in an assignment.

1. Do I understand why I have to read this material? For a test? Report?

2. What do I already know about this subject, topic, issue?

3. What predictions about this material might I make even before I read it?

4. Where else can I get some more information?

5. How much time will I need to learn this?

6. What are some strategies and tactics I can use to learn this?

7. How can I spot an error if I make one?

8. Should I read the first line of a paragraph more than once?

9. Did I understand what I just read?

10. Do I know it well enough to retell it after I finish reading? To answer questions on a test?

To determine if the students are becoming more aware of their own thinking (metacognition), teachers might ask, "How do you think about solving a problem? What steps do you take?"
Teachers might encourage students to

- List the steps and tell where they are in the sequence of a problem-solving strategy.
- Trace the pathways and dead ends they took in the road to a problem solution.
- Describe what data are lacking and their plans for producing those data.

The following is a sequence that might describe persisting through problem solving:

- Sticking to it when the solution to a problem is not immediately apparent and you want to give up and quit
- Employing systematic methods of analyzing a problem
- Knowing ways to begin, knowing what steps must be performed, and when they are accurate or are in error
- Taking pride in their efforts
- Self-correcting
- Striving for craftsmanship and accuracy in their products
- Becoming more self-directed with problem-solving abilities

Checklists

Checklists provide experiences in applying, monitoring, and self-evaluating the performance of the indicators of self-directed learning. Teachers gather students' responses to the question, "What would it look like and sound like if you were thinking flexibly?" Or, "What would it look like or sound like if you were aware of your thinking?" Then the students and teacher use the checklist to observe and record the use of these behaviors and to reflect on the use of the behaviors upon completion of the task. Such observations require practicing self-awareness about one's own and other's skills, styles, and behaviors. It requires that learners operate from data rather than speculation and know when to relinquish their ideas in favor of others (Baker, Costa, & Shalit, 1997). The checklist shown in Figure 4.1 asks students to describe, monitor, and assess their listening skills.

While the students are engaged in the learning activity, they monitor their own and each other's performance. Before the end of the class, the teacher asks the students to reflect on and to describe how the criteria were or were not met. Feelings are explored and indicators of how the team is working more synergistically together are expressed. Teachers may pose such metacognitive questions as

- What decisions did you make about when and how to participate?
- What metacognitive strategies did you employ to monitor your own communicative competencies?
- What were some of the effects of your decisions for you and others in your group?
- As you anticipate future team meetings, what commitments might you make to strengthen the group's productiveness?
- What signals in what other future situations will alert you to the need for these communicative competencies? (Costa & Garmston, 2002, pp. 314–315)

Figure 4.1   How Are We Doing? A Process Checklist for Listening

Strategic Behavior	Often	Sometimes	Not Yet
Listening with understanding			
Verbal			
Restates/paraphrases a person's idea before offering personal opinion			
Clarifies a person's ideas, concepts, or terminology			
Expresses empathy for other's feelings/emotions			
Poses questions intended to engage thinking and reflection			
Expresses personal regard and interest			
Nonverbal			
Faces the person who is speaking			
Establishes eye contact if appropriate			
Nods head			
Uses facial expressions congruent with speaker's emotional message			
Mirrors gestures			
Mirrors posture			

SOURCE: Costa and Kallick (2004).

> The only person you should ever compete with is yourself. You can't hope for a fairer match.
>
> Todd Ruthman

Rubrics

When teachers involve students in developing scoring rubrics, they become clearer about the judgment that determines the quality of the work. Providing rubrics serves several purposes:

1. They remind students of the agreed-upon expectations.

2. They provide a systematic way to chart growth and improvement.

3. They provide an explicit language for goal setting and personal mastery.

Furthermore, a rubric shows stages of development. Everyone is a novice at something. We all suffer the ineptitude of beginning—with a vision of what we would like to be able to do with greater expertise. Most students quickly associate these feelings to athletics. It does not take much prompting for students to remember the first time they—rode a bike, tried to roller blade, played tennis. They have a very concrete vision of what the sport should look like if played well. So it is with the attributes of self-directedness. Figure 4.2 presents a rubric developed by a high school class for monitoring their own clarity and precision.

Letters

Sometimes writing a letter to a particular audience helps students become aware of their thinking, styles, and capabilities. As they formalize their perceptions about how they are working, they are able to become more personal. This student writes a letter to next year's teacher.

There are things to celebrate about having me in your classroom.

I am good at

_____

_____

There are things that I might need help with in your classroom. I have difficulty with

_____

_____

What really makes me feel excited about learning is

_____

_____

Figure 4.2 Analytic Rubric for Monitoring Clarity and Precision

	Clarity	Seeks Accuracy	Precision of Language	Temporal Detail
Expert	Consistently creates works that are free of confusing elements.	Consistently pays close attention to detail when appropriate. Checks information against all important sources. Recognizes inaccuracies quickly and makes corrections. Desires to add greater clarity to work.	Consistently communicates information by providing a clear main idea or theme with rich, vivid, powerful, and detailed support. Spontaneously defines terms, checks for understanding; pursues idea until understanding is achieved.	Consistently plans for and communicates duration, recurrence, simultaneity, and sequence for events. Plans for and expresses relationship between both long- and short-range outcomes.
Practitioner	Creates work free of confusion.	Consistently pays attention to detail. Checks several sources. Recognizes and corrects major inaccuracies.	Consistently communicates information by providing a clear main idea or theme with supporting data. Define terms when probed.	Usually plans for and communicates most of the time dimensions of duration, recurrence, simultaneity, and sequence for events. Plans for and expresses relationship between both long- and short-range outcomes.
Apprentice	Sporadically creates work free of confusion.	Sporadically attends to detail. Checks several sources. Recognizes errors but fails to correct them. Seldom reviews for accuracy.	Sporadically communicates information by providing a clear main idea with support. Defines terms with little detail or description.	Often omits time several time dimensions in planning. Can include and express time dimensions or short-/long-range goal relationships only when probed or questioned.
Novice	Work is vague, unclear, and confused.	Pays little attention to detail. Fails to check several sources. Overlooks major inaccuracies. Seems satisfied with errors. Fails to review for accuracy.	Omits support for ideas, opinion, or claims. Uses vague terminology without definition.	Is unaware of how much time an event will take. Is unable to sequence events. Cannot describe what events will occur simultaneously. Is episodic in thinking.

SUMMARY

We must make our good intentions a reality. It is insufficient to merely name our expectations through a vision or a set of learner expectations. We must make certain that what we value we explicitly address in the classroom through curriculum design, thoughtful instruction, and opportunities for assessment and reflection. Students need the opportunity to look back at their work and learn how to look forward to the next work with new plans and strategies for improvement. Too often, we hear students say—"I already finished that work!" as if doing the task, rather than experiencing learning from the accomplishment of the task, is what is most significant. When teachers focus on self-direction, the question is reversed. It is, "What have I learned and who am I becoming?" Striving for excellence is a life task, not a singular event to satisfy a teacher. We want to see students develop a love of learning and not feel solely dependent on the judgment of others to determine the value of what they are learning. Given many opportunities over time, students will continuously assess themselves and build the strength and humility of continuous learning.

REFERENCES

Baker, B., Costa, A., & Shalit, S. (1997). Norms of collaboration: Attaining communicative competence. In A. Costa & R. Liebmann (Eds.), *The process-centered school: Sustaining a Renaissance community* (pp. 119–142). Thousand Oaks, CA: Corwin Press.

Costa, A., & Garmston, R. (2002). *Cognitive Coaching: A foundation for Renaissance schools.* Norwood, MA: Christopher-Gordon.

Costa, A., & Kallick, B. (2000). *Habits of mind: A developmental series.* Alexandria, VA: Association for Supervision and Curriculum Development.

Costa A., & Kallick, B. (2004). *Assessment strategies for self-directed learning.* Thousand Oaks, CA: Corwin Press.

Marzano, R. J., & Kendall, J. S. (1998). *Awash in a sea of standards.* Aurora, CO: Mid-continent Research for Education and Learning.

PART II

The Mind-Full Curriculum

Many educators are forming a new understanding of what a basic skill is. We are realizing that there is a prerequisite to the "basics"—the ability to think . . . to behave intelligently . . . finding comfort, agreement, and rededication in some common goals—that the process is as important as the product.

Arthur L. Costa

CHAPTER FIVE

Maturing Outcomes

With Robert J. Garmston

> New frameworks are like climbing a mountain—the larger view encompasses, rather than rejects, the earlier more restricted view.
>
> Albert Einstein

Decisions made by policy makers, teachers, and curriculum workers about what should be taught in our schools will shape the minds of our children. The character of their minds, in turn, will help shape the culture in which we all live. Schools serve children best when they broaden the meanings children know how to pursue and capture (Eisner, 1997).

In this chapter we present a systematic map of educational outcomes, intended for use by educational leaders. The map represents increasingly broader levels of curricular and instructional decision making. While we do not reject a more restricted view, we value, as Eisner does, that the broader the meanings which children know how to pursue shapes their minds and ultimately will create citizens who are better able to contribute uniquely to our democratic society and a global community.

Constraints which narrow educators' focus will be described and leadership strategies intended to expand and enlarge the thinking of staff, curriculum policy makers, and the community will be suggested.

Our hope is to offer future citizens a curriculum, developed around broad outcomes and focused on enduring, essential, transdisciplinary

SOURCE: Printed with permission from *Encounter: Education for Meaning and Social Justice,* 11(1), 10–18. www.great-ideas.org/enc.htm

learnings which are as appropriate for adults as they are for students, and are congruent with the vision of continuous, lifelong learning and with the mission of a learning organization.

A MAP OF INCREASINGLY BROADER, MORE ENCOMPASSING EDUCATIONAL OUTCOMES

From examining the literature on instructional objectives, teachers' cognitive processes, and exploring our own experiences, we surmise that there are at least five nested levels of outcomes, each one broader and more encompassing than the level within and each representing greater authenticity. They are summarized below (see Figure 5.1).

1. *Outcomes as Activities:* Inexperienced teachers may exhibit episodic, teacher-centered thinking and simply be satisfied to accomplish activities. For beginning teachers, for whom everything is new, the cognitive demands of the classroom may be more than the working mind is designed to accommodate. Their own survival and keeping students engaged from period to period and day to day often dictate their instructional choices. Their decisions include, What do I want to accomplish in this lesson? What will I do to make it happen? What will my students be doing if they are accomplishing it? Teachers might describe an outcome as, "Today in social studies I'm going to show a video tape on Mexico." Success is measured in terms of did I make it through the lesson, were students on task, and did they pay attention?

2. *Outcomes as Content:* As teachers increasingly gain familiarity with classroom procedures, their students, and themselves, mental energy is freed to consider the cumulative affects of these activities—what concepts and principles are students learning? While teachers maintain interest in day-to-day activities, they are now employed as vehicles to learn content. Teachers ask: What concepts or understandings do I want my students to know as a result of this activity? What will I do to help them understand? How will I know they understand the concepts? In the Mexican history lesson, for example, the video tape is used as a means of helping students understand the principal causes for Mexico's struggle for independence from Spain. The teacher's focus is on what concepts and understandings students will know and how that knowledge will be recognized and assessed.

3. *Outcomes as Processes:* As teachers continue to mature, content begins to be selected for its generative qualities (Perrone & Kallick, 1997). Content becomes a vehicle for experiencing, practicing, and applying the processes needed to think creatively and critically and are basic to lifelong problem solving: observing and collecting data, forming and testing hypotheses, drawing conclusions, and posing questions.

Figure 5.1   Maturing Outcomes Map

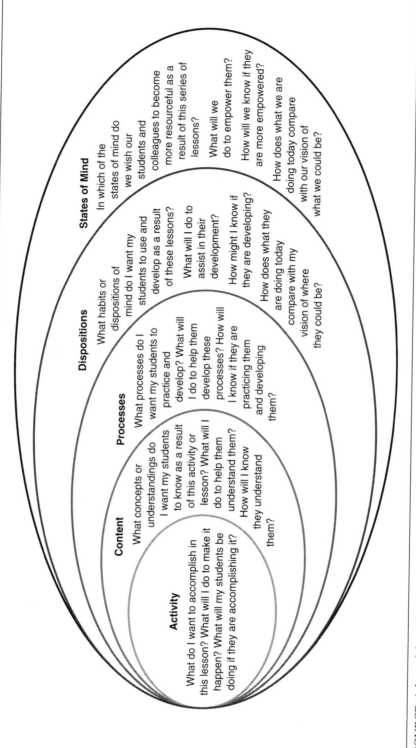

SOURCE: Adapted from Costa and Liebmann (1997b).

Process outcomes are of greater valance than the outcomes of subject-specific content because to be literate in the content, students must know and practice the processes by which that content came into being (Paul & Elder, 1991; Tishman & Perkins, 1997). At this level, teachers decide, What processes do I want my students to practice and develop? What will I do to help them develop those processes? How will I know if they are practicing and developing them? In extending the Mexican history example: students plan a research project to support their theories that the heroes of the Mexican Revolution were as courageous and brave as those of the American Revolution. Students present an exhibit demonstrating their understandings and develop rubrics for judging the exhibits and working together effectively. Additionally, they reflect on and evaluate themselves both individually and collectively as to how well they met the criteria of both the project's completion and for cooperative group work.

4. *Outcomes as Dispositions:* With increased maturity, systems thinking emerges about outcomes. When a vision is shared, an entire staff transcends grade levels and subject areas. Panoramic outcomes are more likely to be achieved because they are reinforced, transferred, and revisited throughout the school, at home, and in the community.

The transcendent qualities of systems thinking about outcomes may be found in dispositions or habits of mind: enhancing ones' capacities to direct and control persistence, managing impulsivity, creativity, metacognition, striving for precision and accuracy, listening with empathy, risk taking and wonderment (Costa, 1991; Tishman & Perkins, 1997). All teachers, regardless of subject area or grade level, can agree on these desirable qualities. Persistence is as valued in social sciences as it is in music, math, and physical education. Creative thinking is as important to science as it is in the auto shop and the arts.

With a focus on dispositions, the historical isolation, disparity, and episodic nature of curricular outcomes are minimized. Furthermore, the dispositions are as applicable to developing adult capacities for effective problem solvers and continuous learners as they are to students. All members of the learning organization continue to become more thoughtful. The outcomes for students and the work culture of the school become congruent and synonymous.

Activities are still taught. Content is selected for its generative nature, processes are practiced, but they now accumulate into grander, more long-range outcomes. Instructional teams decide, What dispositions do we want students to develop and employ? What will we do to assist their development? How might we work collaboratively to determine if students are developing such dispositions over time? What will we see or hear in student behaviors as evidence of their growth? How might we practice and assess our own growth toward these habits of mind through our work together?

In the Mexican history lesson, the teacher builds metacognitive capabilities by having students consciously discuss and employ the skills of listening with understanding and empathy. Operational definitions of these dispositions are generated and observers collect evidence of the group's performance of these skills. Upon completion of the project, students evaluate their own performance using feedback from the observers. Students draw causal relationships not only among the effects of their collaborative skills and task achievement but also between empathy and the sources of revolutionary movements. Questions are asked such as, What metacognitive strategies did you employ to manage and monitor your listening skills during your work in teams? The emphasis is on internalizing these dispositions as individual and community-wide norms and all staff members plan for such dispositions to be encountered and transferred across various disciplines and learning situations.

5. *Outcomes as Mind States:* We consider five human capacities, or mind states, as catalysts—energy sources fueling human thinking, learning, and behaviors as the next level of outcomes. They are the wellsprings nurturing all high-performing individuals, groups, and organizations (Costa & Garmston, 1994). They are the beacons toward increasingly authentic, congruent, and ethical behavior.

As educational outcomes, we want not only our students and our colleagues but also ourselves to amplify the resources of

1. *Efficacy:* the human quest for continuous, lifelong learning, self-empowerment, mastery, and control. We have the capacity to make a difference through our work, and we are willing to take the responsibility to do so.

2. *Flexibility:* the human capacity to perceive from multiple perspectives, and endeavor to change, adapt, and expand their repertoire of response patterns. We have and can develop options to consider about our work and we are willing to acknowledge and demonstrate respect and empathy for diverse perspectives.

3. *Craftsmanship:* the human yearning to become clearer, more elegant, precise, congruent, and integrated. We can continually strive for excellence, and are willing to work to attain our own high standards and pursue ongoing learning.

4. *Consciousness:* the unique human capacity to monitor and reflect on their own thoughts and actions. We monitor what and how we are thinking about our work in the moment and are willing to be aware of our actions and their effects on others and the environment.

5. *Interdependence*: the human need for reciprocity, belonging, and connectedness and to become one with the larger system and community of which they are a part. We will all benefit from our participating in, contributing to, and receiving from learning relationships and are willing to create and change relationships to benefit our work.

Teachers might facilitate learning and drawing upon the mind states by having students analyze functional and dysfunctional groups: what are the resources they can draw upon to become more flexible, efficacious, conscious, craftsmanlike, and interdependent? Students are invited to display the behavior patterns of each and then inquire as to the probable mind states from which such behaviors evolve. From these learnings students draw implications and generalizations about the effects of cooperation and listening in life situations and the mind states necessary to achieve highly effective group work in organizations and in society. They revisit the Mexican history lesson analyzing the mind states of major leaders and groups.

At this level, outcomes are drawn not only from the mind states of consciousness, flexibility, interdependence, craftsmanship, and efficacy, but also from the ways these interact with the school's expressed values, culture, and mission. The staff decides, In which mind states do we wish students and colleagues to become more resourceful? What will we do to capacitate their development? How will we know when the mind states are amplified? How does what we are doing today compare with our vision of what could be?

Staff and students learn to draw upon the five mind states to organize and direct their resources as they resolve problems, diagnose human frailty in themselves and others, plan for the most productive interventions in groups, and search out the motivations of their own and other's actions. They become the desirable meta-outcomes not only for staff, students, and community but for each of us as well. The desired outcomes for us and those we hold for others become as one.

WHAT KEEPS PERSPECTIVES NARROW?

Educational leaders are presented with a dilemma: how to think big when so many forces influence us to think small; how to establish powerful, authentic outcomes of this magnitude when well-meaning policy makers, zealous parents, and community leaders encourage schools to narrow the focus of their educational outcomes. Several examples of limiting signals include

- National goals and assessments resulting from political expediency instead of reasoned values.

Making a national goal of and assessing students' reading and math at fourth and eighth grade levels to compare scores with other nations makes a public statement that quality education means improving scores on tests of reading and math skills (Kamii, Clark, & Dominick, 1994). (Increasing numbers of research studies, however, indicate that higher test scores result from using process-oriented, conceptually based instruction.)

- Mandated curriculums and traditional assessments of student's discreet microperformances based on reductionist theory.

Decades of Newtonian-oriented, behavioristic principles of learning focus us on student's performance of minute skills and low-level knowledge rather than broader, more essential outcomes.

- The self-sealing logic of past and current systems of outcomes.

Much like a dog chasing its tail, the level of adopted outcomes sets the intent and instrumentation of assessments. This cycle seals systems into a mindset that outcomes are significant because they are easily and immediately measured, barring consideration of working for more enduring, long-range outcomes.

- Our historical obsession with the disciplines as separate stores of knowledge to be acquired, which places boundaries on content and keeps school staffs divided.

The organization of curriculum into static compartments may be a helpful classification system for allocating time, writing textbooks, hiring and training teachers, or organizing university departments. This archaic conception of the disciplines, however, conveys an obsolescent and myopic view of what constitutes knowledge (Costa & Liebmann, 1997a).

- School and district change efforts using an episodic, activity-based approach.

Proudly striving to keep abreast of educational improvement practices, some schools adopt an array of innovations (block scheduling, inclusion, cross-grade groupings, interdisciplinary instruction, technology, mentoring, whole language, etc., etc.). Teachers and administrators soon become overwhelmed integrating all the disparate pieces. Knowledge-vigilant organizations, however, view school change from a broader perspective as a process of revealing and emancipating human and organizational resourcefulness.

- Cognitive immaturity.

Another, and most elusive proposition, relates to the cognitive capacity required to comprehend, value, and simultaneously hold and work for educational outcomes that meet the test of authenticity described above.

Such cognitive complexity may be attainable only by persons in later developmental stages of cognitive growth (Kegan, 1994).

HOW LEADERS SUPPORT MATURING OUTCOMES

How can educational communities, constrained and limited by existing mindsets, curriculum, and mandated assessments, mature in their capacity to think about more potent, multiple, simultaneous, and complex outcomes? Educational leaders, maintaining their focus on the bigger picture, can support their organization, staff, and community to think in broader terms.

Developing Cognitive Complexity

The pathway from novice to expert educator is an evolving journey toward the peak of one's capacity—a highly evolved human, capable of operating interdependently, while maintaining and remaining true to a clear sense of personal identity; growing toward greater mental complexity and away from perceiving the self as separate from others and at the center of the universe. As adults in this culture evolve through the systems by which meaning is made, they progress from the interpersonal—in which they internalize uncritically the values and beliefs of others. They seek validation from external criteria and their personal identity is defined by relationships to people and ideas.

A beginning teacher's focus on activities may be representative of this initial stage of meaning making. In time, and with mediation, humans evolve into the institutional stage—they have relationships but are not defined by them. Now they become self-authoring, self-standard setting, and are validated by internal criteria. They develop their own psychic-institution, and, like all institutions, they expend energy trying to protect their boundaries resulting in self-sealing logic and limited flexibility (Kegan, 1994). Still other teachers—but not all adults, Kegan cautions—achieve this transition to the next stage: the post-institutional (and rarely before age 40).

In this most advanced stage of human development, teachers are committed to continual inquiry and occupy a consciously interdependent relationship with their environment. They are open to questions, possibilities, conflict, and reconstruction of their own assumptions, practices, and ways of being. Gifted and burdened with these complexities and perspectives, teachers work to develop students in similar directions of self-assertiveness and integration (Garmston & Lipton, 1996).

Maturing teachers, who live in a rich school culture of complexity, creativity, and collaboration, operate at multiple levels of authentic outcomes simultaneously as lessons are planned, as students' needs are considered, as the immediate and long-range goals of the curriculum are assessed, and as the environment of the school and classroom are arranged. Educators who function at broader, more complex levels of personal development think beyond the immediate purposes of a lesson and envision the potential of fully functioning human beings. These attributes become integrated into outcomes for themselves, students, colleagues, their organization, and the community.

The Maturing Outcomes Map

Anthropologist Gregory Bateson (1972) formulated an early notion of relating systems of learning to human growth. Dilts (1994) then applied this form of systems thinking to education. (See Figure 5.1 previous.) The major concepts are

1. Any system of activity is a subsystem embedded inside of another system. This system is also embedded in an even larger system and so on.

2. Learning in one subsystem produces a type of learning relative to the system in which one is operating.

3. The effect of each level of learning is to organize and control the information on the level below it.

4. Learning something on an upper level will change things on lower levels but learning something on a lower level may or may not inform and influence levels above it.

Staffs begin to realize that authentic outcomes are subsystems embedded inside other subsystems. In such arrangements, different types and magnitudes of learning occur relative to the system in which one is operating. Each more overarching, complex, and abstract level has a greater impact upon the learning of the level within it. Since each level affects the interpretation of the levels below, changing meaning on an upper level changes decisions and actions at lower levels; changing something at a lower level, however, does not necessarily affect the upper levels.

When teachers deliberately adopt and assesses dispositions as outcomes, for example, it changes the design of their activities, determines their selection of content, and enlarges their assessments. The bigger the circle in which the outcomes live, the more influence they exert on the values of each learning.

If we wish to influence an element deeper within the system, each tiny adjustment in the environment surrounding it produces profound effects on the entire system. This realization allows us to search beyond the dispositions for systems to which humans naturally aspire in their journey of human development, which, if affected, would also influence one's capacity to learn (Garmston, 1997).

Using the maturing outcomes as a strategic, metacognitive map, leaders can identify the current level of thinking about outcomes in a discussion or in a product. Leaders can choose to work within the existing level of thought or to mediate a group's or individual's thinking toward a broader, more encompassing level.

STRATEGIES FOR GENERATING MORE COMPLEX, ENCOMPASSING THOUGHT

Examples within four leadership interventions are explored: managing, modeling, monitoring, and mediating.

Managing

Leaders who have the capacity to manage resources can make deliberate decisions about the use of those resources to broaden, heighten, and enhance outcomes. Leaders will be alert for opportunities to intervene in such a way as to broaden groups or individual's outcomes by

• *Clarifying core values.* Leaders can articulate beliefs about how students learn in documents that drive conversations, decisions, assessments, and reporting in all curriculum and instructional practices. They will activate committees to stay current with emerging literature and findings in order to contrast and align present practices with most recent findings. Agreements about student expectations can be derived from thoughtfully facilitated school-community conversations linking what is known about learning.

• *Assessing at higher levels.* Since what is inspected communicates what is expected, thoughtful leaders can design and report assessments at the level above where a group or individual is operating. Teachers naturally assess achievement at the same level as their outcomes. Content level assessment, for example, measures skills and knowledge achievement. Processes, dispositions, and mind states, however, require multiple assessments: portfolios, interviews, performances, and direct observation. To monitor and assess student's development of dispositions requires data to be accumulated systematically, over time, and from multiple perspectives (Marzano, Pickering, & McTighe, 1993). Development of mind state resourcefulness requires assessments of characterization (Krathwohl, Bloom, & Masia, 1964) and self-evaluation under conditions of duress and conflict (Bloom, Englehart, Furst, Hill, & Krathwohl, 1956).

• *Directly instructing.* Leaders can teach about nested levels of increasingly complex outcomes through staff development programs, as a prelude to the work of any curriculum group, as a framing device in deliberations about instruction and assessment practices, as a communication to parents about school goals, and in orientations for new faculty (Saphir & Gower, 1988).

• *Deliberately structuring.* The confluence of multiple perspectives enriches the thought within groups. Leaders can, therefore, design group assignments and composition by timing and defining tasks so that stakeholders from diverse levels of maturity, beliefs, and styles must collaborate. Teachers from different disciplines might be paired in peer coaching and other collaborative arrangements. A diffusion of knowledge and assumptions about learning occurs when teachers from different disciplines plan together, observe in each other's classroom, share responsibilities for student learnings, or are assigned the same students for multi-year periods.

School leaders can structure environments to maximize certain forms of interactions. Multiple classrooms intentionally designed around a common teacher workroom enhances interdependence. A single lab, shared by all science teachers and students, increases connection making among all the sciences. Schools can be designed so as to build flexibility into the very walls and passages of the edifice, making it necessary for the staff, students, and community to function in interdependent ways (Saban, 1997).

Modeling

Leaders must walk the talk. Probably the most powerful intervention is for leaders to behave in a manner consistent with their beliefs and values. Staff, students, and community members are constantly alert to cues which signal congruence between the stated beliefs and values and the overt behavior of the leader.

Leaders model by publicly stating their outcomes in the broadest terms and explain their actions in relation to the five mind states. They specify the behaviors on which they are working, make public the rationale for choosing them, and ask others to monitor and provide feedback about their skills, effectiveness, and congruence with stated values (Hayes, 1995). Such leadership is invested in people at all levels of the organization as they perform their multiple functions of planning, coordinating, communicating, influencing, coaching, consulting, and assessing (Garmston & Wellman, 1995).

Monitoring

Leaders constantly monitor themselves, their interactions with others, the allocation of available resources, and the environment for indicators of the level of outcomes being described, cited, reinforced, or valued.

- *Self-monitoring* implies asking one's self, what are my intentions and motives at this moment? It means keeping in mind the map of the interaction (see Figure 5.1). Self-monitoring implies being aware of one's own words, values, and actions.

- *Monitoring metaphors* means listening to others' words and implicit thoughts about lesson design or staff development plans as indicators of the level at which they are currently operating. Developing banks of synonyms and related words and phrases for each level of the map helps groups remain alert for indicators of the levels of thinking (Zimmerman, 1997). Table 5.1 presents examples of such words and metaphors for each of the five levels.

Table 5.1   Words and Metaphors for Five Levels of Thought

Level of Thought	*About*	*Words and Metaphors as Indicators*
Activities	Objectives:	To "Pay attention, participate, complete, on task, take notes. . . ."
	Assessments:	Teacher observation, counting, recording
Content	Objectives:	To "Know about, understand, comprehend grasp, remember. . . ."
	Assessments:	Quizzes, tests of knowledge
Processes	Objectives:	To "Infer, conclude, criticize, to explain, to interpret, hypothesize, to reason, to analyze, to support with evidence . . ."
	Assessments:	Performances, applications, exhibitions
Dispositions/ Habits of Mind	Objectives:	To "Develop perseverance, to manage impulsivity, to be reflective, to become more intellectually strategic. . . "
	Assessments:	Demonstrations over time, anecdotals, rubrics, portfolios, checklists, self-assessments, self-descriptions using metacognitive maps
Mind States	Objectives:	To "Draw upon resources; to employ capabilities and maps, to demonstrate beliefs and values; to act in accordance with . . . "
	Assessments:	Characterization self-assessment of own performance under duress, self-evaluation using an internal set of criteria, seeking feedback from others

- *Monitoring the allocation of resources* means being alert to where money and time is being invested. By paying attention to the level of outcomes and intentions of published materials, computer programs, curriculum guides, descriptions of staff development opportunities, etc., leaders can select those which will raise and broaden the level of thinking by staff and community.

Mediating

To mediate is to interpose oneself between a set of learners and the environment and, through nonjudgmental questioning, paraphrasing, and clarifying, draw attention to data, the consideration of which, engages and transforms thinking and meaning (Feuerstein, Feuerstein, & Schur, 1997). From such transformed meaning comes a reexamination of practices and their congruence with values.

This arrangement of systems and subsystems of maturing outcomes provides a map around which leaders can strategically design linguistic interventions intended to mediate others' progressively more psychologically encompassing and impactful levels of abstraction than the level currently being addressed. Table 5.2 presents questions that can be asked to raise the consciousness about each of the levels.

BEYOND CURRENT THINKING

In our journey we've described five transcendent levels of maturing outcomes from activity to content and processes through dispositions and states of mind. We hold each level not only as outcomes in and of themselves but as vehicles and enablers of more transcendent virtues as well. As the instructional focus is enlarged, the outcomes for students and the work culture of the school become congruent and synonymous; the staff employs these same mind states as decisions are made, meetings conducted, parent conferences held, and instruction planned. Staff members monitor their own mind states as they gather feedback about their achievements, their effects on others, and set continually higher standards for themselves.

We believe there are additional levels beyond. Biographies of remarkable and virtuous people from the sciences, the arts, politics, and social services, whose personal development seemed to move beyond the mind states, further enlarges our vision. They display a personal set of virtues—a spiritual quality. We call this sixth level "ideals"—encompassing not only the mastery of processes, dispositions, and mind states, but transcending these in pursuit of universal goals. The real challenge to the maturing organization is to be faithful not only to the external goals but to measure up to the interior goals. To reach for what is beautiful, what is good, what is true; what unites and does not divide. We believe the ideals for which humans

Table 5.2   Questions Intended to Raise Consciousness About Levels of Outcomes

When you hear the level of the lesson to be	And you want to raise it to	Leaders mediate by asking such questions as
Activity	Content	How will students benefit from engaging in this activity? What concepts (big ideas) (principles) do you want students to learn as a result of these activities?
Content	Processes	How will students demonstrate their understanding of these concepts? How will students apply these concepts in future lessons? In what cognitive processes will students engage during these learnings?
Processes	Dispositions	What habits do you want students to form as a result of engaging in these processes? What enduring learnings will students gain from engaging in these processes?
Dispositions	Mind States	What do you want students to carry forth to future life situations? How will students feel more resourceful (empowered) as a result of this learning?
Mind States	Ideals	What personal values are students forming as a result of these learnings? How will this help your students become better human beings?

at the highest stages of development strive is the integration of external outcomes and those outcomes within ourselves. Trying to make ourselves better, purer, more beautiful and more loving persons; concerned with uniting and not dividing (*Gifts From the Fire*, 1991).

REFERENCES

Bateson, G. (1972). *Steps to an ecology of mind.* New York: Chandler.

Bloom, B. (Ed.), Englehart, M., Furst, E., Hill, W., & Krathwohl, D. (1956). *Taxonomy of educational objectives. Handbook 1: Cognitive domain.* New York: David McKay.

Costa, A. (1991). The search for intelligent life. In *The school as a home for the mind* (1st ed.). Thousand Oaks, CA: Corwin Press.

Costa, A., & Garmston, R. (1994). *Cognitive Coaching: A foundation for Renaissance schools.* Norwood, MA: Christopher-Gordon.

Costa, A., & Liebmann, R. (1997a). Difficulties with the disciplines. In *Envisioning process as content: Towards Renaissance curriculum* (pp. 21–31). Thousand Oaks, CA: Corwin Press.

Costa, A., & Liebmann, R. (1997b). Towards Renaissance curriculum: An idea whose time has come. In *Envisioning process as content: Towards Renaissance curriculum* (pp. 1–21). Thousand Oaks, CA: Corwin Press.

Dilts, R. (1994). *Effective presentation skills.* Capitola, CA: Meta Publications.

Eisner, E. (1997, January). Cognition and representation: A way to pursue the American dream? *Phi Delta Kappan, 78*(5), 348–353.

Feuerstein, R., Feuerstein, R., & Schur, Y. (1997). Process as content in education particularly for retarded performers. In A. Costa & R. Liebmann (Eds.), *Supporting the spirit of learning: When process is content* (pp. 1–22). Thousand Oaks, CA: Corwin Press.

Garmston, R. (1997, Spring). Nested levels of learning. *Journal of Staff Development, 18*(2).

Garmston, R., & Lipton, L., with Kaiser, K. (1996). The psychology of supervision: From behaviorism to constructivism. In G. Firth & E. Pajak (Eds.), *Handbook of research on school supervision.* New York: Macmillan.

Garmston, R., & Wellman, B. (1995, April). Adaptive schools in a quantum universe. *Educational Leadership, 52*(7), 6–12.

Gifts from the fire: The ceramic art of Brother Thomas. (1991). Video production on the life of Brother Thomas. Boston: Pucker Gallery.

Hayes, C. (1995, Spring). Public coaching as a tool for organization development. *Journal of Staff Development, 16*(2), 44–49.

Kamii, C., Clark, F., & Dominick, A. (1994, May). The six national goals: A road to disappointment. *Phi Delta Kappan,* 672–677.

Kegan, R. (1994). *In over our heads: The mental demands of modern life.* Cambridge, MA: Harvard University Press.

Krathwohl, D., Bloom, B., & Masia, B. (1964). *Taxonomy of educational objectives: Handbook II: Affective domain.* New York: David McKay.

Marzano, R, Pickering, D., & McTighe, J. (1993). *Assessing student outcomes: Performance assessment using the dimensions of learning model.* Alexandria, VA: Association for Supervision and Curriculum Development.

Paul, R., & Elder, L. (1991). All content has a logic: That logic is given by a disciplined mode of thinking. Part 1. *Teaching Thinking and Problem Solving, 16*(5), 1–4.

Perrone, V., & Kallick, B. (1997). Generative topics for process curriculum. In A. Costa & R. Liebmann (Eds.), *Supporting the spirit of learning: When process is content* (pp. 23–34). Thousand Oaks, CA: Corwin Press.

Saban, J. (1997). Process pervades the organization: Capturing the spirit. In A. Costa & R. Liebmann (Eds.), *The process centered school: Sustaining a Renaissance community* (pp. 172–188). Thousand Oaks, CA: Corwin Press.

Saphir, J., & Gower, R. (1988). *The skillful teacher.* Carlisle, MA: Research for Better Teaching.

Tishman, S., & Perkins, D. (1997, January). The language of thinking. *Phi Delta Kappan, 78*(5), 368–374.

Zimmerman, D. (1997). Constructing the metaphors for process. In A. Costa & R. Liebmann (Eds.), *The process centered school: Sustaining a Renaissance community* (pp. 1–9). Thousand Oaks, CA. Corwin Press.

CHAPTER SIX

Mapping Forward

> The pursuit of truth and beauty is a sphere of activity in which we are permitted to remain children all our lives.
>
> Albert Einstein

W hile meeting with some grade-level groups of a small but progressive K–12 school district, the kindergarten teachers proudly described how they work diligently to kindle a love of learning in their youngsters, preparing them for their demanding journey throughout future school and life experiences. But, alas, they bemoaned the slump in enthusiasm that many children experience around the fourth to fifth grade. Somehow, as children become more "schooled," their sense of wonderment may be drummed out of them. Often the most successful test takers are adolescents who are sleepwalking through their lives, focusing on trivial matters and, by adulthood, are locked into narrow, inflexible, and humorless ways of thinking.

Such indifference to learning may be due to the hormonal secretions of maturation, shaped by peer pressure, influenced by culture, or even modeled by parents. We also realize that learning societal conventions and mandates such as the delay of gratification, consideration of others, and following rules requires the young child to learn to manage his/her own impulses. An irrelevant curriculum, high-stakes testing, or uninspired instruction might also contribute to the problem. Regardless of the source, the greatest challenge for educators is to sustain that passion for learning. In a similar manner that we take responsibility for ensuring that "no child

SOURCE: Reprinted by permission. Costa, A. L. (2005, November 15). Sustaining Children's Zest for Learning. *ASCD Express*, 1(3). Alexandria, VA: Association for Supervision and Curriculum Development.

is left behind" due to language deficiencies, physical handicaps, diverse culture, or dysfunctional family life, so too must we ensure that children's innate quest for learning is nurtured and protected as they progress through school.

The purpose of this chapter is to plea for *"forward mapping"*—planning ahead to ensure that the innate zest for learning that is characteristic of young children is built upon and sustained throughout their school experience; that each person who interacts with the learner regardless of grade level, instructional responsibility, or content, be committed to sustaining that child-like exuberance with which each normal brain is endowed.

MAPPING

Grant Wiggins and Jay McTighe (1998), who probably built upon the early work of Franklin Bobbitt, have coined the term "Mapping Backwards" to indicate the need to map back from an assessment to the lessons and activities that will prepare students to be successful. Drawing on the psychological principles of Edward Thorndike, Bobbitt wrote

> Education that prepares for life is one that prepares definitely and adequately for these specific activities . . . the abilities, attitudes, habits, appreciations and forms of knowledge that men need. These will be the objectives of the curriculum. They will be numerous, definite and particularized. The curriculum will then be that series of experiences which children and youth must have by way of attaining these objectives. (Bobbitt, 1918, p. 14)

To think "retrospectively" about what skills and content are prerequisite to successful attainment and performance of desired end-of-lesson, end-of-unit, or end-of-course outcomes makes great sense and is a logical process of curriculum dialogue, design, and decision making.

Mapping backwards to assessments, however, may be only a part of the process. We need also to *map forward* to maintain students' enthusiasm for learning—a prerequisite for all future life endeavors.

Children come fully equipped with an insatiable drive to explore and experiment. Unfortunately, the primary institutions of our society are oriented predominantly toward controlling rather than learning; rewarding individuals for performing for others rather than cultivating their natural curiosity and impulse to learn.

Peter Senge (1990)

WHAT TRAITS ARE WORTHY OF MAPPING FORWARD?

At least 10 "innate" natural learning dispositions characterize the young child and are powerful predictors of a student's subsequent success. They should become a consistent focus of instruction, monitoring, assessment, and reporting throughout a student's school experience. If students acquire and sustain these attributes early in their school years and are consistently reminded of their value, they will most likely continue learning long after they've graduated (Popham, 2005).

1. Natural Curiosity

> The one real objective of education is to have a person in the condition of continually asking questions.
>
> Bishop Medell Creighton

Children come to school with an inclination to question. Illustrative of this inquisitiveness, the following dialogue approximates a conversation overheard recently between an exasperated mother and a tenacious two-year-old at an adjacent table in a fast-food restaurant:

MOTHER: "Jason, sit down."

JASON: "Why?"

MOTHER: "Because you need to finish your lunch."

JASON: "Why?"

MOTHER: "Because we want to go shopping."

JASON: "Where?"

MOTHER: "At the mall."

JASON: "What's a mall?"

MOTHER: "It's a place where you can walk around and look in store windows and buy things."

JASON: "What things?"

MOTHER: "We need to buy you some new shoes."

JASON: "Why?"

MOTHER: "Jason, sit down and eat your french fries!"

As children become more alert to discrepancies and phenomena in their environment they naturally inquire into their causes: "Why do cats purr?" "How high can birds fly?" "Why does the hair on my head grow so fast, but the hair on my arms and legs grows so slowly?" "Why is the sky blue?" "Where do poems come from?" "What are some alternative solutions, other than wars, to international conflicts?"

Sometimes students are reluctant to ask questions for fear of displaying ignorance and come to depend on others to solve problems and to find answers. They lack a strategy of questioning and seldom evaluate the power and effectiveness of their questioning processes and sequences.

"Closed questions" that have a single answer or that can be answered "yes" or "no" provide minimal appeal to inquire. Open questions employ tentative language and plurals. "What *might* be *some alternatives* . . . ? What *hunches do* you have in mind that *might* explain . . . ? Such language cues stimulate hypothetical thinking, alternatives, and multiplicity of responses.

> Someone asked the Nobel Laureate, I. I. Rabi, why he became a physicist rather than a doctor or a lawyer or a tailor like his father. Rabi explained that his mother made him a scientist without ever intending it. Every other Jewish mother in Brooklyn would ask her child, "So, what did you learn in school today?" But not his mother. She always asked, "Izzi, what good questions did you ask today?"
>
> John Barell (1988)

2. Constructing Self-Meaning

The brain of the young child has tremendous capacity and desire to make or elicit patterns of meaning. Infants are in a constant state of exploration into everything they can lay their hands, eyes, and lips on. They live in a state of continuous discovery: dismayed by anomaly, attracted to novelty, compelled to mastery, intrigued by mystery. They derive personal and concrete feedback from their tactile/kinesthetic adventures. Their brains are actually being transformed with each new experience. The reality they are organizing into greater levels of complexity is influenced by the constructive processes of the brain.

Young humans don't get ideas, they make ideas. Knowledge is a constructive process rather than a finding. It is not the content, rather it is the activity of constructing that content that gets stored in memory. Because meaning making is not a spectator sport, our perceptions of learning need to shift from educational outcomes that are primarily collections of facts and sub-skills to include the development of students' identities as conscious, flexible, efficacious, and interdependent meaning makers. Instead of having learners acquire *our* meanings we must have faith in the processes of children's construction of their own and shared meanings through individual activity and social interaction. This is a real challenge to the basic educational framework with which most schools are comfortable (Kamii & Housman, 1999).

Meaning is enhanced when teachers show that they value students' points of view, cause students to question their own and others' assumptions, challenge students with relevant problems, teach toward big ideas and enduring concepts, and engage students in assessing their own learnings.

3. Naiveté: Remaining Open to Learning

Young children are in a continuous learning mode. Their naiveté, in combination with their inquisitiveness, allows them to constantly search for new and better ways, always striving for improvement, always growing, always learning, always modifying themselves.

A great mystery about adults, however, is that we confront learning opportunities with fear rather than mystery and wonder. We seem to feel better when we know rather than when we learn. We defend our biases, beliefs, and storehouses of knowledge rather than inviting the unknown, the creative, and the inspirational. Being certain and closed gives us comfort, while being doubtful and open gives us fear.

Employing a curriculum of fragmentation, competition, and reactiveness, young students are trained to believe that deep learning means figuring out the truth rather than developing their capabilities for effective and thoughtful action. They are taught to value certainty rather than doubt, to give answers rather than to inquire, to know which choice is correct rather than to explore alternatives.

Creative people, who remain eager to learn, possess the humility of knowing that they don't know, which is the highest form of thinking they will ever learn. Paradoxically, unless learners maintain that naiveté, they will never succeed. So, as the first step, young learners already have what will eventually be the crowning glory of all learning: the humility to know—and admit—that they don't know and not be afraid to find out.

4. Self-Initiating: Internal Motivation

"I can do it myself!" Children strive to become autonomous, self-initiating, unique individuals. Children spend countless hours riding bicycles, playing baseball, mastering video games, and becoming engrossed in books. With their interest captured, they can focus for hours. They beg for five more minutes for playing or reading their favorite book. While children bring this natural motivation to school, their engagement typically drops as they progress through school. For students' motivation to thrive, they need authentic choices to awaken their natural interest and caring adults who make them feel supported and who help in making connections between their current learning and their prior knowledge (Carter, 2004).

That teachers must "motivate" students is a myth. Rather, teachers must create conditions that liberate and sustain students' natural, internal motivations. Teachers can do this by allowing students to pursue topics in which they are interested, having students work in groups, engaging all the senses, using technology, and providing rich tasks that challenge the intellect and engage their drive to create.

Schools tend to teach, assess, and reward convergent thinking and the acquisition of content within a limited range of acceptable answers. Life in the real world, however, demands multiple ways to do something well. A fundamental shift is required from valuing right answers to knowing how to behave when we *don't* know answers—knowing what to do when confronted with those paradoxical, confusing, discrepant, and sometimes overwhelming situations that plague our lives. We want students to learn how to develop a critical stance with their work: inquiring, thinking flexibly, and learning from another person's perspective.

5. Faith in Their Own Abilities

Efficacy is the quest for self-empowerment and mastery of our environment. Children have an abiding belief that they will succeed. If a child feels little efficacy, then blame, withdrawal, rigidity, and fear of failure are likely to accompany complex thinking and problem solving. With robust efficacy children are likely to expend more energy in their work, persevere longer, set more challenging goals, continue in the face of barriers, and learn from their experiences. Thus they enhance their problem-solving capacities over time.

For students who lack faith in their own abilities, unlike their peers who are motivated by challenge, avoiding failure becomes more important than striving to succeed. These students are only motivated if they believe the goal is attainable and give up if they think it is beyond their grasp. Inefficacious students attribute their successes and failures to different causes—ability, luck, or level of task difficulty. For students who believe they fail because they are unlucky, they are untalented, or the test was too difficult, helping them understand the connection between effort and success has been shown to make a difference in their learning. Children develop cognitive strategies and effort-based beliefs about their intelligence and higher-order learning when they are continually pressed to raise questions and to accept challenges, to find solutions that are not immediately apparent, to explain concepts, justify their reasoning, and seek information. When we hold children accountable for this kind of intelligent behavior, they take it as a signal that we think they are smart, and they come to accept this judgment. Children become smart by being treated as if they are intelligent already (Resnick & Hall, 1998).

6. Transparency of Self: Congruence
Between Beliefs and Actions

What children think and feel inside is presented on the outside in their behavior, words, and emotions. Adults, on the other hand, experience feelings, thoughts, and opinions, but choose not to expose them to others (Paulson, 1995). As children mature, they are admonished not to express their feelings. "Big boys don't cry." "Nice little girls don't say those things." "You shouldn't feel that way." As they become adults they develop the capacity to mask their emotions.

Integrity is defined as consistency between what people say and what they do and implies that a moral-ethical perspective guides one's actions. Later in life, as adults, these students will be judged by both their beliefs and actions, which requires that their values are validated through observed behavior.

Children are born innocent and pure—with a "clean slate" devoid of values and prejudices. Because all values and biases are products of modeling, investment by adults, the media, and society, the words that adults use, the actions they take in treatment of others, and their responses to problem situations are observed and imitated by children. As Robert Fulghum states, "Don't worry that children never listen to you; worry that they are always watching you!"

7. Sensory Learning: Intake Through All Senses

> I believe, but cannot prove, that babies and young children are actually more conscious, more vividly aware of their external world and internal life, than adults are. I believe this because there is strong evidence for a functional trade-off with development. Young children are much better than adults at learning new things and flexibly changing what they think about the world.
>
> Gopnik, Meltzoff, and Kuhl (1999)

From the moment they're born (and likely before) children are learning. All information gets into the brain through the sensory pathways—ears, eyes, skin, nose, and tongue. Developing most rapidly from birth to three years of age, a child's brain absorbs massive amounts of information and stimuli. Deep inside a baby's developing brain, tiny neurocircuits connect cells at an astonishing rate. Every taste, every touch, every interaction helps or hinders this process. Eventually these neurocircuits will help them speak, solve problems, and learn. But the circuits need to make good connections, and such connections depend on the quality of a child's earliest experiences. The more adults speak, sing, and read to the child, the faster the child's brain develops and the more a child learns. Positive interactions with humans and the environment result in the development of sound circuitry.

Young children naturally engage all their senses as they touch, feel, mouth, and rub various objects in their environment. They will request a story or rhyme be read again and again. They will act out roles and "be" the thing: a father, a flatbed, or a fish. "Let me see, let me see." "I want to feel it." "Let me try it." "Let me hold it." As children progress higher in the grades, however, instruction becomes more abstract, appealing to mainly visual and auditory senses. However, all of the sensory pathways must be kept open, alert, and acute so as to absorb maximum amounts of information from the environment. Otherwise those pathways become withered, immune, and oblivious to sensory stimuli.

As teachers plan lessons, they might search for ways to engage all the senses. In what ways does this lesson provide opportunities for visualizing, moving, hearing, tasting, smelling, and/or touching?

8. Openness to Feedback: Innate Desire to Improve and Achieve

Not only are young children gathering data through their senses, they also possess an innate but underdeveloped ability to observe themselves and their own impact on and control of the environment. An example is when, at about age 2, they discover the power of language as a tool to control and influence others: a question is asked and a response is given; a request is made and the need is fulfilled; a statement is made and a reaction occurs. These capacities for feedback are the building blocks of self-reflection, self-assessment, and self-modification.

Externally introduced feedback from teachers and tests, however, seems to shut down progress toward self-management and self-assessment. On the other hand, when students are involved in their own self-assessment, their learning is greater. The focus should be on increasing each child's capacity to become more self-managing, self-monitoring, and self-modifying (Costa & Kallick, 2004).

Very young children can become adept at developing their own criteria for success, rubrics, and checklists. When teachers involve students in generating their own benchmarks and standards, they become more aware of their own behavior and are more open to self-modification.

9. Playfulness: Finding Humor and Joyfulness

Have you ever watched a child chase a butterfly, play on a merry-go-round, or build then knock down sand castles? From a baby's first smile around their first month of age to their giggles, laughter, and squeals, children delight in finding objects and events humorous.

The salutary effects of humor are well known. The endorphins released during laughter have been shown to reduce feelings of pain, assist in social bonding, give us feelings of pleasure and happiness, and have significant ramifications for our psychological and physical health—even fighting off infections. Humor appears to be a universal coping mechanism we use when faced with stress.

Some students, however, find humor in all the "wrong places"—human differences, ineptitude, injurious behavior, vulgarity, violence, and profanity. They laugh at others yet are unable to laugh at themselves. We must nourish children's whimsical frame of mind being able to laugh at situations and at themselves by finding incongruities, perceiving absurdities, and recognizing ironies.

Not only should teachers help students analyze what makes something humorous, they should vow to have at least one good laugh a day with their students. As Charlie Chaplin said, "A day without laughter is a day wasted."

10. Wonderment and Awe

Rescued after being left to die on Mt. Everest, frost-bitten Dr. Beck Weathers (2001) reported his most important learning—more so than his accomplishments, credits, or degrees. He resolved to be more like young children, to experience his world with wonderment and awe!

Young children are awestruck by most of life's everyday events—the chirp of a cricket or a cell phone conversation with far-away relatives is a source of enchantment. Young children can be observed communing with the world around them, reflecting on the changing formations of a cloud; being charmed by the opening of a bud; sensing the logical simplicity of mathematical order. They find beauty in a sunset, intrigue in the geometrics of a spider web, and exhilaration in the iridescence of a hummingbird's wings. Their environment attracts their inquiry as their senses capture the rhythm, patterns, shapes, colors, and harmonies of the universe.

Some students, however, are overheard complaining, "It's boring." "When am I ever going to use this stuff?" or "Who cares?" By cultivating their sense of wonder they learn compassion toward other life forms as they grow to understand the need for protecting their environment, respecting the roles and values of other human beings, and perceiving the delicate worth, uniqueness, and relationships of everything and everyone they encounter. Wonderment, awesomeness, and passion: these are prerequisites for success.

Teachers often end a unit or lesson with a summary, an evaluation, or a task in which students exhibit their newly gained knowledge. Teachers might also ask such questions as, "Now that we have completed this unit, what will you continue wondering about?" "What intrigues you about this learning?" "What did you find mysterious that still puzzles you?" More important, however, is the teacher's display of his or her own enthusiasm, intrigue, and fascination for the subject. (I love my teacher and my teacher loves science, therefore I love science!)

REMEDIAL ZEST

There are many acceptable ways to remediate skills in reading and math so that no child is left behind: attending summer school, tutoring, online courses, computer-based instruction, etc. Restorative strategies for rejuvenating lost zest for learning, however, are more illusive. As educators, we must remain vigilant of student's continual love of learning and, if it is found waning, institute immediate action to recoup it.

Excellent teachers know how to conserve children's passion. They realize that learning tasks must be relevant and appealing to students' interests, various learning styles, and developmental levels. Superior teachers present challenges that engage students in a variety of authentic, rich activities that require the application of strategic planning, creative approaches, and multiple, complex thinking skills. They cause students to reflect on and apply their learnings to new and novel situations. They also realize that modeling is the most basic form of learning and therefore display their own enthusiasm and eagerness for continued learning.

IN SUMMARY

Drawing upon the skills learned in curriculum mapping (Jacobs, 1997), school staffs will want to map forward by identifying which of these innate learning attributes should be guarded, establishing benchmarks to inform progress along the way, and by composing assessment strategies such as anonymous questionnaires, interviews, rubrics, observations, and child study to monitor the preservation of these learning targets.

Children are born with a natural tendency to learn. They come to school with an inclination to discover, to question, and to wonder. Schooling may contribute to the extinction of that natural inquisitiveness. We must create a culture of vigilance in schools and classrooms where inquiry, investigation, and continuous learning are neither threatened nor extinguished. Through forward mapping, we must take responsibility for protecting and maintaining what is already there—that compelling drive of wonderment which humans carry forth with them throughout life.

> Born original, how comes it to pass that we die copies?
>
> Edward Young, 1687–1765

REFERENCES

Barell, J. (1988, April). *Cogitare*: *Newsletter of the ASCD Network on Thinking Skills.*
Bobbitt, F. (1918). *The curriculum.* Boston: Houghton Mifflin.

Carter, G. (2004, August). Tapping into student motivation. *Infobrief: Newsletter of the Association for Supervision and Curriculum Development.*

Costa, A., & Kallick, B. (2004). *Assessment strategies for self-directed learning.* Thousand Oaks, CA: Corwin Press.

Gopnik, A., Meltzoff, A., & Kuhl, P. (1999). *The scientist in the crib: Minds, brains, and how children learn.* New York: Morrow.

Jacobs, H. H. (1997). *Mapping the big picture: Integrating curriculum and assessment K-12.* Alexandria, VA: Association for Supervision and Curriculum Development.

Kamii, C., & Housman, L. (1999). *Young children reinvent arithmetic: Implications of Piaget's theory* (Early Childhood Education Series, Vol. X). New York: Teachers College Press.

Paulson, D. (1995, January/February). Finding the soul of work. *At Work: Stories Of Tomorrow's Workplace, 4*(1).

Popham, W. J. (2005, February). All about accountability/Students' attitudes count. *Educational Leadership, 62*(5), 84.

Resnick, L., & Hall, M. (1998, Fall). Learning organizations for sustainable education reform. *Journal of the American Academy of Arts and Sciences,* 89–118.

Senge, P. (1990, Fall). The leader's new work: Building learning organizations. *Sloan Management Review,* 7–23. *Tomorrow's Workplace, 4* (1; January/February).

Weathers, B. (2001). *Left for dead: My journey home from Everest.* New York: Random House.

Wiggins, G., & McTighe, J. (1998). *Understanding by design.* Alexandria, VA: Association for Supervision and Curriculum Development.

CHAPTER SEVEN

Changing Curriculum Means Changing Your Mind

> Insanity is continuing to do the same thing over and over and expecting different results.
>
> Albert Einstein

The Irish social commentator George W. Russell stated,

> When steam first began to pump and wheels go round at so many revolutions per minute, what are called business habits were intended to make the life of man run in harmony with the steam engine, and his movements rival the train in punctuality.

In the twenty-first century, this machine-model mentality still serves educators as a rationale for justifying curriculum decisions. Much like a dog chasing its tail, the level of adopted curriculum outcomes sets the intent of instruction and the focus of assessment. This cycle seals systems into a mindset that outcomes are significant because they are easily and immediately measured, barring consideration of working for more long-range, enduring, and essential learnings.

Based on this archaic, nineteenth-century, industrial, reductionist model, we have translated our curriculum and assessments into observable, measurable outcomes and performances. We are fascinated and enamored with

- The amount of time on task
- The number of questions asked at each level of Bloom's *Taxonomy*
- Gain scores on achievement tests
- Class size: numbers of students/ratio of students to adults
- Length of time in school/days in attendance/minutes of instruction
- IQ scores as a basis for grouping
- Percentages of objectives attained
- Numbers of competencies needed for promotion or graduation
- School effectiveness based on published test scores
- Numbers of A's and B's on report cards (often rewarded with cash)

As we enter an era in which knowledge doubles in fewer than five years, and the projection is that by the year 2020 it will double every 73 days, it is no longer feasible to anticipate the future information requirements for an individual. Our increasingly complex world is forcing us to use our brains more. We must think differently and deeply about what learning is of most worth.

> As we let go of the machine models of work, we begin to step back and see ourselves in new ways, to appreciate our wholeness, and to design organizations that honor and make use of the totality of who we are.
>
> Margaret Wheatley (1992)

SHIFTING MENTAL MODELS

The most critical, but least understood, component of school reform is the restructuring of curriculum—it is what drives everything else. We need, in the words of Michael Fullan (1993), to take a "quantum leap" in how we think about and develop curriculum. This chapter invites a shift in how we think about educational outcomes.

Some educators, legislators, and parents are perceptually bound by outmoded traditions, out-of-date laws, past practices, obsolete policies, and antiquated metaphors. Invested in their present ways of working, they believe that if they can just do what they are presently doing *better*— give more money to education, hire more teachers, extend the school year, mandate "high-stakes" testing, "toughen" teacher certification standards, hold schools more accountable—everything will improve.

For most people, changing mental models implies the unknown: the psychologically unknown risks of a new venture, the physically unknown demands on time and energy, and the intellectually unknown requirement for new skills and knowledge. Adopting a new vision demands a shift away from our traditional and obsolescent thinking about learning, teaching, achievement, and talent. The concepts in this chapter invite a shift in our present paradigm from quantity to quality. Changing our mental models will require patience, stamina, and courage.

SEVEN CURRICULUM MIND SHIFTS

What follows are descriptions of seven mind shifts needed for a more quantum conception of curriculum.

1. From Innate Intelligence to Effort-Based Learning

> What is intelligence if not the ability to face problems in an unprogrammed (creative) manner? The notion that such a nebulous socially defined concept as intelligence might be identified as a "thing" with a locus in the brain and a definite degree of heritability—and that it might be measured as a single number thus permitting a unilinear ranking of people according to the amount they possess is a principal error . . . one that has reverberated throughout the country and has affected millions of lives.
>
> Stephen Jay Gould (1981)

Changing our conception of intelligence is a relatively recent event. Such a change, however, is one of the most liberating and powerful forces in the restructuring of our schools, of education, and of society.

At the turn of the century, our society was undergoing great shifts. Masses of foreign immigrants poured into our coastal ports and moved inland to occupy the positions of the job-hungry Industrial Revolution. In retrospect we now realize we were an elitist, racist, and sexist society, fueled by the fear of diluting "Anglo-Saxon purity." A means was needed to separate those who were educable and worthy of work from those who should be relegated to menial labor.

World War I contributed to homogenizing classes, races, and nationalities. There was a need to analyze, categorize, separate, distinguish, and label human beings who were "not like us." Obviously, some means was necessary to measure individuals' and groups' "mental energy" to determine who was "fit" and who was not (Gould, 1981; Perkins, 1995).

With the mentality of mechanism, efficiency, and authority, everything needed to be measured. Lord Kelvin, a nineteenth-century physicist/astronomer stated, "If you cannot measure it, if you cannot express it in numbers, your knowledge is of a very meager and unsatisfactory kind."

Born in this era was the Theory of General Intelligence by Charles Spearman. The theory was based on the idea that intelligence is inherited through the genes and chromosomes and that it can be measured by one's ability to score sufficiently on Alfred Binet's Stanford-Binet Intelligence Test, yielding a static and relatively stable IQ score.

Based in the "efficiency" theories of the day, educators strived for the one best system for educational curriculum, learning, and teaching. In the scene of educational management entered Edward L. Thorndike from Columbia University. He went beyond theory to produce useable educational tools including textbooks, tests, curricula, and teacher training. Thorndike had, and continues to have, a tremendous influence on educational practice. His "associationist" theory suggests that knowledge is a collection of links between pairs of external stimuli and internal mental responses. Learning was thought to be a matter of increasing the strength of the "good" or correct bonds and decreasing the strength of the incorrect ones.

Spearman's and Thorndike's theories still serve educators as a rationale for justifying such standard operating procedures as tracking students according to high and low aptitude, the bell curve, drill and practice, competition, frequent testing, ability grouping, using IQ scores as a basis for special education, task-analyzing learning into separate skills, and reinforcement of learning by rewards and external motivations.

When people view their intelligence as a fixed and unchangeable entity, they strive to obtain positive evaluations of their ability and to avoid displaying evidence of inadequate ability relative to others. The individual's "intelligence" is demonstrated in task performance—they either have or lack ability. This negative self-concept influences effort. Effort and ability are negatively related in determining achievement—having to expend great effort is taken as a sign of low ability.

As Jacob Viner said, "When you can measure it, when you can express it in numbers, your knowledge is *still* of a meager and unsatisfactory kind."

If schools are to break out of this aptitude-centered traditional mentality, we need a definition of intelligence that is as attentive to robust habits of mind as it is to the specifics of thinking processes or knowledge structures—that ability is a continuously expandable repertoire of skills and that through one's efforts, intelligence grows incrementally. Incremental thinkers are likely to apply self-regulatory, metacognitive skills when they encounter task difficulties, to focus on analyzing the task and trying to generate and execute alternative strategies.

When people think of their intelligence as something that grows incrementally, they tend to invest energy to learn something new or to increase their understanding and mastery of tasks. They display continued high levels of task-related effort in response to difficulty. Learning goals are associated with the inference that effort and ability are positively related, so that greater efforts create and make evident more ability.

Children develop cognitive strategies and effort-based beliefs about their intelligence—the habits of mind associated with higher-order learning—when they are continually pressed to raise questions and to accept challenges, to find solutions that are not immediately apparent, to explain concepts, justify their reasoning, and seek information. When we hold children accountable for this kind of intelligent behavior, they take it as a signal that we think they are smart, and they come to accept this judgment. The paradox is that children become smart by being treated as if they already are intelligent (Resnick, 2001).

There is an increasing body of research dealing with factors that seem to shape these habits—factors that have to do with people's beliefs about the relation between effort and ability (Costa & Kallick, 2000; Fogarty, 2002; Perkins, 1995).

2. From Transmitting Meaning to Constructing Meaning

> The brain's capacity and desire to make or elicit patterns of meaning is one of the keys of brain-based learning. We never really understand something until we can create a model or metaphor derived from our unique personal world. The reality we perceive, feel, see and hear is influenced by the constructive processes of the brain as well as by the cues that impinge upon it.
>
> Merlin C. Wittrock (1986)

Meaning making is not a spectator sport. Knowledge is a constructive process rather than a finding. It is not the content stored in memory but the activity of constructing it that gets stored. Humans don't *get* ideas; they *make* ideas.

Meaning making is not just an individual operation. The individual interacts with others to construct shared knowledge. There is a cycle of internalization of what is socially constructed as shared meaning, which is then externalized to affect the learner's social participation. Constructivist learning, therefore, is viewed as a reciprocal process in that the individual influences the group and the group influences the individual (Vygotsky, 1978).

Our perceptions of learning need to shift from educational outcomes that are primarily an individual's collections of subskills to include successful participation in socially organized activities and the development of students' identities as conscious, flexible, efficacious, and interdependent meaning makers. We must let go of having learners acquire *our* meanings and have faith in the processes of individuals' construction of their own and shared meanings through individual activity and social interaction. That's scary, because the individual and the group may *not* construct the meaning we want them to: a real challenge to the basic educational framework with which most schools are comfortable.

3. From Compartmentalized Subjects to Transdisciplinary Learning

> There is an underlying unity . . . one that would encompass not just physics and chemistry, but biology, information processing, economics, political science, and every other aspect of human affairs. If this unity were real . . . it would be a way of knowing the world that made little distinction between biological science, physical science—or between either of those sciences and history or philosophy. Once, the whole intellectual fabric was seamless. And maybe it could be that way again.
>
> George A. Cowan, President of the Santa Fe
> Institute (quoted in Waldrop, 1992)

More than 350 years ago, Renee Descartes (1593–1650) classified knowledge into discrete compartments. He separated algebra from the study of geometry, distinguished meteorology from astronomy, and initiated the concept of hematology.

We are still operating under this obsolescent rubric. The organization of curriculum into these static compartments, while a helpful classification system for allocating time, hiring and training teachers, managing testing, purchasing textbooks, or organizing university departments, has probably produced more problems than benefits:

• Organizing curriculum around the disciplines limits teachers of different departments, grade levels, and disciplines from meeting together, communicating about, and finding connections and continuities among students' learnings.

• Certain disciplines are perceived to be of more worth than others. Through credit requirements, time allotments, allocation of resources, national, state and local mandates, standards, testing, and so on, schools send covert messages to students and the community concerning which subjects are of greater worth. This fractionalization across departments results in incongruent goals among the different people involved.

• The disciplines, as we have known them, may no longer exist. With the advent of increased technology and the pursuit of knowledge in all quarters of human endeavor, the separate disciplines are being replaced by human activities that draw upon vast, generalized, and transdisciplinary bodies of knowledge and relationships applied to unique, domain-specific settings. To be an archeologist today, for example, requires employment of radar and distant satellite infrared photography as well as understanding radioactive isotopes. Professions have combined multiple disciplines into unique and ever-smaller specialties: space biology, genetic technology, neurochemistry, astrohydrology.

- What distinguish the disciplines are their modes of inquiry. Each content has a logic that is defined by the thinking that produced it: its purposes, problems, information, concepts, assumptions, implications, forms of communication, technology, and its interrelationships with other disciplines. What makes a discipline a discipline is a disciplined mode of thinking (Paul & Elder, 1994). The terms *biology, anthropology, psychology,* and *cosmology,* for example, end in *-logy* which comes from the Greek, meaning "logic." Thus, bio-*logy* is the logic of the study of life forms. Psycho-*logy* is the logic of the study of the mind, and so on. All areas of study are topics of interest in which something has to be reasoned out. Mathematics means being able to figure out a solution to a problem using mathematical *reasoning.* Any subject must, therefore, be understood as a mode of figuring out correct or reasonable solutions to a certain range of problems.

- The disciplines deter transfer. Knowledge, as traditionally taught and tested in school subjects, often consists of a mass of knowledge-level content that is not understood deeply enough to enable a student to think critically in the subject and to seek and find relationships with other subjects. Immersion in a discipline will not necessarily produce learners who have the ability to transfer the concepts and principles of the discipline into everyday life situations. Students acquire the idea that they learn something for the purpose of passing the test, rather than accumulating wisdom and personal meaning from the content.

- The separations of the disciplines produce episodic, compartmentalized, and encapsulated thinking in students. When the biology teachers says, "Today we're going to learn to spell some biological terms," students often respond by saying, "Spelling—in biology? No way!" Biology has little meaning for physical education, which has no application to literature and has even less connection to algebra. They may be viewed as a series of subjects to be mastered rather than habituating the search for meaningful relationships and the application of knowledge beyond the context in which it was learned.

- The disciplines, presented as separate organized bodies of content, may deceive students into thinking they are incapable of constructing meaning. Students frequently have been indirectly taught that they lack the means to create, construct, connect, and classify knowledge. They are taught that organized theories, generalizations, and concepts of a particular discipline of knowledge are the polished products created by expert minds far removed from them. Thus students may think they are incapable of generating such information for themselves. While students are challenged to learn the information, the manner in which such information was created and classified often remains mysterious. All they can hope for is to acquire other people's meanings and answers to questions that someone else deems important.

If students are to transfer and apply their knowledge from one situation to another, to draw forth from their storehouse of knowledge and apply it in new and novel situations, the curriculum should capitalize on the natural interdependency and interrelatedness of knowledge.

We need, therefore, to put together teams of teachers who have been artificially separated by departments and to redefine their task from teaching their isolated content to instead developing multiple intellectual capacities of students. Peter Senge (1997) contends that we are all natural systems thinkers, and the findings in cognitive research are compatible and supportive of the need to move from individual to collective intelligence, from disciplines to themes, from independence to relationships.

4. From Knowing Right Answers to Knowing How to Behave When Answers Are Not Readily Apparent

> The habits of a vigorous mind are formed in contending with difficulties.
>
> Abigail Adams

Schools tend to teach, assess, and reward convergent thinking and the acquisition of content with a limited range of acceptable answers. Life in the real world, however, demands multiple ways to do something well. A fundamental shift is required from valuing right answers as the purpose for learning, to knowing how to behave when we *don't* know answers— knowing what to do when confronted with those paradoxical, dichotomous, enigmatic, confusing, ambiguous, discrepant, and sometimes overwhelming situations that plague our lives. An imperative mind shift is essential—from valuing knowledge *acquisition* as an outcome to valuing knowledge *production* as an outcome. We want students to learn how to develop a critical stance with their work: inquiring, thinking flexibly, and learning from another person's perspective. The critical attribute of intelligent human beings is not only having information, but also knowing how to act on it.

By definition, a problem is any stimulus, question, task, phenomenon, or discrepancy the explanation for which is not immediately known. Thus, we are interested in focusing on student performance under those challenging conditions that demand strategic reasoning, insightfulness, perseverance, creativity, and precision to resolve a complex problem.

As our paradigm shifts, we will need to let go of our obsession with acquiring content knowledge as an end in itself and make room for viewing content as a vehicle for developing broader, more pervasive, and complex goals such as personal efficacy, flexibility, craftsmanship, consciousness, and interdependence (Costa & Garmston, 2002).

We must finally admit that process *is* the content. The core of our curriculum must focus on such processes as learning to learn, knowledge production, metacognition, transference, decision making, creativity, and group problem solving. These *are* the subject matters of instruction. Content, selectively abandoned and judiciously selected because of its fecund contributions to the thinking/learning process, becomes the vehicle to carry the processes of learning. The focus is on learning *from* the objectives instead of learning *of* the objectives (Costa & Liebmann, 1997).

5. From Uniformity to Diversity

It is acceptance and trust that make it possible for each bird to sing its own song— confident that it will be heard—even by those who sing with a different voice.

B. Hateley and W. Schnidt (1995)

In simpler times, when citizens seldom ventured farther than a horseback ride from home, our perception of a learning community was one in which all people thought and acted in a similar fashion. In 1847 the first graded school was invented in the United States. Believing that all children were pretty much alike, students were grouped by age and assigned to a grade. Content was allocated to and expected to be taught in each grade level, and, by the end of each academic year, students should have mastered that content. Today we perpetuate this fable of uniformity with "one size fits all" schools, a *common* curriculum and *standardized* tests. We are spending enormous energies specifying and implementing grade-level performance standards and assessment strategies (Eisner, 1999).

Human beings, however, are made to be different. Diversity is the basis of biological survival. Each of us has a unique genetic structure, sole facial features, distinguishing fingerprints, a distinctive signature, a diverse background of experience and culture, and a preferred way of learning and expressing our information and knowledge. We even have a singular frequency in which we vibrate (Leonard, 1978). We know that human development proceeds at a variable rate and that divergence is obvious in the styles, perceptual abilities, and intelligences with which we gather and process information to make meaning from our environment.

Each of us came for a purpose unique to who we are and appropriate to the overall mosaic of life. It is time we value the individual for his or her natural skills and talents instead of trying to create clones all possessing the same abilities.

Noted science educator Paul Brandewein stated, "There is nothing so unequal as the equal treatment of unequals." We need to capitalize on these differences to enhance intellectual growth. Human diversity should naturally increase as students mature and make novel meanings from their learning experiences. Progress would be celebrated by recognizing increased uniqueness rather than comparison with a standard. Open-ended assessments would replace the treachery of standardization, competition, and accountability.

Interdependent learning communities are built not by obscuring diversity but by valuing the friction those differences bring and resolving those differences in an atmosphere of trust and reciprocity. Appreciation for diversity can be choreographed by deliberately bringing together people of different political and religious persuasions, cultures, gender, cognitive styles, belief systems, modality preferences, and intelligences. In an atmosphere of trust, structuring such diversity within decision-making groups not only enhances the decisions that are made but also stretches members' capacity for flexibility and empathy. Our old perceptions of uniformity need to yield in deference to valuing diversity—the true source of power in today's world.

6. From External Evaluation to Self-Assessment

> Are we educating students for a life of tests or for the tests of life?

Evaluation of learning has been viewed as summative measures of how much content a student has retained. It is useful for grading and segregating students into ability groups. It serves real estate agents in fixing home prices in relationship to published test scores.

Since process-oriented goals cannot be assessed using product-oriented measurement techniques, our existing evaluation paradigm must shift as well. Assessment should be neither summative nor punitive. Rather, assessment is a mechanism for providing ongoing feedback to the learner and to the organization as a necessary part of the spiraling processes of continuous renewal: self-managing, self-monitoring, and self-modifying. We must constantly remind ourselves that the ultimate purpose of evaluation is to have students learn to become self-evaluative. If students graduate from our schools still dependent upon others to tell them when they are adequate, good, or excellent, then we've missed the whole point of what self-directed learning is about.

Evaluation, the highest level of Bloom's *Taxonomy* (Bloom & Krathwohl, 1956), means generating, holding in your head, and applying a set of internal and external criteria. For too long, adults alone have been practicing that skill. We need to shift that responsibility to students—to help them develop the capacity for self-analysis, self-referencing, and self-modification. We should make student self-evaluation as significant an influence as external evaluations (Costa & Kallick, 1995).

7. From Motivating Others to Learn to Liberating the Human Innate Passion for Learning

> Children come fully equipped with an insatiable drive to explore and experiment. Unfortunately the primary institutions of our society are oriented predominantly toward controlling rather than learning, rewarding individuals for performing for others rather than cultivating their natural curiosity and impulse to learn.
>
> Peter Senge (1990)

Human beings are active, dynamic, self-organizing systems with an integration of mind, body, and spirit. According to Wheatley and Kellner-Rogers (1996), "Life's natural tendency is to organize. Life organizes into greater levels of complexity to support more diversity and greater sustainability" (p. 3).

One of the purest examples of a self-organizing learning system that organizes into greater levels of complexity is the young child. Infants and toddlers are in a constant state of exploring everything they can lay their hands, eyes, and lips on. They live in a state of continuous discovery: dismayed by anomaly, attracted to novelty, compelled to mastery, intrigued by mystery, curious about discrepancy. They derive personal and concrete feedback from their tactile/kinesthetic adventures. Their brains are actually being transformed with each new experience.

As children mature, the constraints of safety, family expectancies, cultural mores, and public decency demand that the child's natural tendencies of exploration be curbed. This provides both tensions and additional learnings as children become acculturated. Unfortunately, training in mental and emotional passivity starts with the first days of school. Traditional school learning may cause students to perceive that the purpose of acquiring knowledge is for passing tests on the content rather than accumulating wisdom and personal meaning from the content. Students learn to read someone else's static accounts of history, study abstract theories of science, and comprehend complex ideas unrelated to their own life experiences and personal aspirations. They perceive learning to be a game of mental gymnastics with little or no relevant application beyond the school to everyday living, further inquiry, or knowledge production.

From an early age, employing a curriculum of fragmentation, competition, and reactiveness, we are trained to believe that deep learning means figuring out the truth rather than developing capacities for effective and thoughtful action. We are taught to value certainty rather than doubt, to give answers rather than to inquire, to know which choice is correct rather than to explore alternatives.

Thus the child, whose natural tendency is to create personal meaning, is gradually habituated to think they are incapable of generating such information for themselves and that they lack the means to create and construct meaning on their own. Eventually students become convinced that knowledge is accumulated bits of information and that learning has little to do with their capacity for effective action, their sense of self, and how they exist in their world.

We must vow to serve and maintain this natural tendency of humans to inquire, experience, pattern, integrate, and seek additional opportunities to serve the human propensity for learning. A goal of education, therefore, should be to recapture, sustain, and liberate the natural self-organizing learning tendencies inherent in all human beings: curiosity and wonderment, mystery and adventure, humor and playfulness, connection finding, inventiveness and creativity, continual inquiry, and insatiable learning.

IN SUMMARY

> I can't understand why people are frightened by new ideas. I'm frightened of old ones.
>
> John Cage

If we accept that there is currently a shift away from the industrial model of society to a learning society, then our understanding of the focus of education also needs to shift. This change will require a movement away from a measurable, content-driven curriculum to a curriculum that provides individuals with the dispositions necessary to engage in lifelong learning. Simultaneously, the vision of the educator needs to shift from the information provider to one of a catalyst, model, coach, innovator, researcher, and collaborator with the learner throughout the learning process.

Mind shifts do not come easily, as they require letting go of old habits, old beliefs, and old traditions. There is a necessary disruption when we shift mental models. If there is not, we are probably not shifting; we may be following new recipes but we will end up with the same stew! Growth and change are found in "disequilibrium," not balance. Out of chaos, order is built, learning takes place, understandings are built, and gradually, organizations function more consistently as their vision is clarified, as their mission is forged, and their goals operationalized.

In the words of Sylvia Robinson, "Some people think you are strong when you hold on. Others think it is when you let go."

How strong are we?

> Of all forms of mental activity, the most difficult to induce is the art of handling the same bundle of data as before, by placing them in a new system of relations with one another by giving them a different framework, all of which virtually means putting on a different kind of thinking-cap for the moment. It is easy to teach anybody a new fact . . . but it needs light from heaven above to enable a teacher to break the old framework in which the student is accustomed to seeing.
>
> Arthur Koestler (1972)

REFERENCES

Bloom, B., & Krathwohl, D. R. (1956). *Taxonomy of educational objectives. Handbook I. Cognitive domain.* New York: David McKay.

Costa, A., & Garmston, R. (2002). *Cognitive Coaching: A foundation for Renaissance schools.* Norwood, MA: Christopher-Gordon.

Costa, A., & Kallick, B. (1995). *Assessment in the learning organization: Shifting the paradigm.* Alexandria, VA: Association for Supervision and Curriculum Development.

Costa, A., & Kallick, B. (2000). *Discovering and exploring habits of mind.* Alexandria, VA: Association for Supervision and Curriculum Development.

Costa, A., & Liebmann, R. (1997). *Envisioning process as content.* Thousand Oaks, CA: Corwin Press.

Eisner, E. (May, 1999). The uses and limits of performance assessment. *Phi Delta Kappan, 80*(9), 658–660.

Fogarty, R. (2002). *Brain compatible classrooms.* Thousand Oaks, CA: Corwin Press.

Fullan, M. (1993). *Change forces.* New York: Falmer.

Gould, S. J. (1981). *The mismeasure of man.* New York:

Hateley, B., & Schnidt, W. (1995). *A peacock in the land of penguins.* San Francisco: Berrett-Koehler.

Koestler, A. (1972). *The roots of coincidence.* New York: Vintage.

Leonard, G. (1978). *The silent pulse: A search for the perfect rhythm that exists in each of us.* New York: Bantam Books.

Paul, R., & Elder, L. (1994). All content has logic: That logic is given by a disciplined mode of thinking: Part I. *Teaching Thinking and Problem Solving, 16*(5), 1–4.

Perkins, D. (1995). *Outsmarting IQ: The emerging science of learnable intelligence.* New York: Free Press.

Resnick, L. (2001). Making America smarter: The real goal of school reform. In A. Costa (Ed.), *Developing minds: A resource book for teaching thinking.* Alexandria, VA: Association for Supervision and Curriculum Development.

Senge, P. (1990) *The fifth discipline.* New York: Doubleday.

Senge, P. (1997). Foreword. In A. Costa & R. Liebmann (Eds.), *Envisioning process as content* (pp. vii–xii). Thousand Oaks, CA: Corwin Press.

Waldrop, M. M. (1992). *Complexity: The emerging science at the edge of order and chaos.* New York: Touchstone.

Wheatley, M. J. (1992). *Leadership and the new science.* San Francisco: Berrett-Koehler.

Wheatley, M. J., & Kellner-Rogers, M. (1996). *A simpler way.* San Francisco: Berrett-Koehler.

Vygotsky, L. (1978). *Society of mind.* Cambridge, MA: Harvard University Press.

Wittrock, M. (1986). *Handbook of research on teaching* (3rd ed.). New York: Macmillan.

C H A P T E R   E I G H T

Teaching for, of, and About Thinking

> Treat people as if they were what they ought to be, and you help them to become what they are capable of being.
>
> Johann Wolfgang von Goethe

Standing the test of time, a most helpful and enduring guiding organizer for the teaching of thinking is in Ron Brandt's editorial preface to the September 1984 issue of *Educational Leadership.* In it he discusses a balanced program for the teaching of thinking to include three components. I interpret them as follows.

TEACHING *FOR* THINKING

Many authors and psychologists believe that children learn to think long before they come to school and that what educators need to do is to create the conditions for the natural, human inclination to think to emerge and blossom. Leslie Hart, in his book, *Human Brain, Human Learning* (1983), suggested that schools are "brain incompatible." Brewster Ghiselin (1952) and Howard Gardner (1982) in their studies of creativity found that what

SOURCE: Reprinted by permission. Costa, A. L. (2001). Teaching for, of and About Thinking. In A. L. Costa, *Developing minds: A resource book for teaching thinking* (3rd ed., pp. 354–358). Alexandria, VA: Association for Supervision and Curriculum Development.

young children do prior to entering school and what practicing scientists and artists do is more similar than anything that goes on in between. Indeed, Peter Senge (1990) states,

> Children come fully equipped with an insatiable drive to explore and experiment. Unfortunately the primary institutions of our society are oriented predominantly toward controlling rather than learning, rewarding individuals for performing for others rather than cultivating their natural curiosity and impulse to learn. (p. 7)

Teaching *for* thinking simply means that teachers and administrators examine, monitor, and strive to create school and classroom conditions that are conducive to children's thinking. This means that

1. Teachers *pose problems, raise questions*, and *intervene* with paradoxes, dilemmas, and discrepancies that challenge and engage students' minds.

2. Teachers *organize* the classroom for interaction by arranging the environment for large and small group collaborative problem solving.

3. Teachers and administrators *structure* the school environment for thinking—communicating it as a goal, valuing it, making time for it, securing a variety of materials—manipulatives, rich data sources, technology, and raw materials—to support it.

4. Teachers, administrators, and students make it a policy to *gather evidence of, reflect on, evaluate, report, and celebrate growth* in it.

5. Teachers and administrators *respond* to students' ideas in such a way as to maintain a school and classroom climate that creates trust, allows risk taking, is experimental, creative, and positive. This requires nonjudgmental listening to and probing students' and each other's ideas and assumptions.

6. Teachers, administrators, and all the significant adults in the school and home environments strive to improve and *model* the behaviors of thinking that are desired in students.

Accomplishing all of these would be a major undertaking in and of itself. That alone would go far in encouraging students to use their native intelligence. However, there's more. You're not teaching students to think yet.

TEACHING *OF* THINKING

Most authors and developers of major cognitive curriculum projects agree that direct instruction in thinking skills is imperative. Edward deBono (1991); Barry Beyer (1997); Reuven Feuerstein, Y. M. Rand, M. B. Hoffman, and R. Miller (1980); Arthur Whimbey and Jack Lochhead (1999); and

Matthew Lipman (1991) would agree on at least this one point: that the teaching of thinking requires that teachers instruct students directly in the processes of thinking. Even David Perkins believes that creativity can be taught—by design.

Standards of learning are often focused on one or more performances of such thinking operations. Following are some examples taken from the Commonwealth of Virginia's Standards of Learning (1995):

Grade 6 Reading/Literature:

The student will . . .
    Compare and *contrast* author's styles. (p. 68)

Grade 7 Civics and Economics

The student will *compare* the national, state, and local governments with emphasis on their structures, functions, and powers. (p. 90)

Grade 11 Research

The student will *analyze, evaluate, synthesize,* and *organize* information from a variety of sources into a documented paper dealing with a question, problem, or issue. (p. 75)

This may require the analysis of the subject areas or skills being taught in the curriculum, identifying the cognitive abilities prerequisite to mastery of those subject areas or skills, and then teaching those thinking skills directly.

In a science class, for example, the teacher or a lab workbook might pose a question: "What inferences might you draw from this experiment?" This assumes that students know what an inference is and how to make inferences from data. In a social sciences class, the teacher or text might pose the question, "What comparisons do you see in the lives of Abraham Lincoln and Fredrick Douglass?" This assumes that students know how to examine significant characteristics and to find similarities and differences between the two subjects. So that students might successfully complete such assignments, it is prerequisite that they know the procedural knowledge of how to compare, how to infer, how to draw logical conclusions, how to make a prediction, and so on.

Critical thinking skills might be taught directly during a social studies unit on the election process. Steps in the problem-solving process might be taught directly during math and science instruction. The qualities of fluency and metaphorical thinking might be taught directly during creative writing.

Nothing yet has been taught about the application of these thinking skills beyond the context in which they were learned in various thinking tasks such as information production, decision making, and problem solving. Such thinking tasks are also found in Standards of Learning. An example from Virginia illustrates the focus on thinking tasks that require the application of specific thinking operations and skills:

Grade 5 Computation and Estimation

The student will *create and solve problems* involving addition, subtraction, multiplication and division of whole numbers using paper and pencil, estimation, mental computation, and calculators. (p. 11)

While students may be able to perform the steps in the problem-solving process and correctly distinguish between classification and categorization, the question still remains, Do the students, however, have any inclination to use these skills in real-life situations? There's more.

Teaching of thinking not only includes teaching the steps and strategies of problem solving, creative thinking, and decision making, it also includes habituating those attitudes, dispositions, or habits of mind that characterize effective, skillful thinkers. Such habits are formed over time by encountering and applying them in a variety of settings and contexts.

Taking another example from the Virginia Standards of Learning (p. 33):

Students will be able to
Develop scientific dispositions and habits of mind including

- Curiosity
- Demand for verification
- Respect for logic and rational thinking
- Consideration of premises and consequences
- Respect for historical contributions
- Attention to accuracy and precision
- Patience and persistence

Teaching *of* thinking, therefore, means that these cognitive skills, operations, and dispositions are taught *directly*. Even with all of this—creating conditions for thinking and teaching it directly—there is still more.

TEACHING *ABOUT* THINKING

Teaching about thinking is composed of at least four components: (1) brain functioning, (2) metacognition, (3) great thinkers, and (4) epistemic cognition. A brief explanation of these may be helpful.

1. *Brain Functioning.* All of us, particularly adolescents, are fascinated by the intricacies, complexities, and marvels of our own bodies. Recently,

increasing neurobiological research has shed new light on how our brains work. Teaching *about* thinking would include investigating such curiosities as, How do we think? How does memory work? What causes emotions? Why do we dream? How do we learn? How and why do mental disorders occur? What happens when part of the brain is damaged? Such resources as Restak's book, *The Brain* (1984); Nancy Margulies's book, *Inside Brian's Brain* (1996); Susan Barrett's *It's All in Your Head* (1996); and Kapil Gupta's *Human Brain Coloring Book* (1997) would be helpful. Recent public television programs and the series, *The Brain*, have heightened this awareness; this series is available for use in schools. (See also, "The Brain," 2007.)

2. *Metacognition.* Being conscious of our own thinking and problem solving during the act of thinking and problem solving is known as metacognition. It is a uniquely human ability occurring in the neocortex of the brain. Interestingly, it has been found that good problem solvers do it—they plan a course of action before they begin a task, they monitor themselves during the execution of that plan, they back up or adjust the plan consciously, and they evaluate themselves upon completion. All of this is referred to as metacognition.

Metacognition in the classroom might be characterized by having discussions with students about what is going on inside their heads while thinking is occurring; comparing different students' approaches to problem solving and decision making; identifying what is known, what is needed to be known, and how to produce that knowledge; or having students think aloud while problem solving.

Metacognition instruction would include learning how to learn, how to study for a test, and how to use strategies of question asking before, during, and after reading. It might include helping students become acquainted with their own and others' learning styles, knowing about the intelligences in which they excel, their own learning preferences–visually, auditorily, kinesthetically—and what strategies to use when you find yourself in a situation that does *not* match your best learning modality.

3. *Great Thinkers.* Students should be exposed to others—scientists, artists, composers, anthropologists, philosophers—who solve problems well and whose products of creative and critical thought have left a significant and lasting impact on society: Einstein, Van Gogh, Mozart, da Vinci, Gandhi, Newton, Darwin, Pasteur, Franklin, Edison. Their logic, creativity, perseverance, and risk taking are models of the types of behavior we wish to instill in our youth.

It would be desirable if students would respect these traits in others—not only in such noteworthy scientists, artists, and historians—but also become sensitive to and appreciative of the productive and efficient thinking and problem solving of others on whom they depend for rationality: mechanics who use efficient and precise ways of repairing automobiles, parents who deal with irrationality by withholding their impulsivity, entrepreneurs who search for creative ways to offer innovative services and products, and, yes, even teachers who plan, monitor, evaluate, and strive to perfect their instructional skills.

4. *Epistemic Cognition.* Epistemology is the study of how knowledge is produced and the methods of inquiry of the various disciplines of science, anthropology, psychology, art, drama, poetry, economics, history, and so on. It might include discussions of such epistemological questions as

How does what scientists do differ from what artists do?

What are the processes by which scientific truths are discovered and proven?

What are the processes of inquiry used by anthropologists as they live with and study a culture?

What goes on inside a maestro's mind as he or she conducts an orchestra?

What was it about Mozart's genius that allowed him to "hear" a total musical composition before writing it down?

What is that process by which poets create?

Why can't we use processes of scientific inquiry to solve social problems?

Epistemic cognition is the study and comparison of the methods of the great artists, scientists, and scholars and the differential processes of investigation, inquiry, and creativity that underlie their productivity.

As an example, to engage epistemic cognition, the Michigan State Assessment of Educational Performance poses this question about global problems to students:

Select two problems shown on the graphic organizer (Figure 8.1). For each problem selected, describe how any one of the social scientists would look at that problem.

Matthew Lipman's program, "Philosophy for Children" (1991), is especially well suited for this. Other resources include David Perkins, *The Mind's Best Work* (1981); Carol Madigan and Ann Elwood, *Brainstorms and Thunderbolts* (1983); and Gardner, *Art, Mind, and Brain* (1982).

IN SUMMARY

A well-balanced program of teaching thinking, therefore, includes all three components:

1. *Teaching* for *thinking:* Creating, monitoring, and amplifying environmental conditions that maximize the possibility that innate thinking capacities will happen

Figure 8.1   Graphic Organizer

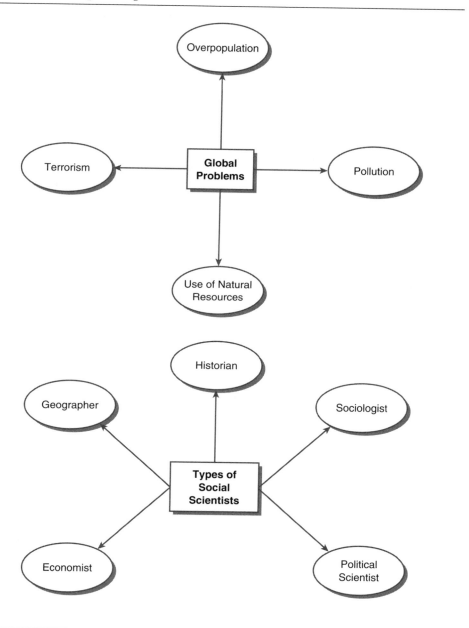

SOURCE: Costa (2001), p. 357.

2. *Teaching* of *thinking:* Directly, including the teaching of specific cognitive operations, how to perform thinking tasks—such as problem solving and decision making—skillfully, as well as habituating the dispositions or habits of mind that characterize skillful thinkers

3. *Teaching* about *thinking:* The attributes, conditions, and processes of human thought

REFERENCES

Barrett, S. (1996). *It's all in your head.* Minneapolis: Free Spirit.

Beyer, B. K. (1997). *Improving student thinking: A comprehensive approach.* Boston: Allyn and Bacon.

The brain: A user's guide. (2007, January 29). *Time* (entire issue).

Commonwealth of Virginia. (1995). *Standards of learning for Virginia public schools.* Richmond: Commonwealth of Virginia, Board of Education.

Costa, A. L. (2001). Teaching for, of, and about thinking. In A. L. Costa, *Developing minds: A resource book for teaching thinking* (3rd ed.; pp. 354–358). Alexandria, VA: Association for Supervision and Curriculum Development.

deBono, E. (1991). The CoRT Thinking Program. In A. Costa (Ed.), *Developing minds: Programs for teaching thinking.* Alexandria, VA: Association for Supervision and Curriculum Development.

Feuerstein, R., Rand, Y. M., Hoffman, M. B., & Miller, R. (1980). *Instrumental enrichment: An intervention program for cognitive modifiability.* Baltimore: University Park Press.

Gardner, H. (1982). *Art, mind, and brain.* New York: Basic Books.

Ghiselin, B. (1952). *The creative process.* New York: New American Library.

Gupta, K. (1997). *Human brain coloring book.* Princeton, NJ: Princeton Review.

Hart, L. (1983). *Human brain, human learning.* New York: Longmans.

Lipman, M. (1991). Philosophy for children. In A. L. Costa (Ed.), *Developing minds: Programs for teaching thinking* (Vol. II; pp. 35–38). Alexandria, VA: Association for Supervision and Curriculum Development.

Madigan, C., & Elwood, A. (1983). *Brainstorms and thunderbolts: How creative genius works.* New York: Macmillan.

Margulies, N. (1996). *Inside Brian's brain.* Tucson, AZ: Zephyr.

Perkins, D. (1981). *The mind's best work.* Cambridge, MA: Harvard University Press.

Restak, R. (1984). *The brain.* New York: Bantam Books.

Senge, P. (1990, Fall). The leader's new work: Building learning organizations. *Sloan Management Review,* 7–23. *Tomorrow's Workplace,* 4(1) (January/February).

Whimbey, A., & Lochhead, J. (1999). *Problem solving and comprehension.* Mahwah, NJ. Lawrence Erlbaum Associates.

CHAPTER NINE

Five Thoughts for a More Thought-Full Curriculum

As we enter an era in which knowledge doubles in less than 5 years, and the projection is that by the year 2020 it will double every 73 days, it is no longer feasible to anticipate an individual's future information requirements. We now have more information than the collective minds in science can understand. Our world has shifted away from an industrial model of society to a learning society. These changes require education to develop individuals with the knowledge, problem-solving skills, cognitive processes, intellectual dispositions, and habits of mind necessary to engage in lifelong learning.

Students in the third millennium must come fully equipped with the skills that enable them to think for themselves, to be self-initiating, self-modifying, and self-directing. They must acquire the capacity to learn and change consciously, continuously, and quickly. They will require skills beyond that of content knowledge. They must possess process skills beyond just fixing problems; rather, they must anticipate what might happen and search continuously for more creative solutions. Our society further recognizes a growing need for informed, skilled, and compassionate citizens who value truth, openness, creativity, interdependence, balance, and love as well as the search for personal and spiritual freedom in all areas of one's life. This demands that the schools' curriculum be open and flexible enough to accommodate these new perspectives.

SOURCE: Reprinted by permission. Costa, A. L. (2001). Introduction in A. L. Costa, *Developing minds: A resource book for teaching thinking* (3rd ed., pp. xv–xviii). Alexandria, VA: Association for Supervision and Curriculum Development.

We are at a time in education when professional educators are being pressured for immediate, measurable results on standardized performances (Colvin & Helfand, 2000). This assumes that if teachers taught academic subjects and if students were to learn and be evaluated on how well they learn the minute subskills in each content area, they would somehow become the kind of people we want them to become (Seiger-Eherenberg, 1991, p. 6). Our desire is to make learning and instruction more reflective, more complex, and more relevant to society's and students' diverse needs and interests now and in their future.

FIVE THOUGHTS ABOUT A THOUGHT-FULL CURRICULUM

Five pervasive themes or patterns may be found in a thought-full curriculum. They provide lenses through which the curriculum may be examined and organized. They may also constitute some "unfinished tasks," providing an agenda for action in building a more thought-full curriculum for a more thought-filled world.

1. Learning to Think

> Iron rusts from disuse; stagnant water loses its purity and in cold weather becomes frozen; even so does inaction sap the vigor of the mind.
>
> Leonardo da Vinci

All of us think. Indeed, we come to this earth with the capacity, ability, and inclination to think. Nobody has to "teach us how to think," just like no one teaches us how to move or walk. We do it innately when we are ready. Thinking, therefore, may be taken for granted.

However, it takes much time and coaching for human movement to be performed with precision, style, and grace. It takes years of practice, concentration, reflection, and coaching to become a superb ballerina, gymnast, or ice skater. Improvement is demonstrated by the increasing mastery of complex and intricate maneuvers performed repeatedly on command with sustained seemingly effortless agility. The distinction between awkwardness and grace is obvious to even the most undisciplined observer.

Like strenuous movement, effective, skillful thinking is also hard work. Similarly with proper instruction, human thought processes can become more broadly applied, more spontaneously generated, more precisely focused, more intricately complex, more metaphorically abstract, and more insightfully divergent. Such refinement also requires practice, concentration, reflection, and coaching. Unlike athletics, however, thinking is most often idiosyncratic and covert. Awkwardness and agility, therefore, are not as easily distinguished in thinking as they are in athletics. Definitions of thought process, strategies for their development, and assessment of the stamina required for their increased mastery are therefore illusive.

A thought-full curriculum serves to forge a common vision among all members of the educational community—educators and parents—of the characteristics of "critical thinkers," dispositions of intelligent human beings, qualities of "thought-full" people, and performances of efficient, effective, creative, and reasoned problem solvers.

Learning to think is enhanced when teachers make thinking skills explicit, labeling cognitive processes and habits of mind when they occur, employing thinking maps and diagrams, and modeling the steps of problem solving and decision making.

2. Thinking to Learn

> Learning is an engagement of the mind that changes the mind.
>
> Martin Heidegger

Meaning making is not a spectator sport. Knowledge is a constructive process rather than a finding. The brain's capacity and desire to make or elicit patterns of meaning is one of the keys of brain-based learning. We never really understand something until we can create a model or metaphor derived from our unique personal world. The reality we perceive, feel, see, and hear is influenced by the constructive processes of the brain as well as by the cues that impinge upon it. It is not the content stored in memory but the activity of constructing it that gets stored. Humans don't *get* ideas; they *make* ideas.

Content, therefore, should not be viewed as an end of instruction, but rather as a vehicle for activating and engaging the mind. Content is selected to serve as a vehicle for experiencing the joy ride of learning.

Furthermore, meaning making is not just an individual operation. The individual interacts with others to construct shared knowledge. There is a cycle of internalization of what is socially constructed as shared meaning, which is then externalized to affect the learner's social participation. Constructivist learning, therefore, is viewed as a reciprocal process in that the individual influences the group and the group influences the individual (Vygotsky, 1978).

Instructional strategies and techniques that encourage successful participation in group activities assist students in constructing their own and shared meanings. Teachers engage students' thinking by posing challenging questions and relevant problems, inviting student assessment of their own learnings, and maintaining a safe, nonjudgmental classroom atmosphere.

3. Thinking Together

> Friendship is one mind in two bodies.
>
> Mencius

A great problem facing education is caused by the fragmentation of thinking and acting—a way of thinking that divides and fails to see the interconnections and coherence of divergent views. Fixated on his or her own certainties, each stakeholder perceives the solution to educational reform from his or her individual perspective. Invested in present ways of working, many educators, parents, legislators, and board members believe that if we can just do what we are presently doing better—give more money to education, purchase more computers, hire more teachers, extend the school year, mandate "high-stakes" testing, reduce class size, "toughen" teacher certification standards, hold schools more accountable—everything will improve. People become convinced that their own perspective on the problem is essentially right and that others have it wrong. But thinking in this way prevents us from gaining a wider perspective—one that would enable all of us to determine what we are missing. This egocentric view hinders serious reflection and honest inquiry.

Therefore, another purpose of a thought-full curriculum is to stimulate dialogue as a means of building an "ecology of thought" (Isaacs, 1999)—a living network of memory and awareness that becomes a complex web linking community members together. This is difficult, because it means temporarily suspending what we individually think—relaxing our grip on our certainties and remaining open to new perspectives, entertaining other's points of view, and being willing to abide by and support the group's decisions arrived at through deep and respectful listening and dialogue. Out of this collective atmosphere, in which we think and work together, unfolds a fresh group intelligence that promotes action toward common goals.

Humans, as social beings, mature intellectually in reciprocal relationships. Collaboratively, individuals generate and discuss ideas eliciting thinking that surpasses individual effort. Together and privately, they express different perspectives, agree and disagree, point out and resolve discrepancies, and weigh alternatives. Because people grow their intellect through this process, collegial interaction is a crucial factor in the intellectual ecology of the school.

The essence of collegiality is when people work together to better understand how to work together. People are more likely to engage and grow in higher-level, creative, and experimental thought when they are in a trusting, risk-taking, and cooperative climate. Risk taking requires a non-judgmental atmosphere in which information can be shared without fear that it will be used for evaluative purposes.

Baker, Costa, and Shalit (1997) identify norms that may serve as standards that are understood, agreed upon, adopted, monitored, and assessed by each participant when working as a contributing member of a group. These norms become the glue that enables groups to engage in productive and satisfying discourse. Such norms include

1. *Pausing.* Taking turns is the ultimate in impulse control (Kotulak, 1997). In a discourse, space is given for each person to talk. Time is allowed before responding to or asking a question. Such silent time allows for more complex thinking, enhances all forms of discourse, and produces better decision making. Pausing is the tool that facilitative group members use to respectfully listen to each other.

2. *Paraphrasing.* Covey (1989) suggests we seek to understand before being understood. Paraphrasing lets others know that you are listening, that you understand or are trying to understand, and that you care.

3. *Probing and Clarifying.* These are effective inquiry skills to use when the speaker expresses vocabulary, uses a vague concept, or employs terminology that is not fully understood by the listener. The use of probing and clarifying is intended to help the listener better understand the speaker. In groups, probing and clarifying increases the clarity and precision of the group's thinking by clarifying understandings, terminology, and interpretations.

4. *Paying Attention to Self and Others.* Meaningful dialogue is facilitated when each group member is sensitive to and conscious of the subtle cues inside themselves and within the group. Paying attention to learning styles, modalities, and beliefs when planning for, facilitating, and participating in group meetings enhances group members' understanding of each other as they converse, discuss, deliberate, dialogue, and make decisions.

Thinking together demands a shift away from the confines of our own obsolescent conception of " me" to a sense of "us." People come to understand that as we transcend the self and become part of the whole we do not lose our individuality but rather our egocentricity. Achieving such an ecology of thought requires patience, stamina, and courage. The benefits, however, are resplendent.

4. Thinking About Our Own Thoughtfulness

I thank the Lord for the brain He put in my head. Occasionally, I love to just stand to one side and watch how it works.

Richard Bolles

Human beings, to the best of our knowledge, are the only form of life with the capacity for metacognition—the ability to stand off and examine their own thoughts while they engage in them. Although the human brain is able to generate reflective consciousness, not everyone seems to use it equally (Csikszentmihalyi, 1993). Thus a broader intent of a thought-full curriculum is heightened consciousness for all of us, not only students.

Thinking involves the whole of us—our emotions, our ways of feeling in the body, our ideas, our beliefs, our qualities of character, and our visions of being. Learning to think begins with recognizing how we are thinking now. Generally we are not all that conscious of how we are thinking. We can begin to think by listening first to ourselves and to our own reactions, to learn to watch how our thoughts encapsulate us. Much of what we think happens simply by virtue of our agreement that it should, not because of our close examination of our bounded assumptions, limited history, and existing mental models.

Descriptions of remarkable performers, effective thinkers, and analyses of the characteristics of efficacious people serve as mental disciplines not only for our students, but for each of us as well. When confronted with problematic situations we all must learn to habitually monitor our reactions by asking ourselves, "What is the most *intelligent thing* I can do right now?"

- How can I learn from this? what are my resources? how can I draw on my past successes with problems like this? what do I already know about the problem? what resources do I have available or need to generate?

- How can I approach this problem flexibly? How might I look at the situation in another way? how can I look at this problem from a fresh perspective? Am I remaining open to new possibilities and learnings?

- How can I illuminate this problem to make it clearer, more precise? Do I need to check out my data sources? How might I break this problem down into its component parts and develop a strategy for understanding and accomplishing each step?

- What do I know or not know? what questions do I need to ask? what strategies are in my mind now? what am I aware of in terms of my own beliefs, values, and goals with this problem? What feelings or emotions am I aware of that might be blocking or enhancing my progress?

- How is this problem affecting others? how can we solve it together, and what can I learn from others that would help me become a better problem solver?

Teachers can cause students to reflect on their own thoughtfulness by posing challenging problems and then having students describe their plans and strategies for solving the problem, sharing their thinking as they are implementing their plans, and then reflectively evaluating the effectiveness of the strategies that they employed.

5. Thinking Big

> I learned to make my mind large, as the universe is large, so that there is room for paradoxes.
>
> Maxine Hong Kingston

A thought-full curriculum serves a larger, more spiritual agenda. When the first astronauts went into space and looked back on Earth, they realized that there were no lines on the planet. The scars of national boundaries were gone. Dividing lines disappear when you get enough perspective. And yet, divisions still exist among people, children, nations, institutions, religions, and political ideologies.

A thought-full curriculum, therefore, builds a more thoughtful world as an interdependent learning community; where all people are continually searching for ways to trust each other, to learn together, and to grow toward greater intelligence. By caring for and learning from one another and sharing the riches and resources in one part of the globe to help the less fortunate others achieve their fullest intellectual potential:

• A world community that strives to generate more thoughtful approaches to solving problems in peaceful ways rather than resorting to violence and terrorism to resolve differences

• A world community that values human diversity of other cultures, races, religions, language systems, time perspectives, and political and economic views in an effort to bring harmony and stability

• A world of greater consciousness of our human effects on each other and on the Earth's limited resources in an effort to live more respectfully, graciously, and harmoniously in our delicate environment

• A world of better communication with other peoples, regardless of what language they speak, to employ clear and respectful dialogue rather than weapons to resolve misunderstandings

Teachers support students to "think big" when they inquire into such moral, ethical, and spiritual questions concerned with what makes human beings human; with what is beauty, what is good, and what is just.

A thought-full curriculum, therefore, supports a vision of classrooms, schools, communities, and indeed, a world that are more thoughtful places. We must learn to unite and not divide. As Alan Kay (1990) stated, "The best way to predict the future is to invent it."

If we want a future that is much more thoughtful, vastly more cooperative, greatly more compassionate, and a lot more loving, then we have to invent it. The future is in our schools and classrooms today.

> Destiny is not a matter of chance—it is a matter of choice. It is not a thing to be waited for—it is a thing to be achieved.
>
> William Jennings Bryan

REFERENCES

Baker, W., Costa, A., & Shalit, S. (1997). The norms of collaboration: Attaining communicative competence. In A. Costa & R. Liebmann (Eds.), *The process centered school.* Thousand Oaks, CA: Corwin Press.

Colvin, R. L., & Helfand, D. (2000, July 1). Millions for schools tied to Stanford 9 test scores. *Los Angeles Times*, pp. A20–A21.

Covey, S. (1989). *Seven habits of highly effective people.* New York: Simon and Schuster.

Csikszentmihalyi, M. (1993). *Flow: The psychology of optimal experience.* New York: Harper & Row.

Isaacs, W. (1999). *Dialogue and the art of thinking together.* New York: Doubleday/ Currency.

Kay, A. (1990). *The best way to predict the future is to invent it.* Keynote presentation delivered at the Annual Conference of the Association for Supervision and Curriculum Development. San Francisco, CA.

Kotulak, R. (1997). *Inside the brain: Revolutionary discoveries of how the mind works.* Kansas City, MO: Andrews McMeel.

Seiger-Eherenberg, S. (1991). Educational outcomes for a K-12 curriculum. In A. Costa (Ed.), *Developing minds: A resource book for teaching thinking.* Alexandria, VA: Association for Supervision and Curriculum Development.

Vygotsky, L. S. (1978). *Mind in society: The development of higher psychological processes.* Cambridge, MA: Harvard University Press.

PART III

Mindful Dialogue

Quality conversation among all inhabitants is a hallmark of the School that is becoming a Home for the Mind. They continually seek to improve their capabilities to listen to one another with understanding and empathy, to disagree gracefully, to take another's point of view, and to value each other's style differences.

Arthur L. Costa

C H A P T E R   T E N

Through the Lens of a Critical Friend

With Bena Kallick

You are seated in the darkened "dilating" room, waiting for the ophthalmologist to bring you into the office. The routine is familiar. Sit in the chair. Place your forehead against the machine. Tell whether you see the letters better or worse as the doctor changes the focusing lenses. This could be an analogy for assessment.

It is only when you change the lens through which you view student learning—or your own practice—that you discover whether a new focus is better or worse. But if you never change the lens, you limit your vision.

Sometimes your frustration mounts and you ask, "Can't you just tell me the right prescription?" Furthermore, you need another person to continually change your focus, pushing you to look through multiple lenses in order to find that "just right" fit for you, the ultimate owner of the glasses. But it is not entirely a matter of science. It requires the subjective perspective, "Which looks better or worse to *you?*"

As we work to restructure schools, we must increasingly ask the right questions and collect the appropriate evidence: we are constantly refocusing our work. The visit to the ophthalmologist suggests that no one perspective on student learning will be sufficient to assess a student's capabilities and performances. It might also suggest that assessment feedback should provide as clear a vision as possible about the learning performance *in the*

SOURCE: Reprinted by permission. Costa, A. L., & Kallick, B. (1993, October). Through the lens of a critical friend. *Educational Leadership, 51*(2), 49–51. Alexandria, VA: Association for Supervision and Curriculum Development.

> Assessment feedback should provide as clear a vision as possible about the learning performance *in the eyes of the learner.*

eyes of the learner. And, it illustrates how assessment requires someone who will provide new lenses through which learners can refocus on their work, namely, a critical friend.

CRITICAL FRIENDS

The role of critical friend has been introduced in many school systems that see themselves as learning organizations and know that learning requires assessment feedback (Senge, 1990). A critical friend provides such feed-

> Every student—and educator, too—needs a trusted person who will ask provocative questions and offer helpful critiques.

back to an individual—a student, a teacher, or an administrator—or to a group. A critical friend, as the name suggests, is a trusted person who asks provocative questions, provides data to be examined through another lens, and offers critique of a person's work as a friend. A critical friend takes the time to fully understand the context of the work presented and the outcomes that the person or group is working toward. The friend is an advocate for the success of that work.

> We often forget that Bloom refers to critique as a part of evaluation, the highest order of thinking.

Because the concept of critique often carries negative baggage, a critical friendship requires trust and a formal process. Many people equate *critique* with *judgment,* and when someone offers criticism, they brace themselves for negative comments. We often forget that Bloom refers to critique as a part of evaluation, the highest order of thinking (Bloom et al., 1956).

Critical friendships, therefore, must begin through building trust. The person or group needs to feel that the friend will

- Be clear about the nature of the relationship, and not use it for evaluation or judgment;
- Listen well: clarifying ideas, encouraging specificity, and taking time to fully understand what is being presented;
- Offer value judgments only upon request from the learner;
- Respond to the learner's work with integrity; and
- Be an advocate for the success of the work.

THE CRITICAL FRIENDS PROCESS

Once trust has been established, the critical friend and the learner meet together in a conference. Time for this conference is flexible, but we found it useful to limit the conference to 20 minutes. Once critical friends are accustomed to the structure, the time may be shortened. One successful process to facilitate conversation is the following:

1. *The learner* describes a practice and requests feedback. For example, a teacher might describe a new problem-solving technique, or a student might describe a project being considered.

2. *The critical friend* asks questions in order to understand the practice described and to clarify the context in which the practice takes place. For example, the friend may ask the learner, "How much time did you allow for the students to do problem solving?" or "What do you hope other people will learn from your project?"

3. *The learner* sets desired outcomes for this conference. This allows the learner to be in control of the feedback.

4. *The critical friend* provides feedback about what seems *significant* about the practice. This feedback provides more than cursory praise; it provides a lens that helps to elevate the work. For example, the teacher's critical friend might say, "I think it's significant that you're asking students to do problem solving because it will help them become more self-directed." The student's critical friend might say, "I think your project will be significant because you are trying to bring a new insight into the way people have understood the changing role of women in the United States."

5. *The critical friend* raises questions and critiques the work, nudging the learner to see the project from different perspectives. Typical queries might be, "What does the evidence from your students' work indicate to you about their capacity to do problem solving?" or "When you do this project, how will you help others follow your presentation?" One second grade student said to his partner, "You might want to glue the objects. It needs to be neater."

6. *Both participants* reflect and write. The learner writes notes on the conference—an opportunity to think about points and suggestions raised. For example, the learner may reflect on questions such as, "Will changes make this work better or worse?" "What have I learned from this refocusing process?" The critical friend writes to the learner with suggestions or advice that seem appropriate to the desired outcome. This part of the process is different from typical feedback situations in that the learner does not have to respond or make any decisions on the basis of the feedback. Instead, the learner reflects on the feedback without needing to defend the work to the critic.

CRITICAL FRIENDS IN MANY SETTINGS

Critical friends are useful in various educational situations: in classrooms, in staff development meetings, and between administrators.

In the Classrooms. Students use the critical friends process in the classroom for feedback on their writing, project work, and oral presentations. The process provides a formal way for students to interact about the substantive quality of their work. They read one another's texts as peer editors and critics. Their conferences make the role of assessor part of the role of learner.

In Staff Development. Teachers use critical friends to plan and reflect on their own professional development. A critical friends group can consist of as many as six people who meet and share practices, perhaps every other week. Some teachers do this during their planning time. Although only one person may have time to share a practice in each meeting, instead of the usual show-and-tell sharing, the critical friends process allows teachers to understand one another's work at a deeper level.

Between Administrators. Administrators often find themselves too busy to reflect on their practices. In addition, they are isolated from one another. To counteract these tendencies, some administrators have designed critical friendships into their working relationships, calling upon colleagues for critique. One superintendent called upon her board from time to time to be her critical friends.

The purpose of this new role of critical friend in assessment is to provide a context in which people receive both critical and supportive responses to their work. For example, a superintendent was recently called to make a presentation to her board. She was warned that certain members of the board were difficult. When she entered the meeting, the superintendent said that she hoped the board would not sit as a panel of judges but rather as a group of critical friends who would help her ask the best possible evaluation questions for the proposed project. The board, taken off guard, responded favorably. During reflection time, members were able to offer their concerns. As a result, in the privacy of the superintendent's own reflection, she was able to reassess her work in light of the issues that were raised.

The art of criticism is often overlooked in school life. In theater, literature, and dance, a good critic can maintain and elevate the standards of performance. In fact, most performing artists have an outside editor built into their work, and over time, they internalize criticism sufficiently so that they are able to become more sharply self-evaluative (Perkins, 1991).

Introducing the role of critical friends into the layers of a school system will build a greater capacity for self-evaluation as well as open-mindedness to the constructive thinking of others. As we begin to look through many lenses, we learn to ask the question, "Better or worse?" Critical friends help us change our lenses and ask this question.

REFERENCES

Bloom, B. S., et al. (1956). *Taxonomy of educational objectives: Handbook 1: Cognitive domain.* New York: David McKay.

Perkins, D. N. (1991). What creative thinking is. In A. L. Costa (Ed.), *Developing minds: A resource book for teaching thinking* (Vol. 1, rev. ed.). Alexandria, VA: Association for Supervision and Curriculum Development.

Senge, P. (1990). *The fifth discipline: The art and practice of the learning organization.* New York: Doubleday.

CHAPTER ELEVEN

Cognitive Coaching^{SM}

Conversations That
Mediate Self-Directedness

With Robert J. Garmston

> While it causes considerable anguish for us, no one can compel others to learn. The gate of learning can only be unlocked from the inside. We cannot open that gate either by admonition, argument or emotional appeal.
>
> Marilyn Ferguson[1]

Cognitive coaches consistently, congruently, and with clear intention work toward the mission of Cognitive Coaching^{SM}: "to produce self-directed persons with the cognitive capacity for high performance both independently and as members of a community."[2]

They use selected verbal and nonverbal behaviors in efforts to promote the development of self-directedness and excellence in their own and others' performance.

Cognitive coaches draw upon a wide range of supportive knowledge from research in the neurosciences, studies of interpersonal behavior, and cognitive psychology. Knowing the mission and building on these foundations, the identity of a coach becomes that of a mediator—facilitating the cognitive growth of others toward the achievement of this mission.

SOURCE: Adapted from Costa, A., & Garmston, R., *Cognitive Coaching: A Foundation for Renaissance Schools,* copyright © 2002, pp. 157–167. Reprinted with permission from Christopher-Gordon Publishers.

In this chapter, we describe what it means to assume the identity of a mediator; define self-directedness; stress the importance of structured, professional conversations as a means of enhancing and enlarging another person's perceptions, beliefs, and concepts; and illustrate how a coach's conscious use of certain verbal and nonverbal skills can engage and transform (mediate) another person's cognitive growth.

BEING A MEDIATOR

The word *mediate* is derived from the word *middle*. Therefore, mediators interpose themselves between a person and some event, problem, conflict, challenge, or other perplexing situation. Based on the work of Reuven Feuerstein's "Mediated Learning Experience,"[3] the mediator intervenes in such a way as to enhance another person's self-directed learning.

Feuerstein suggests that human learning is a matter of strengthening internal knowledge structures. Planning for and reflecting on experience activates these knowledge structures. With mediation, existing knowledge structures can be made more complex through more connections. The structures also can be altered to accommodate new understandings, or they can be made obsolete because some new experience has caused the creation of a new knowledge structure. This sifting and winnowing of prior knowledge structures constitutes learning.

As Feuerstein states,

> Mediated learning is an experience that entails not just seeing something, not just doing something, not just understanding something, but also experiencing that thing at deeper levels of cognitive, emotional, attitudinal, energetic, and affective impact through the interposition of the mediator between the learner and the experienced object or event (stimuli). In such a context, learning becomes a deeply structured and often a pervasive and generalizable change.[4]

Mediators influence the intensity, flow, directionality, importance, excitement, and impact of information coming to the awareness of the person being coached. One way they do that is by posing questions that bring consciousness to the visual, auditory, and kinesthetic systems in which experiences are held. This activates the neural pathways of the original experience, and in looking back, recovers omitted and sometimes valuable information. For example, a teacher might be asked to recall events of a lesson. Should the teacher report only what she remembered seeing, the coach might ask her to elaborate about what she also heard. Such a mediated learning experience enhances the detail and quality of information necessary for self-assessment. Accuracy in self-assessment is a critical prerequisite to self-directed learning.

Rather than give advice to or solve problems for another person, a mediator helps the colleague analyze a problem and develop his or her own problem-solving strategies. A mediator helps a colleague set up strategies for self-monitoring during the problem-solving process. Acting as a sounding board, a skilled mediator also helps another person become more self-directed with learning. A mediator

- Is alert to the mediational moment—usually when a colleague is faced with a complex task, dilemma, discrepancy, or conflict. Often, the colleague exhibits tension and anxiety, the resolution of which is not immediately apparent.

- Facilitates mental processes for others as they understand more completely their own challenges, make their own decisions, and generate their own creative capacities.

- Invites the colleague to reflect on and learn from the problem-resolving process to find applications in future challenges.

- Helps others become continuous self-directed learners.

- Maintains faith in the human capacity for continuing intellectual, social, and emotional growth.

- Possesses a belief in his or own capacity to serve as an empowering catalyst for others' growth.

Feuerstein (2000) believes that mediation produces new connections in the brain. He states

One of the most interesting and exciting aspects of mediated learning . . . is that the quality of interaction not only changes the structure of behavior of the individual, not only changes the amount and quality of his repertoire, but—according to increasingly powerful sources of evidence from fields of neurophysiology and biochemistry—changes the structure and functioning of the brain itself in very meaningful ways.[5]

Neuroscientist Gerald Edelman proposes that the brain reconstructs itself from experience. One commonly understood example of this is the neural pruning that occurs within the first two years of life, cauterizing neural capacities for distinguishing sounds outside one's own language group.[6] Ornstein claims that "to make a personal change, we have to be able to observe the automatic workings inside ourselves."[7] This requires the kind of consciousness evoked by mediation. He describes the brain as having a neural selection system that wires up the nervous system differently depending on the demands on the organism. Managing and developing the mind is to bring automatic processes into consciousness.

Ian Jutes reports that over the past 20 years, as a result of new scanning techniques and combined with neuroscience and neurobiology research, the brain is highly adaptive, and is constantly reorganizing itself based on the intensity and duration of input or experience. This means, says Jutes, that you can change processing power, and reorganize brain circuitry throughout your life.[8]

What Do We Mean by Self-Directedness?

A self-directed person can be described as being

- *Self-Managing.* They approach tasks with clarity of outcomes, a strategic plan, and necessary data. They draw from past experiences, anticipate success indicators, and create alternatives for accomplishment.

- *Self-Monitoring.* They establish metacognitive strategies to alert the perceptions for in-the-moment indicators of whether the strategic plan is working or not and to assist in the decision-making processes of altering the plan.

- *Self-Modifying.* They reflect on, evaluate, analyze, and construct meaning from the experience and apply the learning to future activities, tasks, and challenges.

Self-directed people are resourceful. They tend to engage in cause-effect thinking, spend energy on tasks, set challenging goals, persevere in the face of barriers and occasional failure, and accurately forecast future performances. They proactively locate resources when perplexed.

Seeking constant improvement, they are flexible in their perspectives and are optimistic and confident with self-knowledge. They feel good about themselves, control performance anxiety, and translate concepts into action.

Structured Professional Conversations

> The talking cure can physically change the brain and anytime you have a change in behavior you have a change in the brain.
>
> Lewis Baxter

In any organization, whether it be educational, corporate, or military, there is a constant "din" of idle chitchat. This is not a criticism but rather reality. Such dialogue is what makes groups congenial: birthdays, births, bad hair days, and bloopers. All essential for welding individuals into bonded groups. It is not necessarily, however, growth producing. We also need structured professional conversations. David Perkins believes that an organization functions and grows through conversations and that the quality of those conversations determines how smart an organization is.[9]

Coaching Skills to Engage Self-Directedness

Being conscious of their purpose to create self-directedness in others, cognitive coaches seize opportunities, both planned and informal, to use their behaviors deliberately to achieve these goals. For example, when a colleague is planning an event such as teaching a lesson, conducting a professional development meeting, anticipating a parent-teacher conference, or envisioning a school board meeting, the cognitive coach carefully constructs and poses questions intended to engage the mental processes of self-management. Those questions are invitational, open ended, and cognitively complex, as shown by the examples in Table 11.1.

Furthermore, the coach poses questions (see Table 11.2) so that during the event, the planner's perceptions will be alerted to cues that would indicate

Table 11.1   Coach's Questions for Self-Managing

Self-Managing People Approach Tasks With	Examples of Coach's Questions:
Clarity of outcomes	What specifically do you want students to know or be able to do as a result of this lesson?
A strategic plan	How does this lesson today contribute to your long-range goals or outcomes for your students?
Necessary data	Given what you know about your students' various learning styles, what alternative strategies are you considering?
Knowledge drawn from past experiences	What effective strategies have you used before in situations like this?
Awareness of alternatives for accomplishment	What might be some alternative instructional strategies you have in mind to accomplish these goals?
Anticipation of success indicators	What might you hear students saying or see them doing that will let you know that you've reached your goals?

whether the strategic plan is working or not and to assist in the conscious application of metacognitive strategies for deciding to alter the plan and select alternatives.

After the event, and if conditions are favorable, the coach will also take advantage of this opportunity to invite reflection and to maximize meaning making from the experience (see Table 11.3). Meaning is made by analyzing feelings and data, comparing results with expectations, finding causal factors, and projecting ahead to how the meaning may apply to future situations.

Table 11.2   Coach's Questions for Self-Monitoring

Self-Monitoring People:	Examples of Coach's Questions:
Establish metacognitive strategies to alert the perceptions for in-the-moment indicators of whether the strategic plan is working or not and to assist in the decision-making processes of altering the plan	What will guide your decisions about . . . ? What are some of your predictions about how this lesson will turn out? What will you be aware of to let you know that this lesson is working?

Table 11.3   Coach's Questions for Self-Modifying

Self-Modifying People:	Examples of Coach's Questions:
Reflect on	As you reflect on this lesson, what feelings (or thoughts, or impressions) do you have about it?
Recall Evaluate	What are you recalling that leads to those impressions? What is your sense of the lesson's effectiveness?
Analyze	What might be some factors that contributed to the lesson's success? How does what happened in the lesson compare to what you predicted would happen?
Construct meaning from the experience	As a result of this lesson, what insights or new learning are you forming?
Apply the learning to future activities, tasks, and challenges	As you anticipate future lessons of this type, what big ideas will you carry forth to those situations?

COACHING TOOLS THAT BUILD TRUST AND RAPPORT

Coaches know that the neocortex of the brain shuts down by degrees under stress. The greater the stress, the greater the shutdown.[10] Under great stress, we lash out, run away in terror, or freeze up. Physical rapport, subtleties of body language, voice tone, pausing, implied value judgments, and embedded presuppositions in our language all have an effect on the comfort and thinking of others. To communicate with skill and grace, the cognitive coach communicates with the total body-brain system. The systems that process nonverbal signals and feelings are as important to thinking processes as they are to establishing a trusting relationship necessary for self-reflective learning.

Trust is about the whole of a relationship; rapport is about the moment. Trust is belief in and reliance on another person's consistency, skills, and integrity developed over time. Rapport is comfort with and confidence in someone during a specific interaction. While rapport may be naturally present, cognitive coaches consciously seek it when they are meeting a parent, student, or colleague for the first time. Cognitive coaches know they cannot manipulate someone into a relationship of trust and rapport, but they can draw on specific nonverbal and verbal behaviors to nurture the relationship.

For example, direct eye contact, a concerned voice, and facial expression are better at conveying empathy than are words.[11] In addition, the coach's matching of gestures, postures, or voice qualities contributes to rapport. Some scientists refer to this phenomenon as "mental state resonance" when people are in a form of alignment. Taken together, these have an enormous impact on feelings of connectedness and rapport. Such an alignment permits a nonverbal form of communication that the other person is being "understood" in the deepest sense; they are "feeling felt" by another person.[12] Under these conditions, permission is being tacitly given for coaching. The safer one feels, the greater the access to neocortical functioning.[13]

When people experience stress, there is an altered blood flow and changes in activity patterns in the brain. The body-mind functioning is minimized. The person is less flexible and more predictable, and survival patterns override pattern-detection and problem solving. People "lose their train of thought" and resourcefulness. The coach knows that all communications are important and pays attention to physical signals. States of even mild stress show up in the body. Alert to these cues, coaches use this information to modify their own behavior. Noticing nervousness, they may scan body systems—their own and the colleague's—looking for areas of congruence. Where mismatching occurs, the coach will come into nonverbal alignment to help the colleague.

Response Behaviors

Skillful coaches intent on engaging the mind are aware of employing and monitoring their own use of certain nonjudgmental response behaviors. Their intent is to enhance the quality of communications, model skillful listening, and create a feeling of trust and rapport with their colleagues. While nonverbal communications may convey much of the meaning in an exchange, the words coaches choose—and how they state them—also have a strong effect. Coaches create a nonjudgmental environment in which others feel safe to experiment and risk. This environment can be partially created through the response behaviors of silence, acknowledging, paraphrasing, probing, providing data, and structuring.

Pausing (Silence, Wait-Time). Using wait-time before responding to or asking a question allows time for more complex thinking, enhances dialogue, and improves decision making. Pausing during the conversation allows the listener to breathe while the message is delivered. This enhances message delivery and acceptance. Breathing is essential for supporting cognition. Importance of breathing can best be understood by recognizing that the human brain is approximately 3 percent of body mass and can consume up to 37 percent of the oxygen. When we hold our breath, the carbon dioxide levels in the blood increase. The body reacts to the carbon dioxide increase much in the same way that it responds to threat by releasing hormones that support the fight-or-flight response. In addition, the human brain is hardwired to detect threat, which results in decreasing blood flow to the frontal lobes and increasing flow to the brain stem. When we hold our breath or perceive a threat, thinking is negatively impacted.[14] Action, not thought, becomes the priority. Pausing in appropriate places during the delivery of content supports group breathing and establishes a low-threat environment, thus allowing both presenter and audience to think more clearly and effectively.[15]

Sometimes periods of silence seem interminably long. But if trust is the goal, teachers must have the opportunity to do their own thinking and problem solving. A coach's silence after asking a question communicates, "I regard you as sufficient; I trust your processes and knowledge; also I trust that you know best the time you need to formulate a response."

Paraphrasing. One function of a paraphrase is to acknowledge another person's communication. In this sense, paraphrasing is a strong trust builder. When people feel they are being understood, they breathe more deeply. Deeper breathing provides more oxygen to the brain. As stated earlier, oxygen is an essential resource for thinking. At another level, we believe that a series of empathic paraphrasing changes blood chemistry and helps to maintain the person being coached in a resourceful state.

Paraphrasing lets others know that the coach is listening, that he or she understands or is trying to understand them and that the coach cares. Since a well-crafted paraphrase communicates, "I am trying to understand you— and therefore, I value what you have to say" and establishes a relationship between people and ideas, questions preceded by paraphrases will be perceived similarly. Questions by themselves, no matter how artfully constructed, put a degree of psychological distance between the asker and the asked. Paraphrasing aligns the parties and creates a safe environment for thinking.

Mediational paraphrases reflect the speaker's content and the speaker's emotions about the content and frame a logical level for holding the content. The paraphrase reflects content back to the speaker for further consideration and connects that response to the flow of discourse emerging within the group. Such paraphrasing creates permission to probe for details and elaboration. Without the paraphrase, probing may be perceived as interrogation.

To paraphrase effectively, coaches must

• *Listen and observe* carefully to calibrate the content and emotions of the speaker.

• *Signal their intention* to paraphrase. This is done by modulating intonation with the use of an approachable voice and by opening with a reflective stem. Such stems put the focus and emphasis on the speaker's ideas, not on the paraphraser's interpretation of those ideas.

For example, reflective paraphrases should not use the pronoun "I." The phrase "What I think I hear you saying . . ." signals to many speakers that their thoughts no longer matter and that the paraphraser is now going to insert his or her own ideas into the conversation. Instead, the following paraphrase stems signal that a paraphrase is coming:

• You're suggesting . . .
• You're proposing . . .
• So, what you're wondering . . .
• So, you are thinking . . .
• Um, you're pondering on the effects of . . .
• So, your hunch is . . .

Choose a logical level with which to respond. There are three broad categories of logical levels.[16]

1. Acknowledge and clarify content and emotion. If the paraphrase is not completely accurate, the speaker will offer corrections: "So, you're concerned about the budgeting process and way to get input early on."

2. Summarize and organize by offering themes and containers to organize several statements or separate jumbled issues. This is an especially important form of paraphrase to use when multiple speakers contribute to a topic: "We all seem to be concerned about two issues here. One is

resource allocation and the other is the impact of those decisions on student learning."

3. Shift focus to a higher or lower logical level. Paraphrasing within a flow of discourse often moves through a sequence of acknowledging, summarizing, and shifting focus to a higher or lower logical level. Paraphrases move to a higher logical level when they name concepts, goals, values, and assumptions: "So a major goal here is to define fairness in the budgeting processes and compare those criteria to the operating values of the school." Paraphrases move to a lower logical level when abstraction and concepts need grounding in details: "So 'fair' might mean that we construct a needs assessment form for each department to fill out and submit to the site for public consideration."

Acknowledging. To acknowledge is not to agree but to signal "I got your communication" or "I got your communication and am understanding it from your viewpoint." In North American cultures, this is accomplished by nodding the head or using "subverbals" like the phrase "uh huh." Not all cultures use these cues, however.

Probing and Clarifying. Clarifying signals that the coach cares enough to want to understand what a colleague is saying. Clarifying is not meant to be a devious way of redirecting what a person is thinking or feeling. It is not a subtle way of expressing criticism of something the colleague has done. The intent of probing and clarifying is to help the coach better understand the colleague's ideas, feelings, and thought processes relevant to the mediator. However, clarifying not only assists the coach's understanding, it also sharpens the perceptions and understandings of the person being coached.

Clarifying that is proceeded by a paraphrase helps make clear that the probe for more detail is for understanding, not judgment or interrogation. Clarifying contributes to trust because it communicates to a colleague that his or her ideas are worthy of exploration and consideration; their full meaning, however, may not yet be understood.

Providing Data. The sense of being trusted is a potent aphrodisiac to motivation and self-directed learning. Carol Sanford writes, "The ability to be self-correcting or self-governing is dependent on the capability to be self-reflecting [and] to see one's own processes as they play out. . . ."[17] To support this aim, processes for feedback must be conducted within a system the person being coached has helped create. Sanford adds that feedback should be done based only on a previously arranged agreement that specifies the principles and arenas to be covered.

As one of the main objectives of Cognitive Coaching is to nurture the teacher's capacities for processing information by comparing, inferring, or drawing causal relationships, data provided by the coach must be rich and readily available for the teacher to process. To contribute to the maintenance of trust, data should meet several conditions.

- Data must be requested.
- Data must be stated in observable terms.
- Data must be relevant.
- Data must allow for interpretation by the colleague, not the coach.

Information must be presented in a nonjudgmental, behaviorally descriptive fashion and after the teacher has recalled as much as she can. "During the first five minutes of the lesson, five students shared their recollection of yesterday's lesson." Or, "Of the six students you wanted me to observe, Natasha spoke four times, Tyrone spoke two times, Nuyen spoke once, and the remaining three not at all. What do you make of that?" Having offered data, the coach does not interpret but rather asks the teacher to construct meaning. Receiving data is in itself rewarding[18] and is the source of energy for self-improvement.[19]

Structuring. A safe, trusting relationship exists when your colleague knows what is expected. When expectations are unclear, people spend their energy and mental resources interpreting cues about what the other person wants and detecting any hidden agendas. With structuring, the coach clearly and deliberately communicates expectations about the purposes for and use of resources such as time, space, and materials. Structuring generates a common understanding of the purposes for the conversation, the roles the coach should play, time allotments, the most desirable location for the conference, and the placement of the coach during the observation.

What's the Payoff?

Cognitive Coaching has been continually practiced, refined, and developed for more than 20 years. Much research has been conducted, and the benefits of these forms of meditative conversations have been documented:[20]

1. Cognitive Coaching was linked with increased student test scores and other benefits for students.

2. Teachers grew in teaching efficacy.

3. Cognitive Coaching impacted teacher thinking, causing them to be more reflective and to think in more complex ways.

4. Teachers were more satisfied with their positions and with their choice of teaching as a profession.

5. School cultures became more professional.

6. Teachers collaborated more.

7. Cognitive Coaching assisted teachers professionally.

8. Cognitive Coaching benefited teachers personally.

IN SUMMARY

Why self-directed learning? In one study reported by Carol Sanford,[21] team members in a corporate setting listened to feedback from peers, supervisors, and subordinates about how to be better workers. The hypothesis is that if they got quality feedback about their performance, they would be able to improve the effectiveness of their teamwork. The exact opposite occurred, with feedback undermining the goals of producing improved performance. As a result the company initiated systems of self-reflection and self-assessment for employees.

In another study, 9- and 10-year-old students were asked to self-assess behaviors on which they were working. In one group, students reported self-assessments to teachers who reflected back what students were saying and then added a few observations of their own. In another group, students reported self-assessments and teachers listened, paraphrased, and sometimes would ask questions to clarify meaning. In the first group, the ability to accurately self-assess declined as students became more dependent on the teacher for an assessment of their behaviors. In the group in which teachers only reflected their understanding of student reports, accuracy increased. Self-assessment also led to improvements in student behaviors.

Cognitive Coaching enhances the capacity for accuracy in self-assessment. This is the foundation resource for self-directed learning for both adults and students. Becoming a mediator of others' cognitive growth, however, takes time and practice to consciously employ these behaviors in the flow of conversations. It sometimes means relinquishing old habits and identities. However challenging this is, the benefits outweigh the tasks of "unlearning" what had become habitual. Coaches experience greater feelings of power and satisfaction in observing others become more self-reliant[22] and resourceful and applying these tools and skills in their own personal lives at home and in the community.

NOTES

1. Ferguson, M. (1980). *The Aquarian Conspiracy.* Los Angeles: J. P. Tarcher.

2. Costa, A., & Garmston, R. (2002). *Cognitive Coaching: A Foundation for Renaissance Schools.* Norwood, MA: Christopher-Gordon, p. 16.

3. Feuerstein, R. (2000). Mediated learning experience. In A. Costa (Ed.), *Teaching for Intelligence II: A Collection of Articles.* Thousand Oaks, CA: Corwin Press.

4. Ibid., 275.

5. Ibid.

6. Edelman, G. (1987). *Neural Darwinism: The Theory of Neuronal Group Selection.* New York: Basic Books.

7. Ornstein, R. (1991). *The Evolution of Consciousness: Of Darwin, Freud, and Cranial Fire—The Origins of the Way We Think.* New York: Prentice Hall Press, 224.

8. Jutes, I. (2006, October 21). *Understanding the Digital Kids: Teaching and Learning in the Digital Age.* The InfoSavvy Group Presentation at the Leadership Conference of the Near East and Southeast Asia International Schools. Muscat, Oman.

9. Perkins, D. (2002). *King Arthur's Round Table.* New York: Wiley.

10. Closing down of the neocortex is described by many authors: Damasio, A. R. (1994). *Descartes' Error: Emotion, Reason, and the Human Brain.* New York: G.P. Putnam's Sons; Goleman, D. (1995). *Emotional Intelligence: Why It Can Matter More Than I.Q.* New York: Bantam Books; Kotulak, R. (1997). *Inside the Brain: Revolutionary Discoveries of How the Mind Works.* Kansas City, MO: Andrews McMeel.

11. Burgoon, J., Buller, D., & Woodall, W. (1996). *Nonverbal Communication: The Unspoken Dialogue* (2nd ed.). New York: McGraw-Hill, 138.

12. Caine, G., & Caine, R. (2001). *The Brain, Education and the Competitive Edge.* Lanham, MD: Scarecrow Press.

13. See Damasio, *Descartes' Error.* See also: Csikszentmihalyi, M. (1993). *The Evolving Self: A Psychology for the Third Millennium.* New York: Harper Collins; Damasio, A. (2000). *The Feeling of What Happens: Body and Emotion in the Making of Consciousness.* Orlando, FL: Harcourt; Pert, C. (1997). *Molecules of Emotion: The Science Behind Mind-Body Medicine.* New York: Simon & Schuster.

14. Zoller, K. (2005). The New Science of Non-verbal Skills. In R. Garmston (Ed.), *The Presenter's Fieldbook: A Practical Guide* (pp. 119–138). Norwood, MA: Christopher-Gordon.

15. Garmston, R. (Ed.). (2005). *The Presenter's Fieldbook: A Practical Guide.* Norwood, MA: Christopher-Gordon.

16. Costa, A., & Garmston, R. (2005). *Cognitive Coaching Foundation Seminar: Learning Guide.* Revised by James Ellison and Carolee Hayes. Norwood, MA: Christopher-Gordon, 37.

17. Sanford, C. (1995). *Feedback and Self-Accountability: A Collision Course.* Battle Ground, WA: Springhill Publications, 3.

18. Bandura, A. (1997). *Cognitive Functioning in Self-Efficacy: The Exercise of Control.* New York: Freeman, 212–258.

19. Garmston, R., & Wellman, B. (1999). *The Adaptive School: A Sourcebook for Developing Collaborative Groups.* Norwood, MA: Christopher-Gordon.

20. Edwards, J. (2004). *Cognitive Coaching*[SM]*: A Synthesis of the Research.* Highlands Ranch, CO: Center for Cognitive Coaching.

21. Sanford, *Feedback and Self-Accountability,* 3.

22. Ibid.

CHAPTER TWELVE

Norms of Collaboration

Attaining Communicative Competence

With William Baker and Stanley Shalit

Thought is largely a collective phenomenon.

Of all the attributes of effective thinkers, universally and cross-culturally, the capacity for communicative competency is paramount (Bowers, 1987). It is the most needed and probably least taught skill in schools or homes. Communicative competency is basic to the resolution of any problem or disagreement. When people have not learned this discipline, they resort to self-centered or ethnocentric means to resolve problems: separation, divorce, or abusiveness in settling domestic disputes; filibustering in politics and meetings; terrorism, street violence, hate crimes, wars between nations, terrorism, and ethnic cleansing.

This chapter demonstrates how the Norms of Collaboration serve as the webbing to link discourse in meetings and group interaction. At first, we focus on two forms of discourse: dialogical and dialectical discourse. Later we discuss other forms of discourse.

AUTHORS' NOTE: The evolution of the Norms of Collaboration is a result of long deliberation and refinement over time by Robert J. Garmston, John Dyer, Laura Lipton, Peg Luidens, Marilyn Tabor, Bruce Wellman, and Diane Zimmerman. For their assistance and dedication we are deeply appreciative.

Our purpose is to support educators, parents, and community leaders in understanding the dynamics of different forms of discourse and encouraging them to nurture communicative competency as a means of redesigning, restructuring, and renegotiating the culture of our schools, communities, and society.

DIALOGICAL AND DIALECTICAL DISCOURSE

What Is Dialogical Discourse?

Dia comes from the Greek word that means "through, between, or across two points," and *logos* means "the word." Thus *dialogue* means a verbal interchange and a sharing of ideas, especially when open and frank. The goal of dialogical discourse is to seek knowledge, mutual understanding, harmony, or a meeting of minds. Dialogical discourse involves an extended exchange between different points of view, cognitive domains, or frames of reference. Whenever we consider concepts or issues deeply, we explore their connections to other ideas and issues from different points of view. A dialogue can be among any number of people, not just two. Even one person can have a sense of dialogue within him- or herself. Dialogue connotes a stream of meaning flowing among, through, and between us.

What Is Dialectical Discourse?

Dialectical discourse intends to test the strengths and weaknesses of opposing points of view. Court trials, negotiations, debates, and arguments are dialectical in form and intention. They pit idea against idea, reasoning against counter-reasoning in order to get at the truth of a matter.

Dialectic is the art and practice of examining opinions or ideas logically through talk—often by the method of question and answer—so as to determine their validity. Like dialogue, *dia* comes from the Greek, meaning "through, between, or across two points"; *legein* means "to choose, to talk, or to choose between two points." The terms *dialogical* and *dialectical* have come to mean something quite different. The goal of dialectical discourse is to win, convince, or persuade. Hegel believed that for every thesis there was an opposing point of view, or *antithesis*, leading to an understanding of and reconciliation of opposites. This concept of the dialectic gives rise to debates, negotiations, court trials, and compromises; the intent is that one side wins and the other loses (Paul, 1991).

OTHER FORMS OF DISCOURSE

Dialogical and dialectical discourse are only two forms of group interaction or communication. Other forms of discourse have different structures and intentions. Some well-known forms of discourse for group interaction are lecture, discussion, deliberation, debate, conversation, and therapy. All these forms of discourse can readily be observed in meetings. Sometimes, all these forms of discourse occur in a single meeting. In a meeting where all forms are occurring, chaos or harmony can be observed. Chaos occurs when self-centered behavior dominates and members are not conscious of the effects of the modes of discourse on themselves or others. Harmony occurs when the Norms of Collaboration are consciously or unconsciously used to weld the discourse together, resulting in all members at the meeting feeling a strong sense of satisfaction and accomplishment.

Each form of discourse has a different structure. Each has a different intent. And each can be used successfully or unsuccessfully. We describe the most common forms of discourse so that the reader can consider these in relation to dialogical and dialectical discourse.

Lecture. Lecture is characterized by an emphasis on individuals in a meeting presenting data, information, positions, conclusions, issues, and recommendations. The intent is to inform or convince others of the validity and reasonableness of what is being presented.

Discussion. Discussion in meetings emphasizes the introduction of a wide variety of individual perspectives. During discussion, individuals offer data, knowledge, their ideas, information, rationales for positions on issues, and frequently try to convince others to take on their position. The intent is to talk about something in a constructive and amicable manner. When discussion goes awry, the root of the word predominates. *Cussion* comes from the Latin *cussio,* which means "to shake violently." It is the source for our words *concussion* ("to shake together") and *percussion* ("to strike"). Members talk past one another and little understanding occurs.

Deliberation. The primary intent of deliberative discourse is to analyze and understand the data, knowledge, positions, ideas, or issues together in order to determine the best course of action. An important aspect of deliberation is dialectical discourse. Frequently, deliberative discourse results in decisions. The intent is to reach a deeper understanding of the content and the group members' attitude toward that content in order to decide upon a group course of action.

Conversation. Conversational discourse takes place in meetings when members relate personally to the data, knowledge, positions, ideas, or issues to arrive at decisions that are congruent with their values and feelings. The intent is on building or maintaining relationships rather than attending to the topic. The conversation can be far ranging with seemingly little focus.

Dialogues. Dialogues have the primary intent of expanding the permutations and possibilities of the ideas, knowledge, and issues in order to discover new solutions.

Therapeutic Discourse. Sometimes referred to as sensitivity training or encounter groups, therapeutic discourse is characterized by an emphasis on drawing out, feeding back, and analyzing individuals' affective states during meetings. The intent is to relate individuals' affective states to what is occurring during the meeting. Individuals decide publicly or privately on a private course of action.

The predominate characteristics of these modes of group talk can be located in the "Dialogical Discourse" column in Table 12.1. Again, the Norms of Collaboration will enhance these forms of discourse.

Contrasting Dialogical and Dialectical as Opposite Ends of a Continuum

Although dialogical and dialectical discourse may be considered as being in opposition to each other, we consider dialogical and dialectical to be at opposite ends of a continuum of discourse and place the other forms of discourse along the same continuum. Where a type of discourse falls on a continuum often relates to whether the form of discourse is or is not being used successfully. However, only in the most formal group meetings can such a continuum be observed. Examples include when parliamentary rules are in place; when a therapist controls a session; or when a facilitator insists on people using a particular mode of discourse at any time. When people of good will get together, one can observe that the Norms of Collaboration weld the meeting together by producing the webbing for participants to move seamlessly from one mode of discourse to another.

Table 12.1 shows that both forms of discourse are useful, but it is in the dynamics of shifting from one mode of discourse to another that groups grow, make new leaps, come to terms, or arrive at consensus. By using what we call the "Norms of Collaboration," an individual member of the group can facilitate the shifting from one form of discourse to another.

THE EIGHT NORMS OF COLLABORATION

The following eight Norms serve as standards that are understood, agreed upon, and adopted for use by each participant when working as a facilitating and contributing member of a group. They are the glue that enables school and community groups to engage in productive and satisfying discourse. Unlike a rule, which someone else monitors, a norm is a guide that each group member uses to monitor his or her own participation. Once norms are agreed upon, each member assumes others will use them as well. Time should be allocated for reflection on the use of these norms by members of the group, for drawing relationships between their use and the group's, and for planning for continued improvement in the use of these norms in the future.

Table 12.1   Elements of Dialogical and Dialectical Discourse

Dialogical Discourse	Dialectical Discourse
Different views are presented as a way of discovering a new view.	Different views are presented and defended in search of the best view to support a decision.
There is a free and creative exploration of complex and subtle issues.	An issue is analyzed and dissected from many points of view.
Finding common ground is the goal.	Winning is usually the goal (one's view prevails) but must take second priority to coherence and truth.
One suspends personal views in order to understand the other's views. There is evidence of deep listening and empathizing.	There is a ping-ponging back and forth of something between us.
There is playfulness with ideas.	Decisions are made.
Two or more sides collaborate toward common understanding.	Two sides oppose each other and attempt to prove each other wrong or their own position right.
One listens to the other side(s) in order to understand, find meaning, and find agreement.	One listens to the other side in order to find flaws and to counter its arguments.
Participants enlarge and possibly change their points of view.	Participants affirm their own points of view.
The positions and issues become more complex.	The positions and issues become more simplified.
Assumptions are revealed, examined, and reevaluated.	Assumptions are defended as truth.
Introspection of one's own position is invited.	Critique of the other position is produced.
It is acceptable to change one's position.	It is a sign of weakness and defeat to change one's position.
The skills of synthesis and flexibility are stressed.	The skills of analysis and persistence are stressed.
There is the possibility of reaching a better solution than either of the original solutions.	One's own position is defended as the best solution and excludes other solutions.
Participants strive for multiplicity in perspective.	Participants strive for singularity in perspective.

1. Pausing

In a discourse, space is given for each person to talk. Time is allowed before responding to or asking a question. Such silent time allows for more complex thinking, enhances all forms of discourse, and produces better decision making. Pausing is the tool that facilitative group members use to respectfully listen to each other.

2. Paraphrasing

Lets others know that you are listening, that you understand or are trying to understand, and that you care. An effective paraphrase expresses empathy by reflecting both the feelings and the content of the message.

A paraphrase sends four messages:

a. I am listening to your ideas.

b. I understand your thinking.

c. I am trying to understand your thinking.

d. I care about your thinking.

There are many types of paraphrases. We think they can be categorized into four basic types, each having a slightly different intention, but they often blend into one another. The important factor about the paraphrase is that it is one of the most critical tools to use to gain understanding. Our colleague, Bob Garmston, has introduced the concept that the paraphrase is the tool that a competent communicator uses to gain permission to ask a question of others.

Types of Paraphrase

I. *Empathizing:* An acknowledgment and reflection of emotions

Original statement: "Taking care of Joan has been a difficult situation for me, what with all the other work I have to do! It gets in the way of many other tasks. I just feel so fragmented, trying to handle everything! I'm at the point of quitting!"

Example: "You're *overwhelmed* and *frustrated* with taking care of Joan!"

II. *Summarizing:* A shortening of a longer communication in your own words

Example: "So, taking care of Joan has been hard for you what with all your other tasks!"

III. *Synthesizing:* A statement that lifts or lowers the logical level of the original

Example: "So, taking care of Joan has taken you to an extreme position of escaping the obligation!"

Reflection stems to consider:

"You're suggesting..."   "You're thinking..."
"You're understanding him to mean...."   "You're wondering..."
"You're feeling..."   "You're hoping..."
"So your idea is that..."   "Your goal is to..."

IV. *Group Paraphrase:* The power of the group paraphrase is a skill to be nurtured. A group paraphrase infers the intent of most people in the group and is stated concisely with the appropriate intonation. When a group paraphrase captures the spirit of the group, it most likely helps the group move to a next stage or into its desired action. When it misses, individuals, often more than one at the same time, offer additional information that suggests a next step for the group, or it just falls on deaf ears and the group continues doing what is has been doing.

Classic Group Paraphrases

The punctuation is an attempt to capture the intonation.

- "What we seem to be agreeing on is..."
- "I guess we've just about beaten that one to death?!"
- "Are we agreeing to...?!"

- "In other words, we're..."

- "Looks like most of us here would..."
- "I guess we're ready for a vote?!"
- "What seems to be coming through is..."
- "What we seem to be saying is..."

---

3. Probing and Clarifying

Probing and clarifying is an effective inquiry skill to use when the speaker expresses vocabulary, uses a vague concept, or employs terminology that is not fully understood by the listener. The purpose of clarifying is to invite the speaker to make clearer, to elaborate, to become more precise in their meaning. The use of probing and clarifying is intended to help the listener better understand the speaker. In groups, probing and clarifying increases the clarity and precision of the group's thinking by clarifying understandings, terminology, and interpretations.

Some examples of probing and clarifying include

> "Help me understand what you mean by . . ."
> "What will the participants be doing if we take this course of action?"
> "Which students specifically?"
> "When you say this class is better, better than what?"
> "When you say 'the administrators,' which administrators do you mean?"
> "What do you mean by 'appreciate'?"

4. Putting Your Ideas On and Pulling Them Off the Table

Groups are most productive when everyone shares their thoughts, dreams, mistakes, assumptions, and opinions. Facilitative members engage in productive discourse when they are clear about the intentions or goals of the group and what the group is attempting to accomplish. They offer ideas, opinions, information, and positions. They attempt to keep their suggestions relevant to the topic at hand. There are times, however, when continuing to advocate a position might block the group's functioning. Most of us can remember a time when we were advocating a position and our advocacy was falling on deaf ears. Had we been using the next norm, Paying Attention to Self and Others, we would have known it was not flying. Yet we continued to advocate. Knowing when to pull your ideas off the table may be as important as getting them on the table.

The Greek word *koinonia* means "(fellowship) to participate"—partaking of the whole and taking part in it; not merely the whole group but the *whole* (Bohm, 1990). It is important for everyone to be heard!

5. Paying Attention to Self and Others

Meaningful dialogue is facilitated when each group member is sensitive to and conscious of themselves and of others. Being aware of and watching all the subtle cues of what's happening inside you and what's happening in the group. Being aware of the stance of their body, their body language, posture, gesture, and language. Interestingly, this develops automatically in dialogue as it is all part of communication—verbal as well as nonverbal.

When group members pay attention to themselves they are aware of what they are saying, how it is said, and how others are responding. Paying attention to learning styles, modalities, and beliefs when planning for, when facilitating, and when participating in a group meeting enhances group members' understanding each other as they converse, discuss, deliberate, dialogue, and make decisions. Managing emotions is a critical part of paying attention to self and others. Being sensitive to one's own and others' emotions and discovering underlying causes that produce those emotions enhances group work and decision making.

6. Presuming Positive Intentionality/Positive Presuppositions

People operate on internal maps of their own reality and therefore we assume that they act with positive intentions. This assumption promotes and facilitates meaningful dialogue. Using positive presuppositions assumes and encourages positive actions.

Our language contains overt and covert messages. The deeper meanings we interpret from the language of others is not always communicated by the surface structure of our words and syntax. The subtle (and often not so subtle) way in which the embedded presuppositions in our language can be hurtful or helpful to others (Costa & Garmston, 2002; Elgin, 1980).

Example: "Even Bill could get an A in that class."

Presuppositions: Bill is no great shake as a student.

The class is not difficult.

Limiting Presuppositions

"Do you have an objective?"   "Why were you unsuccessful?"
"What two things went well?"   *"If only you had listened!"*

Empowering Presuppositions

"What are some of the goals that you have in mind for this meeting?"
"As you consider your alternatives, what seems most promising?"
"How will you know whether the meeting is successful?"
"What personal learnings or insights are you carrying forward to future situations?"

---

7. Providing Data and Nonjudgmental Feedback

Providing Data

Groups exercising high levels of communicative competence act on information rather than hearsay, rumor, or speculation. Data serves as the energy sources for group action and learning. Seeking, generating, and gathering data from group members as well as a variety of other primary and secondary sources enhances individual and group decision making. Some examples might be

Using secondary sources: "Let's look up the definition in the dictionary to make certain we all understand what we mean when we use this term."

Using the group as a database: "Let's take a straw poll and find out how the group is feeling about this issue at this point."

Conducting research: "Let's design and conduct an interview to gather data from a random sample of community members about this issue."

Experimentation: "If our hypothesis is correct, then students' performance on tasks of higher-level thinking should increase over the years. How might we collect such evidence?"

Turning to experts: "Let's pose these questions to Judge Smith, who has worked with these cases for many years."

Drawing on research: "According to the research report number 589–3 by the National Center for Teaching Thinking, such forms of higher-level questioning do enhance these types of students' performance on tests of reasoning by as much as 9 percentage points."

Providing Nonjudgmental Feedback

Nonjudgmental feedback is a process whereby concrete and specific factual information about a group's thinking, decisions, and actions are provided so that the group can use the information for self-validation, self-correction, or self-modification. What is essential and unique about nonjudgmental feedback is that it represents the setting aside of judgment. Critical characteristics of nonjudgmental feedback are

- It's based on observation.
- It's concrete.
- It's specific.
- It's honest.
- It relates to strengths.
- It relates to needs.
- It invites self-correction.
- It's useful for self-validation.
- It's useful for self-modification.

Examples: "Everyone in our group offered an opinion today. Mary paraphrased three times. Jerry clarified Ralph's assumptions twice. Our dialogue continued for 27 uninterrupted minutes. We stayed on track except for one time when we talked about . . . !"

8. Pursuing a Balance Between Advocacy and Inquiry

Advocating a position as well as inquiring into another's position assists the group to continue learning. Senge, Ross, Smith, Roberts, and Kleiner (1994) suggest that in order to grow and learn, an organization needs to practice balancing advocacy and inquiry. They maintain that group members need to do the following when advocating their views:

- Make their reasoning explicit, explaining how they arrived at a view, what it is based on
- Encourage others to explore their views by asking questions like "Are there any gaps in my thinking?" "Does this make sense?"
- Invite others to provide different views: "Are there different conclusions?" "What other data should we gather?" "Are there other ways of viewing this?"
- Actively inquire into others' views that differ: "What is your view?" "How did you arrive at your view?" "What data are you using to support your view?"

When inquiring into other members' views, a facilitative participant should

- State his or her assumptions clearly when making assumptions about others' views
- State the data upon which these assumptions are based
- Not ask questions if they're not genuinely interested in the other's response (Senge et al., 1994)

During a meeting, when a group is engrossed in a dialogical discourse, exploring ideas, one member of the group can shift the discussion into a dialectical discourse by using one or more of the Norms of Collaboration, such as a combination of a paraphrase and probe to analyze and decide which ideas to accept or reject. On the other hand, a facilitative participant might use the Norm of Collaboration of paraphrasing to synthesize what has been going on in a dialectical discourse to invite understanding, integrating and harmonizing the group's thinking, and encourage generation of new and divergent solutions and directions.

WHY USE THE NORMS OF COLLABORATION?

Focusing on the Norms of Collaboration Enhances the States of Mind[1] of Individuals and the Group

Using the Norms of Collaboration increases *consciousness*. Applying the Norms of Collaboration causes us to think about what is being said, how it should be said, and what reaction it evokes. We monitor how well we understand what is being said and what we are doing to further the discourse. We monitor our own feelings, choose words and terminology to fit our audience, and select among alternative choices of words and pathways. We suppress and hold in abeyance our own feelings, emotions, judgments, impulses, and desires in order to allow others to express theirs. The skillful participant in a meeting, one with high communicative competence, demonstrates an awareness of what is occurring by employing the Norms of Collaboration regardless of the form of discourse being used.

The Norms enhance *craftsmanship.* They build skillfulness in the behaviors of listening: questioning, attending, clarifying, paraphrasing, and pausing. They demand precise language and clarification of terms, beliefs, and values. The Norms facilitate an increase in the group's communicative competence by encouraging members to spend the necessary time to gain deeper understanding.

The Norms produce *flexibility.* They require allocentric and empathic listening so as to understand the other person's point of view. They also demand drawing on and developing alternative forms of expression and response patterns. The Norms demand that participants pay attention to the varying beliefs, values, and styles of other members of the group. In doing so, members select from a broad repertoire of language to respond to the differences expressed within the group.

The Norms evoke increased feelings of *efficacy.* Using the Norms causes us to feel in control; they cause us to self-evaluate, self-monitor, and self-analyze our own listening and communicative competencies. They produce a feeling of mastery within us because we realize that we have powerful ideas to contribute and that the collective meaning of the group is enhanced when we each contribute our individual assumptions and opinions.

Groups who adopt the Norms develop greater *interdependence.* Using them builds a reciprocity with others and contributes to a sense of community understanding, group meaning, trust and bonding within members of the group.

Implementing the Norms of Collaboration builds *holonomy.* Discourse occurs between the individual and the group. Through harmony of the individual and the group, the whole moves toward coherence. Thus, in such a group one can observe both a collective and individual mind; like a stream, the flow moves between them (Bohm, 1990).

Employing the Norms of Collaboration Builds Culture

They assist the group to renegotiate the ways it works together to *solve problems and form decisions.*

David Bohm (1990) describes the chaos that frequently occurs in groups when people do not engage in dialogue. He uses the metaphor of a laser to suggest that group power, like a laser, can produce communicative competence. We suggest that the Norms of Collaboration serve as the webbing that produces the same effects that he describes. In fact, his description is an excellent description of what occurs when the Norms of Collaboration are in action.

> The power of a group . . . could be compared to a laser. Ordinary light is called "incoherent," which means that it is going in all sorts of directions, and the light waves are not in phase with each other so they don't build up. But a laser produces a very intense beam which *is* coherent. The light waves build up strength because they are all going in the same direction. This beam can do all sorts of things that ordinary light cannot.
>
> . . . Ordinary thought in society is incoherent—it is going in all sorts of directions with thoughts conflicting and canceling each other out. But if people were to think together in a coherent way, it would have tremendous power. That's the suggestion. If we have a dialogue situation—a group which has sustained dialogue for quite a while in which people get to know each other . . . then we might have such a coherent movement of thought, a coherent movement of communication.

A culture is people thinking together. As individuals share meaning, they negotiate and build a culture (communicative competence through the Norms of Collaboration). As groups become more skillful in employing the Norms of Collaboration, the Norms create a renegotiation of the organization by pervading the value system, resulting in the changing of the practices and beliefs of the entire organization. By employing the Norms, the group mind illuminates issues, solves problems, and accommodates differences. By using the Norms, the group builds an atmosphere of trust in human relationships, and trust in the processes of interaction, and trust throughout the organization. The Norms facilitate the creation of a shared vision (Senge, 1990).

The Norms of Collaboration promote *common communicative behaviors.* In school communities people behave similarly. When one observes an interaction between a secretary and a parent, or a teacher and a student, or a board member and a superintendent, one notices these similarities and can infer from them the basic values of the organization. Margaret Wheatley (1992) describes this phenomenon in terms of the organization having a "fractal quality." In the best of organizations one can watch any member to infer the organization's values.

> The very best organizations have a fractal quality to them. An observer of such an organization can tell what the organization's values and ways of doing business are by watching anyone, whether it be a production floor employee or a senior manager.

There is consistency and predictability to the quality of behavior. No matter where we look in these organizations, self-similarity is found in its people, in spite of the complex range of roles and levels.

The Norms of Collaboration promote *collective thought*—thinking together, which is more powerful than individual thought. Schein (1993) refers to this as "Metalogue." It is a harmony of the individual and the collective in which the whole constantly moves toward coherence. Collective thought and interaction with others often results in individual thought. Application of the Norms of Collaboration builds coherence of thought and the tacit or unspoken understandings, agreements, or similarities that come from participating in discourse over time (Bohm, 1990). We might refer to this participatory consciousness as "co-cognition"—developing, monitoring, and expressing our thoughts together (Costa & O'Leary, 1991).

The Norms contribute to the *intellectual growth* of the group's participants. Through discourse, ideas are presented and shaped, data are gathered and accommodated, differences in perceptions are understood and resolved, a variety of points of view are interpreted and understood, and differences in values and feelings are accommodated. When the Norms are used during dialectical discourse to facilitate explanation, justification, or persuasion, the group grows intellectually. The Norms do the same during dialogical discourse to facilitate participants moving beyond their assumptions, thus creating new connections, new courses of action, and new meaning.

Vygotsky (1978) describes this phenomenon of the group dynamic influencing the growth of individual intelligence by talking about inter- and intrapsychological growth. He believes that every function in cultural development appears twice: first, on the social level, and later on the individual level; first between people (interpsychological), and then inside (intrapsychological). This applies equally to voluntary attention, to logical memory, and to the formation concepts. All the higher functions originate as actual relationships between individuals.

The process that Vygotsky describes is a subtle process. The knowledge that results from group interaction is rarely spoken by members of the group. Instead, one infers the knowledge. Sometimes a member does identify a tacit understanding the group has achieved. The group acknowledges that or denies that it has the understanding. The process the member uses to reflect the unspoken, tacit knowledge usually is a group paraphrase—one of the key Norms of Collaboration.

Tacit means that which is unspoken, which cannot be described—like the tacit knowledge required to dance. Thinking, according to Bohm (1990), is actually a subtle, tacit process—the concrete processes of thinking are very tacit; the meaning is basically tacit. And what we can say explicitly is only a very small part of it. Thought emerges from this tacit ground, and any fundamental change in thought will come from the tacit ground. So if we are communicating at the tacit level, then thought may be changing. Truth and enlightenment emerge unannounced.

The Norms of Collaboration Contribute to Continual Learning

Learning to apply the Norms together brings *integrity and congruence* to a learning group or organization. As individuals within a group come to understand, practice, develop criteria for, and assess their continual growth in the skills of discourse, they build a culture of continual learning. In fact, we believe they renegotiate their culture. They find that sharing of mind and consciousness is more important than the content of the opinions. While the process may arrive at truth, the process is more concerned with developing individual and group meaning. It is the application of the Norms of Collaboration that keeps individuals, groups, and organizations growing, changing, creating, and learning.

Wheatley (1992) suggests that this is the process of *Autopoesis*, which groups use to maintain their basic structure while growing.

> *Autopoesis:* (Greek) Self-production. The characteristic of living systems to continuously renew themselves and to regulate this process in such a way that the integrity of their structure is maintained. It is a natural process that supports the quest for structure, process renewal and integrity.

THE NORMS OF COLLABORATION AND TEAMWORK

As schools and learning organizations work to transform themselves (that is, to renegotiate their culture), collaborative teams need to become skillful in all forms of discourse (that is, develop communicative competency) and to know when each is appropriate. Collaborative teams need to be able to engage in fruitful, exploratory dialogue, proposing ideas, probing their roots, considering evidence, sharing insights, testing ideas, and moving among various points of view. Collaborative teams also need to develop dialectical reasoning skills so that their thinking moves comfortably among divergent points of view or lines of thought assessing the relative strengths and weaknesses of the evidence or reasoning presented. They also need to know how to discuss in order for each to get their ideas into the hopper. And, they need to converse in a manner that allows for each members' values and feelings to be heard and accommodated.

Collaborative work teams use dialectical and dialogical discourse to achieve two different types of decisions:

1. *Focusing in Decisions:* Through dialectical reasoning, a focusing in that seeks a common denominator from among many individual views

2. *Opening up Decisions:* Through dialogue, a way of looking beyond each other's views to agree on something we might not have arrived at alone

A team performing at peak levels aligns its energies—the group functions as a whole. Collaborative teams reflect on, evaluate, and learn from their activities and keep getting better. Such collective learning from experience has four critical dimensions: (1) the need to gather critical data and information, (2) to think insightfully about critical issues, (3) to act in innovative and coordinated ways, and (4) to attend to individuals' values and feelings so that they foster the development of peak team performance within the organization.

The power for such generative learning in organizations comes from the synergy between all forms of discourse. We have referred to this synergy as the "webbing" resulting from the application of the Norms of Collaboration. To capture this synergy, five factors must be present.

1. Team members are on the way to *mastering* the skills that are used in all forms of discourse. They are gaining communicative competency through their use of the Norms of Collaboration.

2. Teams can *distinguish* between the purposes and processes of the different forms of discourse and know when to enlist them.

3. Teams can *engage* the four conditions for communicative competence:
   a. Discussing and understanding what is meant by the different forms of discourse and consciously agreeing to engage in them
   b. Suspending assumptions, value judgments at the appropriate times
   c. Regarding one another as trusted colleagues
   d. Assuming the role of facilitative participants or engaging a temporary facilitator who holds the context of dialogue

4. Teams become *observers, reflectors, and evaluators* of their own thinking and their implementation of the Norms of Collaboration.

5. Teams *monitor* and respectfully *divert* forces opposing productive discourse.

Productive work teams use skills of talking together (that is, communicative competence) and can recognize and redirect verbal moves of defensiveness. Defensiveness moves are not in themselves "negative" but are usually employed to protect one's self or others from discomfort or embarrassment or to protect and defend their own opinions and assumptions.

Mental and Verbal Skills Promoting Productive Discourse

Choosing appropriate forms of discourse

Establishing criteria for effective discourse

Suspending judgments

Employing the eight Norms of Collaboration

Accessing holonomous states of mind: Efficacy, flexibility, craftsmanship, consciousness, interdependence

Working from the balcony: Looking down on the interaction—thinking metacognitively about their discoursing

Recognizing and redirecting forces opposing productive discourse

Group coaching: Planning for, monitoring of, and reflecting on the process

Self- and group monitoring of the Norms of Collaboration

Forces Opposing Productive Team Discourse

Not putting ideas on the table and talking behind the group's back

Smoothing over situations and avoiding advocacy or inquiry

Waging abstraction wars—talk for talk's sake—overintellectualizing

Being patronizing

Unwilling to share personal agendas, assumptions, or principles

Saying "That's interesting"

Sheltering ideas from criticism

Confronting person to squash idea

Playing a "broken record"

Changing the subject

Pulling rank

Digging in heels

Intimidating or attacking persons to suppress ideas

Holding nonnegotiable assumptions

Referring to rules, traditions, or past experiences:
 "It didn't work in '87 and it isn't going to work now."
 "'They' won't let us do that here."
 "We've never done it that way before."

Table 12.2 is the Norms of Collaboration Checklist for monitoring individual and/or group performance of the eight Norms of Collaboration. The intent of the checklist is to record indicators of the performance of each or several of the Norms of Collaboration by individuals during team meetings

(How am I doing?). Individual group members might wish to identify one or more of the Norms for self-improvement, pay attention to their own use of these behaviors, and then seek feedback from group members about how he or she did on that particular Norm.

Another use of the checklist might be for group performance (that is, How are we doing?) (Costa & Kallick, 1995). The group begins by appointing a group process observer (that is, a coach) and identifying which of the Norms they wish to practice during the meeting. The group process observer then clarifies to ensure he or she and the group understands which behaviors they have agreed upon and what they would look like or sound like. During the meeting the group process observer records indicators of the agreed-upon Norms. Upon completion of the meeting, the group process observers gives feedback to the group about their performance of the Norms. These data are discussed, the effects of their use on group effectiveness is illuminated, and strategies for individual and group improvement are planned.

Using the Norms of Collaboration Checklist results in clear feedback. Individuals grow intellectually. Trust grows within the group. Members understand their level of participation in the group. As participants increase their knowledge of communicative competency in groups there is an increased likelihood that they will transfer these Norms to other life situations.

As you can infer from what has preceded, we believe that all forms of discourse, including dialectical and dialogical discourse, must occur if school or community deliberating bodies are to proceed productively and with member satisfaction. We believe that groups talk with each other in at least four different ways. Each of these ways of talking is important for good decision making to occur. Yet, each way of talking has a different intention.

1. Groups hold *discussions* for the primary intent of each member presenting data, knowledge, positions, ideas, or issues.

2. They hold *deliberations* with the primary intent of analyzing and understanding the data, knowledge, positions, ideas, or issues in order to determine the best course of action. The predominate characteristics of these two modes of group talk can be located in the dialectical discourse column described in Table 12.1. Groups hold *dialogues* with the primary intent of expanding the permutations and possibilities of the ideas, knowledge, and issues in order to discover new solutions.

3. They hold *conversations* with the primary intent of relating personally to the data, knowledge, positions, ideas, or issues to arrive at decisions that are congruent with their values and feelings.

Again, the Norms of Collaboration will enhance these forms of discourse.

Table 12.2   Norms of Collaboration Checklist

How Am I Doing?

Norm	Often	Sometimes	Not Yet
1. Pausing			
• Listening attentively to others' ideas with mind and body			
• Allowing time for thought after asking a question or making a response			
• Rewording in my own mind what others are saying to further understand their positions and points of view			
• Waiting until others have finished before entering the dialogue			
2. Probing			
• Posing questions that invite self and others to recall ideas and past experiences, to describe facts, to express opinions and positions			
• Seeking clarification, explanation, interpretation, implications, or consequences			
• Asking for predictions, postulations, extrapolations, imaginations, and new connections			
• Inviting personal connections or relationships, expressing personal values or beliefs, identifying likes and and dislikes, making choices and commitments			
3. Paraphrasing			
• Acknowledging another's contribution			
• Summarizing another's idea			
• Translating another's idea into own words			
• Empathizing with others' feelings			
• Synthesizing the group's thinking or progress			

(Continued)

Table 12.2   (Continued)

Norm	Often	Sometimes	Not Yet
4. Putting Ideas On/Pulling Ideas Off the Table			
• Being clear about the intentions, goals, and outcomes of the group			
• Offering ideas, opinions, information, or positions			
• Removing, rescinding, or changing own ideas, opinions, points of view, and positions			
5. Paying Attention to Self and Others			
• Using visual, auditory, and kinesthetic clues expressed by others			
• Respecting differences in people's preferences, beliefs, values, culture, ethnicity, and so on			
• Maintaining focus on goals and avoiding straying from the topic or issue at hand			
• Viewing situations from own, others', and global perspectives			
6. Presuming Positive Intentionality			
• Assuming that others' intentions are positive and acting as if others mean well			
• Restraining impulsivity under emotional and stressful situations			
• Using positive presuppositions when inquiring and responding to others			
7. Providing Data			
• Asking for information, data, facts			
• Substantiating ideas and opinions with data, facts, and rationale			
• Referring to secondary resources of information			
• Setting up experiments and action research to test ideas			
• Basing actions on best available research			

Norm	Often	Sometimes	Not Yet
8. *Pursuing Balance Between Advocacy and Inquiry*			
• Monitoring the equity of opportunities for participation by all group members			
• Respecting the rights of individual's level of participation in the dialogue			
• Monitoring the relationship between advocacy and inquiry occurring in the group			
• Presenting reasons, logic, and rationale for holding a position and the decision-making processes that led to that position			
• Referring to agreed-upon goals, values, and purposes in arriving at decisions			
• Inquiring of others regarding their reasons and values for holding a position and how they arrived at it			

All groups talk in these four ways to agree on courses of action. All four kinds of talk occur simultaneously, without differentiation. When members are unaware of this phenomenon, chaos, confusion, conflict, fragmentation, and discord results. When groups consciously employ the Norms of Collaboration and are aware of the kind of discourse that is occurring, we believe that harmony, productivity, and satisfaction will result. Since the different kinds of talk have different intentions, one uses the Norms of Collaboration differently depending upon the kind of discourse taking place. We believe that groups can become aware of these different ways of talking. By paying attention to the intentions of individuals and using the Norms of Collaboration most appropriate at the moment, their decision making and group interaction will become more productive and satisfying.

Table 12.3 outlines these four kinds of talk and the ways in which individuals might employ the Norms of Collaboration.

These ways of talking together are not mutually exclusive. One way of talking can lead to another way. They can occur simultaneously. Facilitative members of a group can use them to invite the group into different modes of thought. As group members become more aware of these four ways of talking together, at the appropriate time they can decide to focus on one specific way of talking in order to meet a specific intention.

Table 12.3   Four Ways Group Members Talk Together

Hold a Discussion	Hold a Conversation
Intent: Present data, knowledge, positions, ideas, issues	*Intent*: Relate one's personal values and feelings to the data, knowledge, positions, ideas, issues and make choices that are congruent with one's values and feelings
Focus: All group members get their ideas, knowledge, positions, issues into the discussion (on the table)	*Focus*: Present and explore the feelings, values, and concerns members have
Norms: Group members • *Pause, probe*, and *paraphrase* for clarification and to invite everyone to contribute • All *put their ideas on the table* • *Provide* appropriate *data* to describe and support ideas, etc. • *Pay attention* to *self* and *others* by being aware of how others are receiving ideas, etc. • *Presume* that *each* member *means well* when submitting ideas • *Advocate* their positions • *Inquire* of others to understand their position, not necessarily to agree with it	*Norms*: Group members • *Pause, probe*, and *paraphrase* for empathy and acknowledgement • All *put their ideas on the table* • *Provide data* about their feelings and concerns • *Pay attention* to their own inner voices and others' expressions • *Presume* the *best* of *intentions* about others' feelings and values • *Advocate*: Are clear about their own values and their relationship to the issue or topic at hand • *Inquire*: Seek clarity about others' values and feelings regarding . . . !
Examples "Are you saying that . . . ?" "Joan, what ideas are you thinking of with regard to . . . ?" "Do we have everyone's ideas on the table?" "I'm putting forth this position because . . ." "Tell us about your reasons for presenting this. . . "	*Examples* "You're really concerned about . . . ?" "You believe we should . . . !" "What are you wanting us to do about . . .?" "So you're feeling . . . !" "The course of action you are excited about is . . . !" "What is of most value to you is . . ."

Hold a Deliberation	Hold a Dialogue
Intent: Analyze and understand the data, knowledge, positions, ideas, issues. Make sense of things!	*Intent*: Expand the permutations, possibilities, the what if's; find the new and untried!
Focus: Find the truths and falsehoods, balance and weigh, compare the pros and cons, identify the advantages and disadvantages	*Focus*: Explore new ideas, make new connections, create something new, go beyond the tried and true!
Norms: Group members: • *Pause, probe,* and *paraphrase* to invite explanation, to identify consequences, costs and benefits, and to encourage disequilibrium • *Provide data* by gathering evidence, showing justifications for, presenting arguments for and against • *Pay attention to self and others* to determine the degree of conflict present and to judge how to respond • Actively pursue *inquiry* as they *advocate* the pros and cons of a specific course. They focus on finding out why something will or won't work	*Norms*: Group members: • *Pause, probe,* and *paraphrase* to invite shifts of thought, raise or lower logical levels, seek new ways of thinking, reframing the situation • Seek *information* or *data* that will expand their thinking. They generate many ideas • *Pay attention to others* to build on others' ideas, add to and to support. They view the situation from many perspectives • Wait until the new is fairly well formed before applying *advocacy* and *inquiry* to the situation
Examples "How is what you are saying related to what Jim is saying . . . ?" "Why is that important to do?" "As we think about next steps, which are the most critical to do well?" "Why do we think this is the best way to go?" "What may get in the way of its working?"	*Examples* "What if we were to . . . ?" "If we take X and Y and put them together, where might that lead us?" "If we were the parents in this situation, how might we be viewing it?" "Is there another way to go?"

NOTE

1. For in-depth definitions and examples of five states of mind, see Costa & Garmston (2000), Chapter 6; and Ellison & Hayes (2004), Chapter 2.

REFERENCES

Bohm, D. (1990). *On dialogue.* Dayton, OH: Institute for the Development of Educational Activities.

Bowers, C. A. (1987). *The promise of theory; education and the politics of cultural change.* New York: Columbia University, Teachers College, 31–48.

Costa, A., & Garmston, R. (2002). *Cognitive Coaching: A foundation for Renaissance schools.* Norwood, MA: Christopher-Gordon.

Costa, A., & Kallick, B. (1995). *Assessment in the learning organization: Shifting the paradigm.* Alexandria, VA: Association for Supervision and Curriculum Development.

Costa, A., & O'Leary, P. W. (1991). Co-cognition: The cooperative development of the intellect. In N. Davidson & T. Worsham (Eds.), *Enhancing thinking through cooperative learning.* New York: Teachers College Press.

Elgin, S. H. (1980). *The gentle art of verbal self-defense.* New York: Prentice-Hall.

Paul, R. (1991). Dialogical and dialectical thinking. In A. Costa (Ed.), *Developing minds: A resource book for teaching thinking.* Alexandria, VA: Association for Supervision and Curriculum Development.

Schein, E. H. (1993, Autumn). On dialogue, culture and organizational learning. *Organizational Dynamics, 22*(2), 40–51.

Senge, P. (1990). *The fifth discipline: The art and practice of the learning organization.* New York: Doubleday/Current.

Senge, P., Ross, R., Smith, B., Roberts, C., & Kleiner, A. (1994). *The fifth discipline fieldbook.* New York: Doubleday/Currency.

Vygotsky, L. (1978). *Society of mind.* Cambridge, MA: Harvard University Press.

Wheatley, M. (1992). *Leadership and the new science.* San Francisco: Berrett-Koehler.

CHAPTER THIRTEEN

Getting Into the Habit of Reflection

With Bena Kallick

> Building in frequent opportunities for faculty and students to reflect on their teaching and learning enriches education for all. Life can only be understood backwards; but it must be lived forwards.
>
> —Søren Kierkegaard

A bimonthly school faculty meeting opens with a review of the school's goal and mission statements. The principal asks the staff members to reflect on how their teaching relates to the school's goals. The teachers then might study student work or analyze the results of action-research projects. At other times, some of the faculty might capture and document on computers one teacher's reflections on how her practices have strengthened student performance.

This school immerses its staff in continual learning and growth experiences and considers the practice of reflection as significant to its work as planning is. Rather than regard teaching, faculty activities, and school improvement efforts as unrelated, episodic events, teachers use reflection as an opportunity for constructing meaning from their work. They are

SOURCE: Reprinted by permission. Costa, A. L., & Kallick, B. (2000, April). Getting into the habit of reflection. *Educational Leadership* 57(4), 60–62. Alexandria, VA: Association for Supervision and Curriculum Development.

dedicated to maintaining the continuity of the school's core values, while viewing such events as steps in a spiral of planning, experimenting, gathering evidence, and revisiting and modifying their work experiences (Costa & Kallick, 1994).

In teaching, as in life, maximizing meaning from experiences requires reflection. The act of reflection, particularly with a group of teaching colleagues, provides an opportunity for

- Amplifying the meaning of one's work through the insights of others;
- Applying meaning beyond the situation in which it was learned;
- Making a commitment to modifications, plans, and experimentation; and
- Documenting learning and providing a rich base of shared knowledge.
- In teaching, as in life, maximizing meaning from experiences requires reflection.

Every school's goal should be to habituate reflection throughout the organization—individually and collectively, with teachers, students, and the school community.

Internal and External Voices

The ultimate purpose of reflection is to get us into the habit of thinking about our experiences. Once educators have developed this habit, they start hearing both an internal and an external voice of reflection.

The Internal Voice of Reflection. Self-knowledge involves *what* and *how* you are thinking, even unconsciously. Many people are not used to engaging in the "self-talk" that is necessary for hearing their inner voice. To develop this voice, write in a letter to yourself or a journal what you learned from an experience. Remind yourself of what to anticipate in similar future experiences. Some educators find it helpful to record the steps they used to solve a problem and to comment on how useful those steps were.

The External Voice of Reflection. Sharing reflections on events validates, expands, and enriches our internal conversations. By sharing, we can demonstrate and practice effective listening skills: probe for clarity and understanding, ask thoughtful questions, and share our metacognition. Some ways to develop the capacity for sharing reflections include sitting with colleagues in a circle and having each person offer one reflection on the day's activities, or share thoughts in small groups with a designated recorder who synthesizes everyone's comments to present to the large group. Participants could then offer and analyze problem-solving strategies or share an example of a disposition or a habit of mind displayed by each group member.

The Path to Reflection

Documenting these internal and external conversations through teacher journals or student records helps a faculty measure the organization's progress toward a greater valuing of reflective processes. But before making such assessments, the school needs to create an atmosphere for reflection. Step into any school; it will most likely be lively and noisy. Schools must dedicate time and space for reflection, away from the school issues and the student problems that can fill a day. At the beginning of each faculty, grade-level, or department meeting, take a few minutes to establish it as a time and a place for looking backward and inward, not forward and outward.

Soothing music can signal the change in thinking: We are going to take a break from what we have been doing, stand back, and ask ourselves, What have we learned from doing our work today? On their own, many teachers arrange their planning time to devote a day each to planning the curriculum, discussing students, dealing with parents, handling general logistics, and reflecting on student work. Despite a reflective faculty's best intentions to focus on the past, the tradition in education is to simply discard what has happened and move on to new topics. This episodic approach is reflected in both classroom instruction and assessment and in change efforts as schools frantically strive to stay abreast of an array of educational improvements and mandates. Knowledgeable, vigilant, and reflective organizations, however, view school change from a broader perspective—as a process of revealing and emancipating human and organizational intellectual resourcefulness.

In reflective schools, there is no such thing as failure—only the production of personal insights from one's experiences. To be reflective means to mentally wander through where you have been and to try to make some sense of it. Such mental processes include

- Drawing forth cognitive and emotional information from visual, auditory, kinesthetic, and tactile sources;
- Linking information to previous learnings;
- Comparing the results that were anticipated and intended with the results that were achieved;
- Searching for effects and finding connections among causal factors;
- Acting on and processing the information by analyzing, synthesizing, and evaluating;
- Applying learning to contexts beyond the one in which it was learned and making commitments to plans of action; and
- Thinking about thinking: conducting an internal dialogue (metacognition) about the completeness of, satisfaction with, and interest in the reflective process (Costa & Garmston, 2002).

Strategies for Reflection

Schools should invite both students and educators to reflect on teaching and learning, especially during the school change process, which can be hard on students and educators alike (Wasley, Hampel, & Clark, 1997). Students often give educators insights into the worthiness of the changes that the school is instituting, and reflecting on the changes can help students identify how the changes benefit them. Many strategies may facilitate reflection.

Metacognitive reflections invite thinking about thinking and help students make meaning out of events. Teachers can conduct discussions with students about their problem-solving processes. They can invite students to share their metacognition—to reveal their intentions, strategies, and plans for solving a problem; to describe their mental maps for monitoring their strategies during the problem-solving process; and to reflect on strategies to determine their adequacy. Those who practice metacognition learn to listen to, and explore the implications of, one another's strategies and build such habits of mind as empathy, flexibility, interdependence, and persistence.

Collaborative dialogues held between teachers, between a teacher and students, or among students cause participants to share their reflections and outline their progress toward the mastery of learning tasks (Lee & Barnett, 1994) Time should be set aside at the end of a learning sequence—lesson, unit, school day, or year—for participants to question one another about what they have learned and how they can apply their knowledge and skills in future settings.

In an atmosphere of trust, well-crafted questions allow participants to reveal their insights, understandings, and thought processes: As you reflect on this semester's work, which dispositions were you most aware of in your own learning? What metacognitive strategies did you employ to monitor your progress toward your desired outcomes? What insights have you gained that you will use in the future? The resulting dialogue allows staff and students to model and practice listening habits characterized by understanding and empathy, to communicate clearly, and to compose powerful questions.

Portfolios and journals afford opportunities for staff and students to periodically look back on events throughout their journey toward knowledge. Collecting work provides documentation for comparing students' levels of knowledge and performance at the beginning, middle, and end of a project. Focusing on one or two significant skills or pieces of knowledge lets teachers and students reflect on the significance of what they are learning, apply new knowledge to future situations, and form goals and an action plan to consciously modify behavior.

Providing sentence stems might stimulate more thoughtful reflections during portfolio conferences (where reflection can be modeled) or as an option for those who need a "jump start" for reflections:

- I selected this piece of writing because . . .
- What really surprised me about this writing was . . .
- When I look at my other journal entries, I see that this piece is different because . . .
- What makes this piece of writing strong is my use of . . . Here is one example from my writing to show you what I mean . . .

Models of reflection give students images to mirror. Students need to see adults—parents, teachers, and administrators—reflect on their practice. Such models may also be found in literature. In many novels, central characters take a reflective stance as they consider their actions. Some novels and films use reflection as their way of telling a story. For example, in Marcel Proust's *Swann's Way*, the smell of a *petit madeleine* reminds the main character of his past. In *Wilfred Gordon McDonald Partridge* by Mem Fox, Wilfred discovers that life's meaning can come from the retrieval of powerful memories. As he visits with a group of elderly people, he hears them reminisce about significant events from their past, and he realizes that memories are given meaning through making them explicit to someone else.

Developing habits of continual growth and improvement requires self-reflection. As we as individuals, staffs, and organizations reflect on our actions, we gain important information about the efficacy of our thinking. These experiences let us practice the habit of continual growth through reflection. With meditation, trust, consistent modeling, and practice, we and our students learn to listen to the internal and external voices of reflection, and in the process, our school communities truly learn by doing.

A defining condition of being human is that we have to understand the meaning of our experience.

—Jack Mezirow

REFERENCES

Costa, A., & Garmston, R. (2002). *Cognitive Coaching: A foundation for Renaissance schools.* Norwood, MA: Christopher-Gordon.

Costa, A., & Kallick, B. (1994). *Assessment in the learning organization: Shifting the paradigm.* Alexandria, VA: ASCD.

Lee, G., & Barnett, B. (1994). Using reflective questioning to promote collaborative dialogue. *Journal of Staff Development, 15*(1), 16–21.

Wasley, P. A., Hampel, R. L., & Clark, R. W. (1997). *Kids and school reform.* San Francisco: Jossey-Bass.

PART IV

Toward Mindful Instruction

Cogitare is the language we use to grow intelligent behaviors. . . . Speaking Cogitare simply means that we consciously use our language to evoke thinking in others. . . . Do you speak Cogitare?

Arthur L. Costa

CHAPTER FOURTEEN

What Goes On in Your Head When You Teach?

T he following diagram (see Figure 14.1), which deletes such important concepts as affect, motivation, and perceptual abilities, is an attempt to synthesize many psychologists' and psychobiologists' concepts of human intellectual functioning that can serve as a basis for supervisory decision making. (Being well aware of the limitations of reducing to such a crude model so complex and elegant a concept as the human intellect, this attempt is approached with all due humility.)

The purpose of supervision for intelligent teaching would be to enhance the teacher's innate capacity for using these intellectual functions.

Based on the model in Figure 14.1, information taken in is constantly being interpreted in terms of what is already known. If the new information can easily be understood with familiar knowledge in storage, no problem or challenge exists (Assimilation). If, however, the new information cannot be explained or resolved with the knowledge in short- or long-term memory, a discrepancy is perceived and the information must be processed, action taken to gather more information to resolve the discrepancy, and the ultimate resolution tested for its "fit" with reality (Accommodation). Thus, a problem may be defined as some stimulus or challenge, the response to which is not readily apparent.

SOURCE: Adapted from Costa, A., & Garmston, R., "What goes on in your head when you teach?" in *Cognitive Coaching: A Foundation for Renaissance Schools,* copyright © 2002. Reprinted with permission from Christopher-Gordon Publishers.

Figure 14.1   A Model of Intellectual Functioning

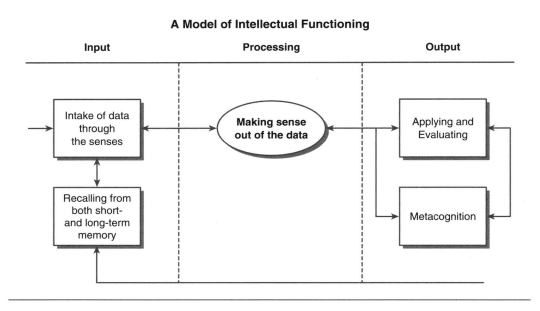

The supervisor's role, then, is crucial as a mediator of intelligent behavior. To stimulate the use of those skills, the supervisor calls attention to discrepancies and poses problems intended to invite more than a memory-type response. To assist a teacher in the resolution of these problems, the supervisor's questions and statements can be designed to elicit specific cognitive functions which produce data, relationships, and generalizations that can be employed to resolve the problem.

Based on this model, we can recast this information processing system into the thought processes of instruction. Basically there are four that roughly correspond to those in the model of thinking above. They are

    I. Planning (The Preactive Stage)

   II. Teaching (The Interactive Stage)

  III. Analyzing and Evaluating (The Reflective Stage)

  IV. Applying (The Projective Stage)

Planning consists of all those intellectual functions performed during that calmer period prior to instruction. *Teaching* includes all those multiple decisions made during the immediacy and spontaneity of the teaching act. They are probably more intuitive and unconscious than the rational decisions of the planning phase. *Analyzing and Evaluating* consists of all those mental processes used to reflect upon, analyze, and judge the teaching act performed in the past. These, too, are probably performed in a more relaxed state and involve "autocriticism" or the ability to stand away from one's self and contemplate one's own intellectual functioning—a uniquely human act. *Applying* involves learning from experience. As a result of the evaluation and analysis phase, commitments are made to use what was learned from the evaluation of teaching in future teaching activities or actions. It involves abstracting from the teaching experience and carrying forth those generalizations to future situations. Each of these four phases of instruction is examined in depth in the following pages.

I. PLANNING—THE PREACTIVE STAGE

Psychologists have found that the human intellect has a limited capacity for handling variables. Miller (1963) described this as "M-Space" or Memory Space. He found that the human being has a capacity for handling and coordinating on the average seven different variables, decisions, or disparate pieces of information at any one time (plus or minus two). This assumes the person has attained the Piagetian stage of formal operations. Not all adults have achieved this stage, however. Therefore, we find that in an average adult population, some may be able only to handle four or so.

It has been found that when humans approach the limits of their capacity, a state of stress begins to set in, as if to feel a "loss of control" because the maximum number of variables controllable is being reached. Much intellectual energy appears to be invested in techniques and systems to simplify, reduce, and select the number of variables with which the intellect has to deal. Planning helps to reduce this stress.

During planning a teacher can describe cues—definitions of acceptable forms of student performance for learning and thus simplify judgments about appropriate and inappropriate student behaviors. The teacher can select potential solutions, back-up procedures, and alternative strategies for those times when a learning activity needs to be redirected, changed, or terminated (Newell & Simon, 1972). Planning is useful because it causes "thought experiments" during which a teacher can mentally rehearse activities to help anticipate possible events and consequences.

Planning calls upon a teacher to view the learning from a student's point of view. It allows the teacher to imagine how this lesson will be perceived and received by the students. Therefore, superior teachers have the capacity to overcome their "ego-centrism" as they are able to place themselves in the position of the learner and view the lesson from multiple perspectives.

Superior teachers seem to have the capacity to operate under two or more classification systems simultaneously. Basically, this means that they can teach toward both immediate and long-range goals simultaneously; they perceive relationships between the day-to-day student behaviors and their cumulative progress toward long-range educational outcomes; and they can prioritize goals and objectives so that they know which student behaviors to reinforce and which to ignore.

Planning a teaching strategy requires task analysis—both structural and operational. Structural analysis is the process of breaking down the content into its component parts, while operational analysis involves a seriation of events into a logical order or sequence (Clark & Yinger, 1979).

Thus, planning may well include the most important decisions teachers make, since this is the design phase upon which rest the other three phases. Planning basically involves four components (Shavelson, 1976, p. 393).

1. *Developing descriptions of students' learning that are to result from instruction.* These are predicted in explicit or observable student behaviors. Zahorick (1975) found this to be of low priority, however.

2. *Identifying the student's present capabilities or entry knowledge.* This information about student abilities is drawn from such sources as previous teaching/learning experiences, data from school records, test scores, and clues from previous teachers, parents, counselors, etc. (Borko, Cone, Russo, & Shavelson, 1979; Shavelson, 1977).

3. *Envisioning the characteristics of an instructional sequence or strategy that will most likely move the students from their present capabilities toward the immediate and ultimately the long-range instructional outcomes.* This sequence is derived from whatever theories or models of teaching, learning, or motivation the teacher has adopted.

4. *Anticipating a method of evaluating outcomes.* The outcomes of this evaluation provide a basis for decisions about the design of the next cycle of instruction.

To handle this "information overload" teachers probably synthesize much of this information into "hypotheses" or best guesses about student readiness for learning. They estimate the probability of successful student behavior as a result of instruction (Coladarchi, 1959, pp. 3–6).

During the planning phase, a wealth of information can be brought to bear because the teacher has the time and lack of pressure to call it from memory. Planning may be done in a formal setting—thinking, writing, and devoting attention to it; or informally, such as while driving to work, washing dishes, upon awakening, etc. The unpressured planning phase is in sharp contrast to the interactive phase of teaching when teachers must respond quickly to the immediate demands of the situation without time to reflect before acting.

This information plays a central role in the decisions teachers make about an overall teaching strategy, including short-range and long-term objectives of instruction, the content and materials to be used, the arrangement of classroom space and social groupings, the time that will be devoted to the several activities, and the acceptability of student performance.

II. TEACHING—THE INTERACTIVE STAGE

O. J. Harvey (1966) described teaching as the second most stressful profession. When a teacher is in the process of constantly interacting with students, he or she is under great pressure and often in a state of uncertainty. This has great influence on the types of decisions a teacher makes (Raiffa, 1970). Thus, while the decision steps in the planning phase model (see Figure 14.2) are similar to those decisions in the interactive stage of teaching, the decisions made during teaching may be either unconscious, spontaneous, planned, or a mixture of each. They are probably modifications of those decisions made during the planning phase. These modifications, however, are made on the spur of the moment. Factors which influence decisions made during interaction are probably not as well defined and as thoroughly considered as alternative teaching strategies and the consequences of each. Insufficient data about students' readiness for learning may be observed or recalled.

Figure 14.2   A Model of Instructional Planning

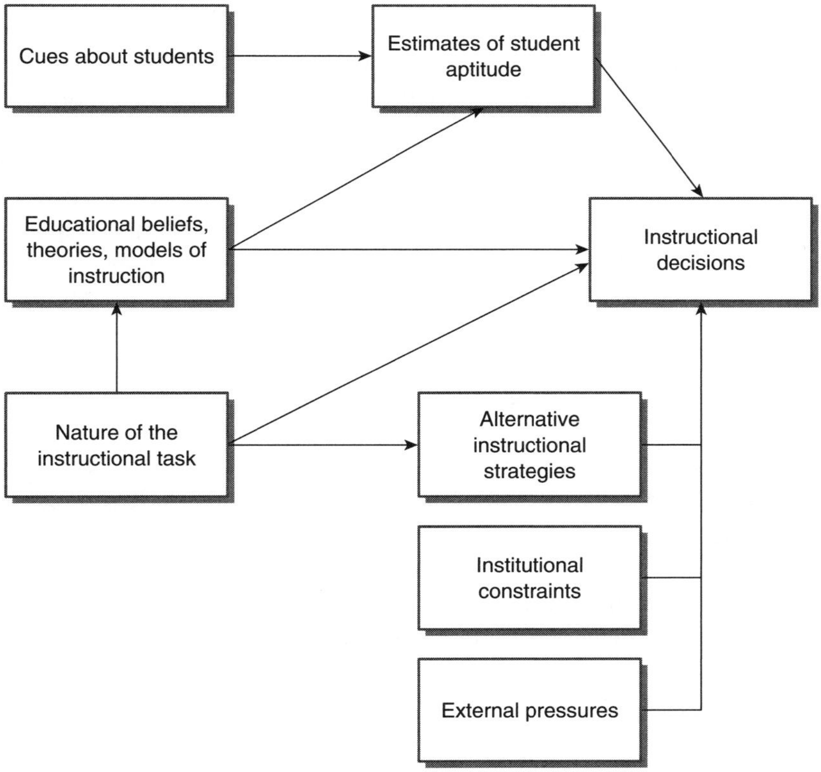

SOURCE: Shavelson & Borko (1977), p. 184. Reprinted by permission.

A teaching strategy is a plan of action. It might be defined in part as a sequentially ordered set of teacher behaviors designed to produce a desired student outcome. Keeping the planned strategy in mind while teaching allows the teacher a backdrop against which to make temporal and comparative judgments and to assess the readiness for more or different learnings. For example, during the beginning of a lesson, much emphasis may be placed upon structuring the task and motivating students to become curious, involved, and focused. Later in the sequence, recall types of thinking might be stressed to review previously learned information and to gather data to be considered later. Still later, higher-level thinking might be invited (Doyle, 1979, p. 54).

Thus, the teacher must make temporal decisions as to when and how fast to move through the steps in the sequence. When are students properly motivated? How much data should be input? When is there an adequate data base on which to predict successful thinking if a higher-level question were to be asked? In the interaction of teaching, a teacher is constantly questioning, probing, observing, and interpreting students' behaviors and making decisions about moving ahead in the sequence or remaining at the present step longer. This sequence of decisions might be diagrammed as in Figure 14.3. (Each of the diamond-shaped boxes represents a decision.)

Thus, a teacher may ask a question as a means of yielding diagnostic information about a student. That information is analyzed in the teacher's mind and a decision made as to which next teacher behavior should be chosen. Should the student's response be praised, extinguished, clarified, or extended? Superior teachers not only know how to ask a range of questions, they also know when to ask them. They know how to select from a repertoire of teacher behaviors and how to predict the outcomes when each is used. Keeping a strategy in mind helps in making these decisions. Without a strategy, classroom interaction is unfocused, random, and chaotic.

A teaching strategy also provides a "screening mechanism" by which teachers can select the relevant and often subtle cues out of the myriad signals that a classroom full of students sends. In order to manage the continual flow of events in the interaction of teaching, the teacher must constantly scan the classroom environment and be alert to cues coming from students. These cues provide an information feedback system on which decisions are based.

As mentioned earlier, however, the human intellect can take in and deal with only a limited amount of data. Information from students is constantly being received through the senses, but teachers' conscious processing of this information can only be directed to a selected number of task-relevant cues. With a strategy in mind, task-relevant cues are noticed more rapidly.

After the teacher sees or hears a particular student behavior (cue), he or she interprets it by either assigning from memory or constructing a particular meaning for it. He or she then either designs or calls from past experience the most appropriate teacher behavior to use in response to

Figure 14.3   Interactive Teaching Decision-Making Flowchart

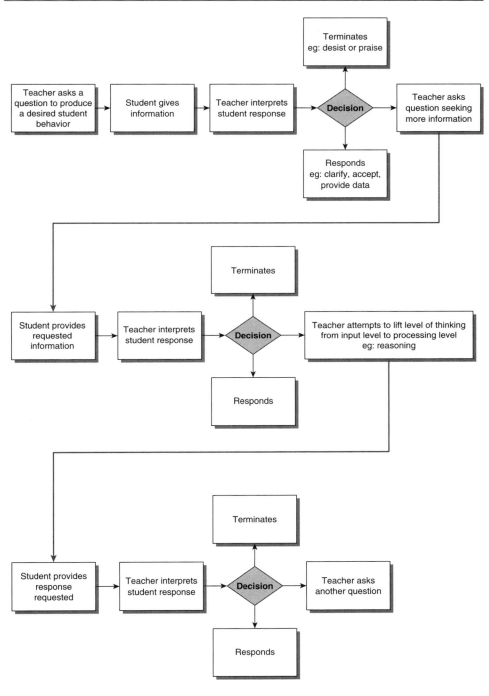

SOURCE: Adapted from Marland (1982).

that student. It is found that teachers possess impressively large amounts of data and perceptions about students. Teachers seldom, however, check on the accuracy of their interpretations about students' cognitive and affective states. The validity of these interpretations and the appropriateness of the next behavior to be used might, therefore, be questionable (Marland, 1982).

Interpretations are also made regarding students with special needs (e.g., disadvantaged, upset, ill, etc.). Thus, teachers often apply compensatory principles in making "special interpretations" for target students. These interpretations may result in unusual teacher behaviors such as praise, granting special favors, using students or their work as models, etc.

Thus, teachers can monitor a classroom for cues that are both conscious and unconscious. Cues are also constantly being received through nonconscious pathways. These cues often "build up" over time and can have great emotional relevance.

Such emotional cues can disrupt conscious information processing. Teachers try to restrain their impulsivity by avoiding strong emotional reactions to classroom events, since emotion tends to preempt attention. Thus, restraint of impulsive or emotional reactions becomes an efficient strategy to reserve the limited capacity for consciously processing the immediate tasks of making classroom decisions (Doyle, 1979, p. 58). Superior teachers probably control their emotional, impulsive reactions to events in (and out) of the classroom.

Routines and management systems are especially helpful in dealing with the information-processing demands of the immediacy, spontaneity, and unpredictability of classroom interaction. Routines reduce the need to attend to the abundance of simultaneous cues from the classroom environment.

Routinizing classroom procedures helps to make the teacher's task more feasible and the students' behavior more predictable. Superior teachers develop routine systems for dealing with many of the classroom-management functions (e.g., taking roll, distributing papers and books, forming groups, passing to recess, etc.), as well as having systematic lesson designs (e.g., spelling, math drills, etc.) and teaching strategies (e.g., questioning sequences, structuring, etc.). When a teacher has established routines, cues that signal discrepancies and abnormalities can be attended to rather than having to deal with all student behaviors all the time (Doyle, 1979, pp. 61–63).

III. ANALYZING AND EVALUATING

The Reflective Stage

Analyzing involves collecting and using understandings derived from the comparison between actual outcomes and the intended outcomes

(Behavioral Objectives) of instruction. If there is great similarity between those behaviors that were predicted during the planning stage and those behaviors that were observed during the interaction stage, then there is a "match" and no discrepancy exists (Assimilation). If, on the other hand, there is a mismatch between student behaviors observed and student behaviors intended, a discrepancy exists which must be resolved or explained (Accommodation). Thus, reasons are given to explain this discrepancy; cause and effect relationships are drawn between instructional situations and behavioral outcomes (Barr & Brown, 1971).

Evaluating involves judging the worth of these decisions made during the planning and interactive phases (Shavelson, 1976, pp. 400–402). During evaluation, some value is placed on the quality of the thinking that the teacher performed before and during teaching. The ability to self-evaluate is what Binet called "autocriticism" (Whimbey & Whimbey, 1976, pp. 116–130). A uniquely human intellectual capacity is our ability to stand apart from, contemplate, and evaluate our own actions. This ability involves a conscious awareness of self-interacting with the real world. It is a teacher's inclination to be aware of their own thinking while they are deciding (Introspection) and to reflect upon their thinking after they've decided (Retrospection) (Clark & Yinger, 1979).

Superior teachers seem to have an internal, rather than external, locus of control. It is one thing for a supervisor to judge the learning outcomes of a teacher's lesson, but what about teachers' estimates of their own success (Harootunian & Yarger, 1981)? Teachers may dismiss or distort information that indicates that students did not learn as a result of their teaching strategy. Teachers may not be entirely rational when they are faced with the possibility that their lesson did not produce desired results; they may be more concerned about maintaining a consistent self-image.

Some studies bear out this point: teachers give themselves credit when there is student improvement, but place blame elsewhere when performance is inadequate. Teachers attribute increase in performance to themselves, but attribute decreases in performance to the environment. (Classroom observers, however, were much less likely to attribute improvement to the teacher and more likely to attribute decreases to the teacher and to student motivation. [Shavelson, 1976, p. 402]).

Thus, teachers who are insecure, or who have low self-esteem, may allow biases to enter their interpretations. Superior teachers, who possess a positive self-image, are more likely to "own" or hold themselves responsible for the outcomes of teaching—whether high or low achievement. *Locus of Control,* therefore, refers to the location where the responsibility for outcomes is placed. Teachers can either assume responsibility for their own actions, or they can place the blame on external forces: parents, genetics, previous teachers, textbooks, students' laziness, etc. (Rohrkemper, 1982).

IV. APPLYING

The Projective Stage

Knowing when to decide seems to be a cognitive skill of teaching. This comes about through experience. Experience alone, however, is not enough unless meaning is ascribed to it and it is applied. Experience then must be compared, differentiated, categorized, and labeled. Such a conceptual system provides a relationship among the many classroom events and the probability of unlikely events. Such a system allows the teacher to recognize and interpret classroom events, departures from routines, and novel occurrences. Thus, the teacher can predict the consequences of possible alternatives and directions of activities. Without this conceptual system, the classroom remains a mass of chaos and confusion. (Since this knowledge comes through experience, it explains why the demands on inexperienced teachers are so intense; their knowledge is both being tested and constructed at the same time. [Doyle, 1979, pp. 65–74]).

Superior teachers, therefore, reflect upon, conceptualize, and apply understandings from one classroom experience to the next. As concepts about teaching accumulate, teachers become more routinized, particularized, predictable, and refined.

Concepts and relationships derived from the analysis and evaluation stage can be extrapolated in making future decisions in planning and interactive teaching. During this application stage, teachers formulate hypothetical statements or future plans. Hypotheses might be characterized by "iffy" thinking. "If I were to do this lesson again, I would . . ." Future-oriented thinking must include such statements as "From now on I'm going to . . ." or "Next time I'll plan to . . ."

Thus, superior teachers seem to make commitments to change their behaviors and strategies based upon self-analysis—gathering and processing the data from their experience and knowledge and projecting forth those relationships to future situations. This step closes the instructional cycle as it serves as a basis for future planning which is in Stage I.

IN SUMMARY

Many of the cognitive or intellectual processes involved in the four components of the instructional act have been examined. To be sure, this does not include all the kinds of teacher decisions or intellectual processes teachers make. It is, however, an attempt to refocus the energies of the supervisor from only the overt behaviors of teaching to include the inner thinking processes of teaching.

REFERENCES

Barr, R., & Brown, V. L. (1971). Evaluation and decision making. *Reading Teacher*, *24*(4).

Borko, H., Cone, R., Russo, D., & Shavelson, R. (1979). Teachers' decision making. In P. Peterson & H. Walberg (Eds.), *Research on Teaching*. Berkeley, CA: McCutchan.

Clark, C., & Yinger, R. (1979). Teachers' thinking. In P. Peterson & H. Walberg (Eds.), *Research on Teaching*. Berkeley, CA: McCutchan.

Coladarci, A. P. (1959, March). The teacher as hypothesis maker. *California Journal of Instructional Improvement, 2*, 3–6.

Doyle, W. (1979). Making managerial decisions in classrooms. In D. Duke (Ed.), *1979 yearbook of the National Society for the Study of Education, Part II*. Chicago: University of Chicago Press.

Harootunian, B., & Yarger, G. (1981, February). Teachers' conceptions of their own success. *ERIC Clearinghouse on Teacher Education*, no. S017 372.

Harvey, O. J. (1966). System structure, flexibility and creativity. In O. J. Harvey (Ed.), *Experience, structure and adaptability* (pp. 39–65). New York: Springer.

Marland, P. W. (1982, January). Paper presented at the Conference on Thinking, University of the South Pacific, Suva, Fiji.

Miller, G. A. (1963, March). The magical number seven, plus or minus two: Some limits on our capacity for processing information. *Psychological Review, 63*(2), 81–97.

Newell, A., & Simon, H. (1972). *Human problem solving*. Englewood Cliffs, NJ: Prentice-Hall.

Raiffa, H. (1970). *Decision analysis: Introductory lectures on choices under uncertainty*. Reading, MA: Addison Wesley.

Rohrkemper, M. (1982). Teacher self-assessment. In D. Duke (Ed.), *Helping teachers manage classrooms*. Alexandria, VA: ASCD.

Shavelson, R. (1976). Teacher decision making. In *The psychology of teaching methods: 1976 yearbook of the National Society for the Study of Education, Part I*. Chicago: University of Chicago Press.

Shavelson, R. (1977, Spring). Teacher sensitivity to the reliability of information in making pedagogical decisions. *American Educational Research Journal, 14*, 144–151.

Shavelson, R., & Borko, H. (1977, Spring). Research on teachers' decisions in planning instruction. *Educational Horizons, 47*.

Whimbey, A., & Whimbey, L. S. (1976). *Intelligence can be taught*. New York: Bantam Books.

Zahorick, J. (1975). Teachers' planning models. *Educational Leadership, 33*, 134–139.

CHAPTER FIFTEEN

Do You Speak *Cogitare?*

Embedded in the vocabulary, inflections, and syntax of the language of adults lie the cognitive processes derived by children. Research over many years has demonstrated the close, entwined relationship of language and thought. From birth, children imitate the sounds, then words, phrases, and thought patterns of the significant adults who mediate their environment (Feuerstein, 1980; Flavell, 1977; Vygotsky, 1962).

Through interaction with adults during children's formative, early years, they develop the foundations of thought that endure throughout their lifetimes. Environments and interactions that demand and provide models of more complex language and thought contribute to the ability to handle complex thinking processes as children mature (Sternberg & Caruso, 1985).

In the past two decades there has been a significant transformation of the American family. With increases in the amount of time passively spent watching television, both parents working or traveling, single-parent families, children giving birth to children, and "latchkey kids," family life sometimes lacks meaningful verbal interaction. Some children are parentally and therefore linguistically deprived. When children enter school lacking the complexity of language and thought needed to master academic demands, they are often disadvantaged (Bronfenbrenner, 1975).

With the recent educational emphasis on the education of the intellect, we wish to have students acquire the ability and inclination to perform discrete thinking skills, cognitive processes, and problem-solving strategies (Ennis, 2001). Success in school and future careers is dependent upon autonomous application of the skills of problem solving, innovation, and decision making.

Educators often assume that students know how to perform these skills. They are asked daily by the teacher or the instructional materials, for example, to summarize, to draw conclusions, to infer, to categorize, or to compare. Yet these processes are often omitted as essential skills to be taught. Students may be at a loss to know what to do when the task is to classify a word list, to infer the author's intent in a reading passage, or to draw conclusions from a set of data.

Adults in the child's environment can subtly and carefully compose language using selected syntax, vocabulary, and inflection to stimulate, engage, and practice desired cognitive processes in children. Teachers can consciously select key cognitive terminology so that students will encounter those words in common, everyday dialogue. We can formulate questions to cause students to exercise certain cognitive functions. We can provide data that students must interpret for themselves. We can remain nonjudgmental so that children must make their own judgments. It is believed that if adults will monitor their own language for the embedment of cognitive terminology and if they will seize opportunities for thinking in the day-to-day interactions of the classroom, a positive effect will result in students' cognitive structures that, in turn, will produce an increase in their academic success.

What follows are some suggestions for monitoring our language and some ways to enhance children's thinking during the daily interactions of classroom life.

THINKING WORDS

Teachers are often heard to admonish students to think: "Think hard!" Students are sometimes criticized for not having the inclination to do so: "These kids just go off without thinking."

The term *think* is a vague abstraction covering a wide range of mental activities. Two possible reasons why students fail to engage in it are (1) the vocabulary is a foreign language to them, and (2) they may not know how to perform the specific skills that term implies. When adults speak *Cogitare*—using specific cognitive terminology and instructing students in ways to perform those skills—they will be more inclined to use them (Astington & Olson, 1990). Table 15.1 provides some examples.

As children hear these cognitive terms in everyday use and experience the cognitive processes that accompany these labels, they will internalize the words and use them as part of their own vocabulary. Teachers will also want to give specific instruction in those cognitive functions so that students possess experiential meaning along with the terminology (Beyer, 2001).

DISCIPLINE

When disciplining children, teachers often make the decisions about which behaviors to desist and which to reinforce. Teachers can speak Cogitare—posing questions that cause children to examine their own

Table 15.1   Speaking Cogitare for Thinking

Instead of saying	Speak Cogitare by saying
"Let's look at these two pictures."	"Lets *compare* these two pictures."
"What do you think will happen when . . . ?"	"What do you *predict* will happen when . . . ?"
How can you put into groups . . . ?"	"How can you *classify* . . . ?"
Let's work this problem."	"Let's *analyze* this problem."
What do you think would have happened if . . . ?"	"What do you *speculate* would have happened if . . . ?"
"What did you think of this story?"	"What *conclusions* can you draw about this story?"
"How can you explain . . . ?"	"What *hypotheses* do you have that might explain . . . ?"
"How do you know that's true?"	"What *evidence* do you have to support . . . ?"
"How else could you use this . . . ?"	"How could you *apply* this . . . ?"

behavior, search for the consequences of that behavior, and choose more appropriate actions for themselves (Bailis & Hunter, 1985). See examples in Table 15.2.

Table 15.2   Speaking Cogitare to Discipline

Instead of saying	Speak Cogitare by saying
"Be quiet!"	"The noise you're making is disturbing us. Is there a way you can work so that we don't hear you?"
"Sarah, get away from Shawn!"	"Sarah, can you find another place to do your best work?"
"Stop interrupting!"	"Since it's Maria's turn to talk, what do you need to do?"
"Stop running!"	"Why do you think we have the rule about always walking in the halls?"

Discussions with children about appropriate behavior, classroom and school rules, and courtesy will be necessary if they are to learn appropriate alternatives. Then, when they occasionally forget, they can go back in their memory for what was learned. Soon they will monitor their own behavior— an important dimension of metacognition (Costa, 1984).

PROVIDE DATA, NOT SOLUTIONS

Sometimes we rob children of the opportunity to take charge of their own behavior by providing solutions, consequences, and appropriate actions for them. If adults would merely provide data as input for children's decision making, we can cause them to act more autonomously, to become aware of the effects of their behavior on others, and to become more empathic by sensing the verbal and nonverbal cues from others. We can speak Cogitare by giving data, divulging information about ourselves, or sending "I" messages, as demonstrated in Table 15.3.

Some children, of course, will be unable to detect these data as cues for self-control. In such cases, we may have to step in and provide more specific directions for appropriate behavior. We can start, however, by allowing the student to control him or herself.

CLASSROOM MANAGEMENT

When communicating instructions on how to perform a task, teachers can speak Cogitare, which will cause students to analyze a task, decide what is needed, then act autonomously. Too often teachers may give all the information so that students merely perform the task without having to infer meaning. Examples of speaking Cogitare are presented in Table 15.4.

Table 15.3   Speaking Cogitare to Provide Data

When children	*Speak Cogitare by saying*
Make noise by tapping their pencils	"I want you to know that your pencil tapping is disturbing me."
Interrupt	"I like it when you take turns to speak."
Whine	"It hurts my ears."
Are courteous	"I liked it when you came in so quietly and went right to work."
Chew gum	"I want you to know that gum chewing in my class disturbs me."

Table 15.4   Speaking Cogitare to Communicate Instructions

Instead of saying	Speak Cogitare by saying
"For our field trip, remember to bring spending money, comfortable shoes, and a warm jacket."	"What must we remember to bring with us on our field trip?"
"The bell has rung; it's time to go home. Clear off your desks, slide your chairs under the desk quietly, and line up at the door."	"The bell has rung. What must we do to get ready to go home?"
"Get 52 cups, 26 scissors, and 78 sheets of paper. Get some butcher paper to cover the desks."	"Everyone will need two paper cups, a pair of scissors, and three sheets of paper. The desktops will need to be protected. Can you figure out what you'll need to do?"
"Remember to write your name in the upper right-hand corner of your paper."	"So that I easily can tell who the paper belongs to, what must you remember to do?"
"You need to start each sentence with a capital and end with a period."	"This sentence would be complete with two additions. Can you figure out what they are?"

PROBING FOR SPECIFICITY

Oral language is filled with omissions, generalizations, and vaguenesses. Our language is conceptual rather than operational, value laden, and sometimes deceitful. Speaking Cogitare causes others to define their terms, become specific about their actions, make precise comparisons, and use accurate descriptors (Laborde, 1984).

Being alert to certain vague or unspecified terms cues our need to speak Cogitare—the language of specifics. These vague terms fall into several categories:

1. Universals, including "always," "never," "all," or "everybody"

2. Vague action verbs: "know about," "understand," "appreciate"

3. Comparators such as "better," "newer," "cheaper," "*more* nutritious"

4. Unreferenced pronouns: "they," "them," "we"

5. Unspecified groups: "the teachers," "parents," "things"

6. Assumed rules or traditions, including "ought," "should," or "must"

When such words or phrases are heard in the speech or writings of others, we speak Cogitare by having them specify, define, or reference their terms, as shown in Table 15.5.

Table 15.5   Speaking Cogitare to Ask for Specifics

When we hear	Speak Cogitare by saying
"He *never* listens to me."	"Never?" "Never, ever?"
"Everybody has one."	"Everybody?" "Who, exactly?"
"*Things* go better with . . ."	"Which things specifically?"
"Things *go* better with . . ."	"Go? Go-how, specifically?"
"Things go *better* with . . ."	"Better than what?"
"You *shouldn't* do that . . ."	"What would happen if you did?"
"The *parents* . . ."	"Which parents?"
"I want them to *understand* . . ."	"What exactly will they be doing if they understand . . . ?"
"This cereal is more *nutritious*."	"More nutritious than what?"
"*They* won't let me . . ."	"Who are 'they'?"
"*Administrators* . . ."	"Which administrators?"

"Critical thinkers" are characterized by their ability to use specific terminology, to refrain from overgeneralization, and to support their assumptions with valid data. Speaking Cogitare by having children use precise language develops those characteristics (Ennis, 2001).

METACOGNITION

Thinking about thinking begets more thinking (Costa, 1984). Having children describe the mental processes they are using, the data they are lacking, and the plans they are formulating causes them to think about their own thinking—to metacogitate. When teachers speak Cogitare they cause the covert thought processes that students are experiencing to become overt. Whimbey (1985) refers to this as "Talk Aloud Problem Solving." See examples provided in Table 15.6.

As teachers probe students to describe what's going on inside their heads when thinking is taking place, students become more aware of their own thinking processes; and, as they listen to other students describe their metacognitive processes, they develop flexibility of thought and an appreciation that there are several logical ways to solve the same problem.

Table 15.6   Speaking Cogitare to Explore Thought Processes

When children say	Speak Cogitare by saying
"The answer is 43 pounds, 7 ounces."	"Describe the steps you took to arrive at that answer."
"I don't know how to solve this problem."	"What can you do to get started?"
"I'm comparing . . ."	"What goes on in your head when you compare?"
"I'm ready to begin."	"Describe your plan of action."
"We're memorizing our poems."	"What do you do when you memorize?"
"I like the large one best."	"What criteria are you using to make your choice?"
"I'm finished."	"How do you know you're correct?"

PRESUPPOSITIONS

Language may be interpreted in terms of its "surface" meaning and its "structural" meaning. *Surface meaning* refers to the word definitions, syntax, semantics, grammar, verb forms, modifiers, and so on. *Structural meaning,* on the other hand, refers to the subtle nuances, connotations, feelings, and images conveyed by the words.

A *presupposition* is a hidden, covert, implicit meaning buried within the structure of the statement or sequence of language. For example: "Even Richard could pass that course." Hidden with the substructure of this sentence are several implied meanings: That Richard is not too bright a student, and further, that the course must be a cinch! Neither of these pieces of information is overtly present in the surface structure of the sentence. It does not say, "Even Richard, who is not too bright a student, could pass that course, which is a cinch!" The implicit meaning or presupposition, however, is blatant (Elgin, 1980).

Over time, these messages "seep" into children's awareness below the level of consciousness. Often they are unaware that such verbal violence is being used against them. They feel hurt or insulted in response to language that may sound, on the surface, like a compliment. Interestingly, people behave in response to other's perceptions of them—they behave as if they are expected to behave that way. Over time, these negative presuppositions accumulate and produce in students poor self-esteem and a negative self-concept as a thinker. Their negative behavior follows.

Interestingly, we can also use *positive* presuppositions. Teachers can purposely select language to convey a positive self-concept as a thinker: "As you plan your project, what criteria for your research report will you keep in mind?" Notice the positive presuppositions: that you are planning, that you know the criteria for the research report, that you can keep them in your mind, and that you can metacognitively apply them as you work.

Teachers never purposely set out to deprecate students' self-esteem. Unconsciously, however, these negative presuppositions may creep into the language of classroom interaction. Teachers who speak Cogitare will monitor their own language for their positive rather than negative presuppositions (see Table 15.7 for examples).

Table 15.7   Speaking Cogitare to Use Positive Language

Instead of saying	Speak Cogitare by saying
"Why did you forget to do your assignment?"	"As you plan for your assignment, what materials will you need?"
"Why don't you like to paint?"	"We need you to paint a picture to add to our gallery of artists."
"Did you forget again?"	"Tell us what you do to help you remember."
"When you will grow up?"	"As we grow older, we learn by reflecting on such experiences as this one."
"Here, I'll give you an easier puzzle; then you'll be successful."	"As the puzzles get more difficult, how will you use planning like this again?"

THE STUDY OF COGITARE

Like any language, Cogitare is dynamic. It can be analyzed, refined, transmitted to others, created, and can become archaic. Students, too, can explore the linguistic structure of Cogitare.

We can, for example, focus on word clusters or syntactical cues within the language that give clues as to what cognitive operations those words evoke. This is sometimes referred to as "discourse analysis." It includes such cognitive processes as concept formation, relationship identification, and pattern recognition.

For example, students can search for relationships as a way of "linking" information. They can find the word or word cluster that cues the thinking process of that relationship. This process is called "relationship identification." It requires students to

Identify separate ideas that are related within a sentence

Identify the type of relationship between the ideas: addition, comparison, causality, sequence, or definition

Identify the linguistic cue for the performance of that cognitive relationship (and, or, but, after, while, and so on)

Table 15.8 presents some of the possibilities.

Table 15.8   Some Analyses Using Cogitare

Cognitive Process	Type of Relationship	Example of Linguistic Cue
Addition	Two ideas go together in the same way.	"He is intelligent *and* he is kind."
Comparison	Common attributes are shared.	"Shawn and Sarah *both* play the violin."
Contrast	Two ideas don't go together.	"He is healthy *but* he doesn't exercise."
Causality	One event causes another.	"Peter went home *because* his work was finished."
Sequence	One event happens before, during, or after another event.	"He went home *then* he went to the library."

It is believed that teaching students to be alert to the cognitive process embedded in written and spoken language can help them become aware of their own language and thought. It can help them decode the syntactic, semantic, and rhetorical signals found in all languages, and it can help them integrate the complex interaction of language, thought, and action (Marzano & Hutchins, 1985).

IN SUMMARY

Our language is a tool. As a tool we can use it to enhance others. Speaking Cogitare simply means that we consciously use our language to evoke thinking in others by

1. Using specific cognitive terminology rather than vague abstract terms

2. Posing questions that cause children to examine their own behavior, search for the consequences of that behavior, and choose more appropriate actions for themselves

3. Giving data, divulging information about ourselves, or sending "I" messages so that students must "process" the information

4. Causing students to analyze a task, decide on what is needed, then act autonomously

5. Causing others to define their terms, become specific about their actions, make precise comparisons, and use accurate descriptors

6. Causing the covert thought processes that students are experiencing to become overt (metacognition)

7. Employing positive presuppositions to enhance students' self-concept as thinkers

8. Helping children study and become alert to the cues in the structure of language that evoke thought processes.

By asking questions, selecting terms, clarifying ideas and processes, providing data, and withholding value judgments, we can stimulate and enhance the thinking of others. Cogitare is the language we use to grow intelligent behavior.

REFERENCES

Astington, S., & Olson, D. (1990). Metacognition and metalinguistic language: Learning to talk about thought. *Applied Psychology: An International Review, 39*(1), 77–87.

Bailis, M., & Hunter, M. (1985, August). Do your words get them to think? *Learning, 14*(1).

Beyer, B. (2001). Practical strategies for the direct teaching of thinking skills. In A. L. Costa (Ed.), *Developing minds: A resource book for teaching thinking.* Alexandria, VA: Association for Supervision and Curriculum Development.

Bronfenbrenner, U. (1975). *Influences on human development.* Hillsdale, IL: Erlbaum.

Costa, A. (1984, November). Mediating the metacognitive. *Educational Leadership, 42*(3), 57–62.

Elgin, S. (1980). *The gentle art of verbal self defense.* New York: Dorset Press.

Ennis, R. (2001). An outline of goals for a critical thinking curriculum and its assessment. In A. L. Costa (Ed.), *Developing minds: A resource book for teaching thinking.* Alexandria, VA: Association for Supervision and Curriculum Development.

Feuerstein, R. (1980). *Instrumental enrichment.* Baltimore, MD: University Park Press.

Flavell, J. (1977). *Cognitive development.* Englewood Cliffs, NJ: Prentice-Hall.

Laborde, G. (1984). *Influencing with integrity.* Palo Alto, CA: Syntony Press.

Marzano, R., & Hutchins, C. L. (1985). *Thinking skills: A conceptual framework.* Aurora, CO: Mid-continent Regional Educational Laboratory.

Sternberg, R., & Caruso, S. (1985). Practical modes of knowing. In E. Eisner (Ed.), *Learning and teaching the ways of knowing. 84th Yearbook of the National Society for the Study of Education.* Chicago: University of Chicago Press.

Vygotsky, L. S. (1962). *Thought and language.* Cambridge: Massachusetts Institute of Technology Press.

Whimbey, A. (1985). Test results for teaching thinking. In A. Costa (Ed.), *Developing minds: A resource book for teaching thinking.* Alexandria, VA: Association for Supervision and Curriculum Development.

CHAPTER SIXTEEN

Teacher Behaviors That Enable Student Thinking

> Act so as to elicit the best in others and thereby in thyself.
>
> Felix Adler

What the teacher says and does in the classroom greatly affects student learning. Certain teacher behaviors influence students' achievement, self-concept, social relationships, and thinking abilities. Teacher behaviors that invite, maintain, and enhance students' thinking in the classroom fall into four major categories:

1. *Questioning* to challenge students' intellect and to help students collect and recollect information, process that information into meaningful relationships, and apply those relationships in different or novel situations. Questions can focus students on their own emotions, motivations, and metacognitive processes.

2. *Structuring* the classroom by arranging for individual, small-group, and total-group interaction; by managing the resources of time, energy, space, and materials to facilitate thinking; and by legitimizing thinking as a valid goal for students.

SOURCE: Reprinted by permission. Costa, A. L. (2001). Teacher behaviors that enable thinking. In A. Costa (Ed.), *Developing minds: A resource book for teaching thinking*. Alexandria, VA: Association for Supervision and Curriculum Development.

3. *Responding* to students so as to create a trusting environment and to help maintain, extend, and become aware of their thinking.

4. *Modeling* in their own behaviors those *desirable* intellectual capacities and dispositions as teachers encounter the day-to-day problems and strategies of the classroom and school.

Classroom interaction generally falls into two categories: *recitation* and *dialogue*. Recitation is characterized by recurring sequences of teacher questions and student answers, where students recite what they already know or are learning through the teacher's questioning. The interaction is teacher-centered because the teacher controls the classroom by asking questions and reinforcing responses. Dialogue, on the other hand, involves group interaction in which students discuss what they don't know, usually by considering a subject from more than one point of view. The teacher, as the facilitator, creates an atmosphere of freedom, clarity, and equality.

This latter form of classroom interaction—dialogue—must be kept in focus as we consider which teacher behaviors are facilitative. Analyses of those instructional strategies intended to enhance thinking, creativity, cooperation, and positive self-worth stress the need for this dialectic discussion strategy.

I. QUESTIONING TO CHALLENGE STUDENTS' INTELLECT

> Learning is an engagement of the mind that changes the mind.
>
> Martin Heidegger, *What Do We Mean?*

Minds are generally engaged through some form of cognitive dissonance, a provocation, or an inquiry. Effective teachers create that dissonance either by raising a point of uncertainty or discrepancy in the content, by pressing the students to raise such points as they try to understand what is being presented, and by challenging students' assumptions or conclusions. Ultimately, engagement occurs through student interest and teachers can set the conditions in which the student's interest is piqued.

Teacher's questions can provide rich invitations for developing such student engagement. Through their questioning strategies, teachers engage and transform the mind. To draw forth, become aware of, practice and apply skillful thinking, learners must be presented with problems and questions, the answers to which are not apparent. Both teachers and students are encouraged to raise their own dilemmas and paradoxes as they consider different points of view. Our purpose is to continuously reinforce the habit of questioning and problem posing as well as increase the possibility for a sense of wonderment and curiosity.

Designing Powerful Questions

Careful, intentional, and productive questioning, therefore, is one of the most powerful tools of effective teachers. When a teacher begins a question with, "Who can tell me . . . ?" there is an immediate signal that only certain students can tell the teacher the answer to the question. If, on the other hand, a teacher begins the question with, "What do we know about . . . ?" the signal is that "we," all of us, probably have something to offer. If questions are posed, the answers to which are already known, there is a tendency for students to "guess what's in the teacher's head" and search for conformity or agreement. But if neither the teacher nor the students know the answers, then there is a sincere and collaborative inquiry—searching together for approaches and solutions. The focus becomes one of developing strategies to resolve the problem and generate alternative answers to the question rather than to conform and produce an answer that will be confirmed or negated by someone of higher authority.

What follows is a discussion of powerful questioning strategies. The intent is to equip teachers with the linguistic skills and metacognitive maps:

- To monitor their own questions;
- To formulate and pose questions which intentionally challenge students' intellect and imagination;
- To purposely draw forth student's awareness and employment of thinking skills, cognitive tasks, and dispositions;
- To model complex questions in their own interaction so students will increase their habit of posing complex questions and develop a questioning attitude.

Some questions may place limits on students' thinking. Limits to thinking are to be avoided if skillful thinking is to be exercised. To heighten awareness of their own questions and to insure that they are not miss-cueing, confusing, or limiting student thought, let us begin by examining some questioning "don'ts" before presenting some questioning "do's."

Some Questioning Patterns to Avoid

There are at least five types of questions which mis-cue students' thinking because they send confusing and mixed messages. They do *not* belong in thoughtful lesson designs:

1. *Verification questions:* The answers to which are already known by you or by the student:

   "What is the name of . . . ?"

   "How many times did you . . . ?"

2. *Closed questions* that can be answered "yes," "no," or "I can."

   "Can you recite the poem?"

   "Who can state the formula for . . . ?"

3. *Rhetorical questions* in which the answer is given within the question:

   "In what year was the War of 1812?"

   "Since when has Mikhail Gorbachev had his birth mark?"

   "How long is the 100-yard dash?"

4. *Defensive questions* which cause justification, resistance, and self-protection:

   "Why didn't you complete your homework?"

   "Why would you do a thing like that?"

   "Are you misbehaving again?"

5. *Agreement questions* the intent of which is to invite others to agree with your opinion or answer:

   "This is really the best solution, isn't it?"

   "Let's do it my way, O.K.?"

   "We really should get started now, shouldn't we?"

   "Who can name the three basic parts of a plant? Root, stems, and leaves, right?"

Composing Powerful Questions: Some Questioning "Do's"

Questions that evoke in students an awareness of and engagement in the mind. They have *three* characteristics (Costa & Garmston, 2005, pp. 48–49):

1. They are invitational.

- *An approachable voice is used.* There is a lilt and melody in the questioner's voice rather than a flat, even tenor.

- *Plurals are used to invite multiple rather than singular concepts:*

   "What are *some* of your *goals?*"

   "What *ideas* do you have?"

   "What *alternatives* are you considering?"

- *Words are selected to express tentativeness:*

  "What conclusions *might* you draw?"

  "What *may* indicate his acceptance?"

  "What *hunches* do you have to explain this situation?"

- *Invitational stems are used to enable the behavior to be performed:*

  "As you consider . . ."

  "As you reflect on . . ."

  "As you plan for . . ."

- *Positive Presuppositions assume capability and empowerment:*

  "What are *some* of the *benefits you will derive* from *engaging* in this activity?"

  "*As you anticipate* your project, what are *some indicators* that you are progressing *and succeeding?*"

2. **They engage specific cognitive operations at various levels of complexity.**
   (Refer to the three levels described below.)

3. **They address external or internal content that is relevant to the learner.**

   - *External Content* might be what is going on in the environment outside the learner:

A lesson content	Another student
A meeting	A project
A playground experience	A home experience

   - *Internal Content* might be what is going on inside the person's mind, heart, or emotion:

Satisfaction	Puzzlement
Frustration	Thinking processes (Metacognition)
Feelings/Emotions	

Levels of Complexity

Questions invite different levels of complexity of thinking. Early in children's lives they learn to be alert to certain syntactical cues to know how to behave or what to think. Teachers will want to deliberately use these linguistic tools to engage and challenge complex thinking in their students' minds. The following poem captures the levels of thinking at increasingly complex levels:

The Three-Story Intellect

There are one-story intellects, two-story intellects, and three-story intellects with skylights.

All fact collectors, who have no aim beyond their facts, are one-story men.

Two-story men compare, reason, generalize, using the labors of the fact collectors as well as their own.

Three-story men idealize, imagine, predict—their best illumination comes from above, through the skylight.

Oliver Wendell Holmes

Oliver Wendell Holmes reminds us that all three levels of thinking are important. Teachers will want to design and pose questions that elicit all three levels of intellect. Figure 16.1 is a graphic representation of Holmes' poem. It might be used as a "mental map" to assist teachers in posing questions. At the first story are the "*data gathering*" cognitive operations; at the second story are the cognitive operations by which meaning is made of the data—the "processing level." The third story of the house invites students to go "beyond the skylights" to speculate, elaborate, and apply concepts in new and hypothetical situations.

Following are some examples of questions that incorporate the criteria for powerful questions described above and that are intended to invite specific cognitive operations at each level of the Three-Story Intellect.

COGNITIVE LEVELS OF QUESTIONS

I. Gathering and Recalling Information (INPUT)

To cause the student to INPUT data, questions and statements are designed to draw from the student the concepts, information, feelings, or experiences acquired in the past and stored in long- or short-term memory. They can also be designed to activate the senses to gather data that the student can then process at the next higher level. There are several cognitive processes included at the INPUT level of thinking. Some verbs that may serve as the predicate of a behavioral objective statement are

Figure 16.1   The Three-Story Intellect House

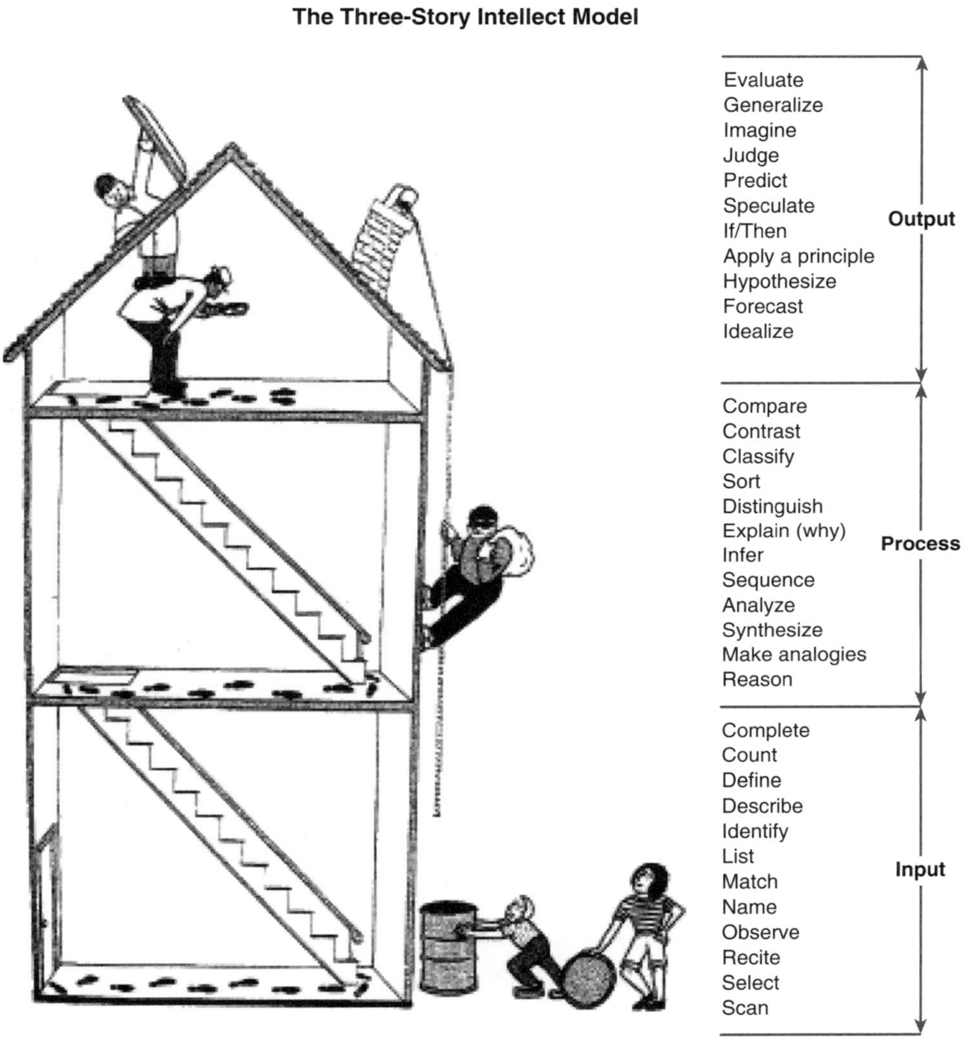

The Three-Story Intellect Model

Output
- Evaluate
- Generalize
- Imagine
- Judge
- Predict
- Speculate
- If/Then
- Apply a principle
- Hypothesize
- Forecast
- Idealize

Process
- Compare
- Contrast
- Classify
- Sort
- Distinguish
- Explain (why)
- Infer
- Sequence
- Analyze
- Synthesize
- Make analogies
- Reason

Input
- Complete
- Count
- Define
- Describe
- Identify
- List
- Match
- Name
- Observe
- Recite
- Select
- Scan

SOURCE: From Costa, A. (1991) Teacher Behaviors That Enable Student Thinking. In A. Costa (Ed.), *Developing Minds: A Resource Book for Teaching Thinking*. Alexandria, VA: Association for Supervision and Curriculum Development. P. 38.

completing	identifying	observing
counting	listing	reciting
defining	matching	scanning
describing	naming	selecting

Examples of questions and statements designed to elicit these cognitive objectives are

Question/Statement	Desired Cognitive Behavior
"Which states bound California?"	Naming
"How does the picture make you feel?"	Describing
"What word does this picture go with?"	Matching
"What does the word 'haggard' mean?"	Defining
"What were the names of the children in the story?"	Naming
"What did you see the man doing in the film?"	Observing
"Which ball is the blue one?"	Identifying
"How does the Gettysburg Address begin?"	Reciting
"How many coins are there in the stack?"	Counting
"Which words in this list are rhyming words?"	Selecting
"The Mexican houses were made of mud bricks called . . . what?"	Completing
"Watch what color it turns when I put the litmus paper in the liquid."	Observing
"List the first four numbers in a set of positive integers."	Listing
"How did you feel about the grade you received in science?"	Recalling

II. Making Sense Out of the Information Gathered (Processing)

To cause the student to PROCESS the data gathered through the senses and retrieve from long- and short-term memory, questions and statements are designed to draw some relationships of cause and effect, to synthesize, analyze, summarize, compare, contrast, or classify the data that he/she has acquired or observed. Following are verbs that may serve as the predicate of a behavioral objective statement if the desired cognitive behavior of students is at the level of processing. Often, when students are doing research projects, they are inclined to copy or paraphrase the text that is in the resource book. When students understand the research is, by definition, inquiry, then they can learn to raise questions that can be answered through their research rather than answer questions of completion. The following list of words can guide students to raise questions at a more complex level. The assignment might read, "In your research, you must be able to answer definitional questions as well as to answer any question you raise that uses one of the following verbs." The verbs that are listed below also serve as good ones to use when you are trying to raise an "essential question" for a given unit of study.

analyzing	distinguishing	making analogies
categorizing	experimenting	organizing
classifying	explaining	sequencing
comparing	grouping	synthesizing
contrasting	inferring	

Examples of questions designed to elicit these cognitive objectives are

Question/Statement	Desired Cognitive Behavior
"In what ways do you see the Civil War like the Revolutionary War?	Comparing
"What suggests to you that Columbus believed he could get to the East by sailing West?"	Explaining
"From our experiments with food coloring in different water temperatures, what might you infer about the movement of molecules?"	Inferring
"How might you arrange the rocks in the order of their size?"	Sequencing
"As you analyze the development of machines, what were some of their effects on the people living at that time?"	Explaining Causality
"How might you arrange in groups the things that a magnet will and will not pick up?"	Grouping
"What other machines can you think of that work in the same way that this one does?"	Making Analogies
"What are some characteristics of Van Gogh's work that make you think this painting is his?"	Distinguishing
"What might you do to test your idea?"	Experimenting
"In what ways are pine needles different from redwood needles?"	Contrasting

"In what ways might you arrange the blocks so that they have a crowded feeling?"	Organizing
"What data are we going to need in order to solve this problem?"	Analyzing
"Arrange the following elements of a set in ascending order: 13/4, 3/2, 5/6, 32/5."	Sequencing
"How does the formula for finding the volume of a cone compare with the formula for the volume of a pyramid?"	Comparing

III. Applying and Evaluating Actions in Novel Situations (OUTPUT)

Questions and statements which cause OUTPUT are designed to have the student go beyond the concept or principle that he/she has developed and to use this relationship in a novel or hypothetical situation. Application invites the student to think creatively and hypothetically, to use imagination, to expose a value system, or to make a judgment. These questions most powerfully lend themselves to the research process because the answers to these questions cannot be found in books or in databases. Students are required to make sense out of the resource material and to answer a question that requires them to invest in the material learned. We often ask this as a "so what?" question. In addition, essential questions can be raised at this level and they can take on a more philosophical tone.

Verbs that may serve as the predicate of a behavioral objective statement if your desired cognitive behavior of students is at the level of application include

Applying a principle	Imagining	Evaluating
Judging	Hypothesizing	Generalizing
Model building	Predicting	Extrapolating
Speculating	Forecasting	Transferring

Examples of questions designed to elicit these cognitive objectives are

Question/Statement	**Desired Cognitive Behavior**
"What do you suppose will happen to our weather if a high pressure area moves in?"	Forecasting
"If our population continues to grow as it does, what so you suppose life will be like in the twenty-first century?"	Speculating

"Drawing on what you know about how heat affects the speed of movement of the molecules, what do you predict will happen when we put the liquid in the refrigerator?"	Predicting
"Imagine what life would be like if there were no laws to govern us."	Imagining
"What might you say about all countries' economies that are dependent upon only one crop?"	Generalizing
"Design some ways to use this bimetal strip to make a fire alarm."	Applying
"How could you use this clay to make a model of a plant cell?"	Model Building
"What would be a fair solution to this problem?"	Evaluating
"As you consider the periodic table and the invention of the microscope, which was more essential to organizing chemistry?"	Judging
"From what we have learned about its characteristics, what other examples of romantic music can you cite?"	Applying a Principle
"What do you think might happen if we placed the saltwater fish in the tank of freshwater?"	Hypothesizing

II. STRUCTURING THE CLASSROOM FOR THINKING

Structuring may be described as the way teachers control such classroom environmental resources as time, space, human energy, and materials. Even the "unstructured" classroom imposes a structure to which students react and within which students interact. In a well-structured classroom where students know the objectives of the lesson, time is used efficiently, the teacher is clear about the directions, the classroom environment conveys a congenial sense of order, and student energies are engaged in meaningful learning tasks which, in turn, produces higher achievement.

Structuring the classroom for thinking should be conscious, deliberate, clear, and based on the desired outcomes for students. Knowing what learning tasks are to be accomplished and what type of interaction is desired, the teacher gives directions, states ground rules, describes objectives, places limits, and creates a classroom organizational pattern intended to best elicit the desired cognitive performance from students. Three central aspects of teacher structuring include

1. The clarity of verbal and written instructions
2. The structuring of time and energy
3. The different ways of organizing and arranging interaction patterns

Instructional Clarity

Teacher: "Why do you think Robert Frost repeated the last line of this verse?"

Student: (No response)

Teacher: (After a long pause) "Well, what feelings did you have as you read the poem?"

Student: "Why don't you just tell us the answer?"

If you are specific in what you expect, then others will be specific in fulfilling your expectations.

Rulon G. Craven

Students expend great amounts of energy trying to figure out teachers' intentions. If the messages and directions presented by the teacher are confused, garbled, and unclear, then students will have a more difficult learning task. Because some students come from homes, previous teachers, or other schools where thoughtful behavior was not valued, they often are dismayed and resistant to the teacher's invitations to think. Such resistance and reluctance to respond would indicate that a program to develop creativity, flexibility, and risk-taking is sorely needed.

If students are to realize that thinking is a legitimate goal of education, then teachers must convey to students that the goal of instruction is thinking, that the responsibility for thinking is theirs, that it is often desirable to have more than one solution to a problem, that it is commendable when students take time to plan, that an answer can be changed with additional information.

Structuring Time and Energy

It is nonsense to say there is not enough time to be fully informed. Time given to thought is the greatest time-saver of all.

Norman Cousins

Achievement correlates highly with the amount of time students are successfully engaged in learning. But an emphasis on thinking cannot be viewed by the student as an isolated event. Students must repeatedly receive cognitive skills instruction and encounter situations that require them to think throughout the school day, across academic content areas, and over extended periods of time. Only then can students transfer, generalize, and apply cognitive skills (Sternberg & Wagner, 1982, pp. 50, 53).

Structuring time alone, however, is inadequate. Schools must also consider the quality of the task during that time: the degree that students' *energies* are engaged. All knowledge arises or is constructed from interactions between learners and their environment. The extent to which teachers mediate the interaction of pupils with instructional materials and with the content of the lesson not only determines how well decision-making and problem-solving skills are learned, it also influences students' attitudes toward the school, the teachers, the content to be learned, and learning itself. In effective learning environments, students are encouraged to become active thinkers, not passive observers. This might include Socratic dialogue led by teachers and students, individual hands-on/heads-on manipulations, and cooperative small-group or total-group investigations.

Structuring Classroom Organizational Patterns for Thinking

The lecture method has long been found wanting in terms of student learning. Early studies have shown that there are vast individual differences in the amount of learning assimilated by students through lecture (Jones, 1923). And Ebbinhous (1913) found that retention dropped from about 60 percent of immediate recall after the lecture to about 20 percent after eight weeks.

Different students need different classroom organizational patterns. Some students learn best individually; some learn best in groups. There are students who can only learn when an adult is present to constantly encourage and reinforce them; others can't learn when another person is nearby. Some students need noise, others need quiet. Some need bright light, some need subdued light. Some need formal settings, others need informal situations. Some need to move, others need to be stationary (Dunn & Dunn, 1978). Less able students seem to do better in highly structured situations where direct help is generous, while more able students seem to prefer less structured situations (Sternberg & Wagner, 1982, p. 51).

What kind of classroom structure, then, produces the greatest achievement of cognitive skills and strategies? Thomas (1980) states

Where the locus of control over learning is entirely vested in the *teacher*, where maximum structure is provided for carrying out learning activities, and where the motivation to perform is provided for through external rewards, praise, and/or fear of reprisal, there is little latitude or opportunity for students to develop a sense of agency and subsequently, to become proficient in using learning strategies. . . . What may be required is an instructional procedure replete with tasks for which strategies have some payoff and perhaps a deliberate attempt to teach and/or allow for the discovery of varieties of cognitive strategies appropriate to these tasks. (Thomas, 1980, p. 236)

Roger and David Johnson (2001) find that students working cooperatively in groups used more higher-level reasoning strategies and greater critical-thinking competencies than students working in competitive and individualistic learning situations.

When higher-level thinking, creativity, and problem solving are the objectives, students must be in a classroom climate where they are in the decision-making role—where they construct strategies to solve problems, where they determine the correctness of an answer based on data they produced and validated, where they play a key part in setting their own goals and devising ways to assess the accomplishment of those goals.

Intrinsic Rather Than Extrinsic Rewards

The reward system in such a classroom should be intrinsic. It must spring from an internal motivation to learn: an intellectual curiosity about phenomena; a proud striving for craftsmanship and accuracy; a sense of being a productive and interdependent member of a community of scholars; and a desire to emulate respected others (Bruner, Goodnow, & Austin, 1956; Lepper & Green, 1978).

Teachers who value internal rather than external rewards, who engage students in structuring their own learning, who realize human variability in learning, and who can teach toward multiple goals use a repertoire of classroom organizational patterns. Classrooms organized for thinking are characterized by

• Individual students working alone, engaged in a task requiring one or more cognitive skills, such as comparing, classifying, sorting, and evaluating. During individual work, teachers monitor students' progress and mediate their experiences.

• Groups working cooperatively, in pairs or small groups, on such collaborative problem solving as planning strategies for group projects, contributing data and ideas to the progress of the project, identifying information that needs to be gathered, devising strategies to generate that information, and evaluating individual and group social skills. During group work, teachers monitor students' progress, assess growth in social and cognitive abilities, and mediate both the intellectual skills required of the task and the cooperative group skills.

- Total-group engagement in listening to presentations by, and interacting with, the teacher, resource people, media, and other students. Such total-group interactive strategies as the Socratic, the dialectic, and class meetings are also employed when the teacher or a student raises a dilemma, problem, or discrepancy for all to participate in debating and resolving.

III. TEACHER RESPONSE BEHAVIORS

> Being listened to is so close to being loved that most people cannot tell the difference.
>
> David Oxberg

The manner in which teachers and administrators respond to students can create and maintain a thoughtful environment that creates trust, allows risk taking, is experimental, creative, and positive. This requires listening to students and each other's ideas, remaining nonjudgmental, and having rich data sources. The following five patterns of response behaviors—using silence, facilitating the acquisition of data, accepting without judgment, clarifying, and empathizing—are employed to create an atmosphere in which students may experience and practice complex and creative thought processes.

Silence (Wait Time)

In some classrooms, the teacher dominates the interaction using a rapid-fire pace and lower cognitive-level questions. The teacher may wait less than one second after posing a question before repeating the question, commenting on a student answer, redirecting the question to a new student, answering the question himself, or starting a new questioning sequence. Students' answers are often terse, fragmentary, or show a lack of confidence with inflected tones. After a student replies, the teacher may wait less than one second before commenting or asking another question. There is little chance for students to have second thoughts or to extend their ideas. Many teachers appear to be programmed to accept one predetermined "right" answer. There is little room left for alternate answers or differing opinions. The message students receive is that "the teacher's way of knowing is the only way of knowing."

Dr. Mary Budd Rowe (1974) first developed the concept of Wait Time in the late 1960s. In observing classrooms, she noticed that some teachers were using "purposeful pauses" as they conducted lessons and class discussions. She noted students making speculations, holding sustained conversational sequences, posing alternative explanations, and arguing over the interpretation of data. She noted positive changes in the affective climate and the quality of classroom interactions. She also noticed an increase in the level of cognitive functioning and academic achievement, and a decrease in the number of behavior problems. Classroom changes with increased wait time include

1. 300–700 percent increase in the length of student responses.

2. The number of unsolicited but appropriate student responses increases.

3. Failures to respond decrease.

4. Confidence increases—there are fewer inflected responses.

5. Speculative responses increase.

6. Teacher-centered show & tell decreases; student-student interaction increases.

7. Teacher questions change in number and kind: The number of divergent questions increases; teachers ask higher-level questions (Bloom's et al. *Taxonomy*, 1956); and there is more probing for clarification.

8. Students make inferences & support inferences with data.

9. Students ask more questions.

Wait Time I is the length of time a teacher pauses after asking a question. Wait Time II is the length of time a teacher waits after a student comments or asks a question. A minimum of three seconds of pausing is recommended. With higher-level cognitive tasks, five seconds or more of wait time may be required to achieve positive results. Wait Time III is pausing and modeling thoughtfulness after the student asks the teacher a question.

It takes time for students to be able to think flexibly or creatively. The use of longer pauses in group discussions provides students with the necessary think time that helps them manage their impulsivity and take responsible risks as they answer questions posed either by the teacher or by the work they are studying.

Dr. Rowe has also examined the use of longer pauses in whole-group lecture settings. Students need mental processing time in information-dense subjects like chemistry, physics, and geology. Her research indicated that retention and understanding increase when 2 to 3 minutes of discussion, note clarification, and question raising with seatmates are provided after every 8 to 10 minutes of instruction.

Facilitating the Acquisition of Data

If learners are to process data by comparing, classifying, making inferences, or drawing causal relationships for themselves, then data must be available for them to process. Facilitating the acquisition of data means that when the teacher perceives that a student needs information, or when a student requests additional information, the teacher provides it or makes it possible for the student to acquire the data, facts, or information needed or requested.

The teacher, therefore, creates a climate that is responsive to the student's quest for information. Teachers do this in a variety of ways:

a. By providing data (feedback) about a student's performance:

"No, three times six is not twenty-four. Three times eight is twenty-four."

"Yes, you have spelled 'rhythm' correctly."

b. By providing personal information or data (self-divulgence). (These are often in the form of "I" messages.):

"I want you to know that chewing gum in this classroom really disturbs me."

"John, your pencil tapping is distracting me."

"The way you painted the tree makes me feel like I'm on the inside looking out."

c. By making it possible for students to experiment with equipment and materials to find data or information for themselves:

"Here's a larger test tube if you'd like to see how your experiment would turn out differently."

"We can see the video again if you want to check your observations."

d. By making primary and secondary sources of information accessible:

"Catherine, this geography database gives information you will need for your report on the world's highest mountain ranges."

"Here's the dictionary. The best way to verify the spelling is to look it up."

e. By responding to a student's request for information:

Student: "What's this thing called?"

Teacher: "This piece of equipment is called a DVD-ROM drive."

f. By surveying the group for its feelings or for input of its information.

"On this chart we have made a list of what you observed in the film. We can keep this chart in front of us so that we can refer to it as we classify our observations."

"Let's go around the circle and share some of the feelings we had when we found out the school board decided to close our school."

g. By labeling a thinking process or behavior:

"That is an hypothesis you are posing, Gina."

"Sharing your crayons like that is an example of cooperation, Mark."

"The question you are asking is an attempt to verify the data."

Data energizes learning and growth and knowledge of results is the most important variable governing the acquisition of skillful thinking.

Accepting Without Judgment

> If you judge people, you have no time to love them.
>
> Mother Teresa

Nonevaluative, nonjudgmental teachers accept what students say and do. When they accept, they give no clues through posture, gesture, or word as to whether a student's idea, behavior, or feeling, is good, bad, better or worse, right or wrong. In response to a student's idea or action, acceptance of it provides a psychologically safe climate where students can take risks, are entrusted with the responsibility of making decisions for themselves, and can explore the consequences of their own actions. Nonjudgmental acceptance provides conditions in which students are encouraged to examine and compare their own data, values, ideas, criteria, and feelings with those of others as well as those of the teacher. While teachers may respond nonjudgmentally in several ways, two types of nonjudgmental accepting responses are described here: acknowledgment and paraphrasing.

Acknowledging

Acknowledgment is responding by simply receiving without judging what the student says. It communicates that the student's ideas have been heard.

Examples of this type of response are

"Um-hmm," "That's one possibility," "Could be," or "I understand" (Passive, verbal, accepting responses).

Nodding the head or recording without change the student's statement on the chalkboard (Passive, nonverbal, accepting responses).

Say, "Thank you." When a student gives you a gift of their thinking, acknowledge it by saying thank you.

Paraphrasing

Paraphrasing is responding to what the student says or does by rephrasing, recasting, translating, or summarizing. Teachers use this response when they want to extend, build upon, compare, or give an example based upon what the student has said. While the teacher may use different words than the student, the teacher strives to maintain the intent and accurate meaning of the student's idea. By paraphrasing, the teacher sends a signal that "I understand you" or that "I am trying to understand you" and that "I care."

Examples of this type of response are

"So your explanation is that if the heat were increased, the molecules would move faster and therefore disperse the food coloring faster."

"I understand. Your idea is that we should all write our legislators rather than send them one letter from the group."

"Shaun's idea is that the leaves could be classified according to their shapes while Sarah's way is to group them by size."

"An example of what you mean was when we arranged our rock collection according to several different classification systems."

Praise Decreases Motivation and Creativity

He who praises everybody praises nobody.

Samuel Johnson

Using rewards and praise as motivators of student learning increases the student's dependency on others for learning rather than finding the learning inherently satisfying or involving the acquisition or exercise of skills which the students value themselves (Deci, 1978, 1995; Kohn, 1994; Lepper & Green, 1978).

Using Praise Judicially

Surprisingly, while many teachers advocate the use of praise such as "good," "excellent," "great," in attempts to reinforce behaviors and to build self-worth, the research on praise indicates that the opposite is more often the case. Thus praise builds conformity. It makes students depend on *others* for their worth rather than upon *themselves*. It has been found to be a detriment to creativity (Kohn, 1987). Some examples of teacher responses that use praise:

"That was a very *good* answer, Linda."

"Your painting is *excellent*."

"You're such a *fine* boy today, Leo."

"Yours was the *best* example that anybody gave."

Although there are problems with the use of praise, it is not being suggested praise be eliminated without consideration. For example, there are times when praise is totally appropriate. Instances where students have accomplished tasks that they might never have accomplished; times when students have successfully managed to obey rules or change behaviors to the benefit of themselves and the class and developmentally appropriate instances that differentiate the need for praise with young children versus students as they grow into adolescence. Praising seems best used with only certain students and for certain tasks.

Give the criteria or rationale for the value judgment.

If praise is given, it is important that the criteria for the praise be described. What makes an act "good," or "excellent" must be communicated along with the praise. Thereby, the student understands the reason or criteria that makes the act acceptable and thus that performance can be repeated.

Help students analyze their own answer.

Teacher: "Jane says San Francisco is the largest city in California. Bill says Los Angeles is the largest. Would each of you please tell us what is the population of the two cities? One way to find out is to compare our data."

Most teachers enjoy rewarding and praising their students. Brophy (1981), however, found that the one person in the classroom for whom praise has the most beneficial effect is, indeed, the teacher. It is understandable, therefore, that research studies showing the detrimental effects of rewards are met with resistance.

While teachers may have good intentions in using praise or rewards, what is more important is how the student interprets it. That determines whether the reward will have its intended effect. Teachers must be sensitive to individual students' interpretation of rewards and praise and will therefore, choose to praise or reward according to the timing, circumstances, and type of rewards and praise to be given.

Clarifying When You Don't Understand

Clarifying is similar to accepting in that both behaviors reflect the teacher's concern for fully understanding the student's idea. While active acceptance demonstrates that the teacher *does* understand, *clarifying* means that you *do not* understand what the student is saying and, therefore, more information is needed.

When a student uses some terminology, expresses a concept or idea, or asks a question that the teacher does not understand, the teacher may wish to *clarify* both the *content* of that idea *and/or* the *process* by which that idea was derived. The teacher may express a lack of understanding of the student's idea and seek further explanation of it. She/he may invite the student to become more specific by requesting the student to elaborate or rephrase the idea, or to seek descriptions of the thinking processes underlying the production of that idea.

The intent of clarifying is to better understand the students' ideas, feelings, and thought processes. Clarifying is *not* a devious way of changing or redirecting what the student is thinking or feeling. It is not a way of directing the class's attention to the "correct answer." Clarifying is often stated in the form of an interrogative but could also be a statement inviting further illumination. For example:

"Could you explain to us what you mean by 'charisma'?"

"What you are saying is that you'd rather work by yourself than in a group. Is that correct?"

"Go over that one more time, Shelley, I'm not sure I understand you."

"You say you are studying the situation. Tell us just exactly what you do when you 'study' something."

"Explain to us the steps you took to arrive at that answer."

By clarifying, teachers show the students that their ideas are worthy of exploration and consideration; the full meaning, however is not yet understood. Clarifying demonstrates that the teacher is interested in values and wants to pursue students' thinking. When a teacher responds to students' comments by encouraging them to elaborate further, students become more purposeful in their thinking and behaving.

Empathizing

Sometimes students come to school from dysfunctional, abusive, drug-dependent, impoverished environments. The emotions and feelings they bring to school affect their learning and motivation.

Empathic acceptance is a response that accepts feelings in addition to cognition. Teachers respond empathically when they want to accept a student's feelings, emotions, or behaviors. Often teachers show empathy when they express similar feelings from their own experiences. Such responses communicate that the teacher not only "hears" the student's idea but also the emotions underlying the idea. Empathic acceptance does not mean that the teacher condones acts of aggression or destructive behavior. Some examples of this type of response are

> "I can see why you're confused. Those directions are unclear to me, too."

> "You're frustrated because you didn't get a chance to share your idea. We've all got to take turns and that requires patience. It's hard to wait when you're anxious to share."

The student enters the room and slams a math workbook on the desk. The teacher responds empathetically to this behavior by saying

> "Something must be upsetting you today. Did you have difficulty with that assignment?"

In total, we use the acronym S.P.A.C.E. to make reference to these behaviors. They can be taught to students, parents, and groups of people meeting to consider school improvement. The use of **S**ilence, **P**roviding data, **A**ccepting without judgment, **C**larifying, and **E**mpathizing can serve as a mental map for building an environment in which thinking can flourish.

IV. MODELING: BEHAVING CONGRUENTLY WITH COGNITIVE GOALS AND OBJECTIVES

> Actions, not words, are the true criterion.
>
> George Washington, *Social Maxims: Friendship* (c. 1790)

Students are quick to pick up the inconsistencies between what a teacher says and what a teacher does. Effective teachers of thinking constantly strive to bring their words, actions, beliefs, values, and goals for students into harmony.

Children acquire much of their behavior, feelings, attitudes, and values not through direct instruction but through imitation of both adult and peer models. Students adopt new behavior patterns or modify their own behavior on the basis of observation alone. Thus, since there is such extended contact between teacher and student, the teacher is one of the most significant and influential models in a student's life.

Modeling tends to reinforce students' perceptions of the values and goals stated by the teacher or by the school, and by exhibiting the kinds of behavior desired in students, adults can strongly influence students' behavior patterns. For example:

- If listening to one another is a valued behavior, teachers who listen to students will greatly enhance the probability of achieving this objective.
- If solving problems in a rational, scientific manner is valued, students must observe teachers and administrators using rational, scientific ways to solve problems that arise in the school or classroom.
- If managing impulsivity is a characteristic of intelligent problem solving, students must witness teachers and administrators reacting calmly and patiently during stressful situations.
- If teachers want students to accept one another's points of view, values, and differences (overcoming egocentrism), they will accept students' differences.
- If teachers want students to become enthusiastic about thinking, they will show enthusiasm for challenges, puzzles, and complex tasks requiring thought.

Emulating others is a basic way of learning. Young people, especially, are very quick to imitate behavior. If we become "do as I say, not as I do" educators, we can make students feet hostile, frustrated, and confused. Our goal as educators should be to facilitate students' development of their own behavior, since in the end, each person is responsible for what he or she does.

REFERENCES

Bloom, B., et al. (1956). *Taxonomy of educational objectives handbook I: Cognitive domain.* New York: David McKay.

Brophy, J. I. (1981, October). *Teacher praise: A functional analysis.* (Occasional Paper no 28). East Lansing: Michigan State University Institute for Research on Teaching.

Bruner, J., Goodnow, J., & Austin, G. A. (1956). *A study of thinking.* New York: Wiley.

Costa, A., & Garmston, R. (2005). *Cognitive Coaching foundation seminar learning guide.* Norwood, MA: Christopher-Gordon, 43–44.

Deci, E. (1995). *Why we do what we do.* New York: Grosset Putnam.

Deci, E. (1978). Application of research on the effect of rewards. In M. Lepper & D. Green (Eds.), *The hidden cost of rewards: New perspectives on the psychology of human motivation.* New York: Erlbaum.

Dunn, R., & Dunn, K. (1978). *Teaching students through their individual learning styles.* Reston, VA: Reston Publishing.

Ebbinhous, H. (1913). *Memory.* New York: Columbia University Teachers College.

Johnson, D., & Johnson, R. (2001). Cooperation and conflict: Effects on cognition and metacognition. In A. Costa (Ed.), *Developing minds: A resource book for teaching thinking* (pp. 451–454). Alexandria, VA: Association for Supervision and Curriculum Development.

Jones, H. E. (1923, November). Experimental studies of college teaching. *Archives of Psychology, 68,* entire issue.

Kohn, A. (1994). *Punished by rewards: The trouble with gold stars, incentive plans, A's, praise and other bribes.* New York: Houghton-Mifflin.

Kohn, A. (1987, September). Art for art's sake. *Psychology Today, 21*(9).

Lepper, M., & Green, D. (Eds.). (1978). *The hidden cost of rewards: New perspectives on the psychology of human motivation.* New York: Erlbaum.

Rowe, M. B. (1974, Spring). Wait time and rewards as instructional variables: Their influence on language, logic and fate control. *Journal of Research in Science Teaching, 11*(2), 81–84.

Sternberg, R., & Wagner, R. K. (1982). *Understanding intelligence; What's in it for educators?* Paper submitted to the National Commission on Excellence in education, Washington, DC.

Thomas, J. (1980, Summer). Agency and achievement: Self-management and self-regard. *Review of Educational Research, 50*(2), 213–240.

CHAPTER SEVENTEEN

Mediating the Metacognitive

Try to solve this problem in your head:

How much is one half of two plus two?

Did you hear yourself talking to yourself? Did you find yourself having to decide if you should take one half of the first two (which would give the answer, three) or if you should sum the twos first (which would give the answer, two)?

If you caught yourself having an "inner" dialogue inside your brain, and if you had to stop to evaluate your own decision-making/problem-solving processes, you were experiencing *metacognition*.

Occurring in the neocortex and therefore thought by some neurologists to be uniquely human, metacognition is our ability to know what we know and what we don't know. It is our ability to plan a strategy for producing what information is needed, to be conscious of our own steps and strategies during the act of problem solving, and to reflect on and evaluate the productiveness of our own thinking. While "inner language," thought to be a prerequisite, begins in most children around age 5, metacognition is a key attribute of formal thought flowering about age 11. Interestingly, not all humans achieve the level of formal operations (Chiabetta, 1976). And as Alexander Luria, the Russian psychologist found, not all adults metacogitate (Whimbey, 1980). We often find students following instructions or performing tasks without wondering why they are doing what they are doing. They seldom question themselves about their own learning strategies or

SOURCE: Reprinted by permission. Costa, A. L. (1984, November). Mediating the metacognitive. *Educational Leadership 42(3)*, 57–62. Alexandria, VA: Association for Supervision and Curriculum Development.

evaluate the efficiency of their own performance. Some children virtually have no idea of what they should do when they confront a problem and are often unable to explain their strategies of decision making (Sternberg & Wagner, 1982). There is much evidence, however, to demonstrate that those who perform well on complex cognitive tasks, who are flexible and persevere in problem solving, who consciously apply their intellectual skills, are those who possess well-developed metacognitive abilities (Bloom & Broder, 1950; Brown, 1978; Whimbey, 1980). They are those who "manage" their intellectual resources well: 1) their basic perceptual-motor skills; 2) their language, beliefs, knowledge of content, and memory processes; and 3) their purposeful and voluntary strategies intended to achieve a desired outcome (Aspen Systems, 1982).

If we wish to install intelligent behavior as a significant outcome of education, then instructional strategies, purposefully intended to develop children's metacognitive abilities, must be infused into our teaching methods, staff development, and supervisory processes (Costa, 1991). Interestingly, *direct* instruction in metacognition may *not* be beneficial. When strategies of problem solving are imposed by the teacher rather than generated by the students themselves, their performance may become impaired. Conversely, when students experience the need for problem-solving strategies, induce their own, discuss and practice them to the degree that they become spontaneous and unconscious, their metacognition seems to improve (Sternberg & Wagner, 1982). The trick, therefore, is to teach metacognitive skills without creating an even greater burden on their ability to attend to the task.

Probably the major components of metacognition are developing a plan of action, maintaining that plan in mind over a period of time, then reflecting back on and evaluating the plan upon its completion. Planning a strategy before embarking on a course of action assists us in keeping track of the steps in the sequence of planned behavior at the conscious awareness level for the duration of the activity. It facilitates making temporal and comparative judgments, assessing the readiness for more or different activities, and monitoring our interpretations, perceptions, decisions, and behaviors. An example of this would be what superior teachers do daily: developing a teaching strategy for a lesson, keeping that strategy in mind throughout the instruction, then reflecting back upon the strategy to evaluate its effectiveness in producing the desired student outcomes.

Rigney (1980) identified the following self-monitoring skills as necessary for successful performance on intellectual tasks:

Keeping one's place in a long sequence of operations;

Knowing that a subgoal has been obtained; and

Detecting errors and recovering from those errors either by making a quick fix or by retreating to the last known correct operation.

Such monitoring involves both "looking ahead" and "looking back." Looking ahead includes

Learning the structure of a sequence of operations, identifying areas where errors are likely;

Choosing a strategy that will reduce the possibility of error and will provide easy recovery; and

Identifying the kinds of feedback that will be available at various points, and evaluating the usefulness of that feedback.

Looking back includes

Detecting errors previously made;

Keeping a history of what has been done to the present and thereby what should come next; and

Assessing the reasonableness of the present immediate outcome of task performance.

A simple example of this might be drawn from a reading task. It is a common experience while reading a passage to have our mind "wander" from the pages. We "see" the words but no meaning is being produced. Suddenly we realize that we are not concentrating and that we've lost contact with the meaning of the text. We "recover" by returning to the passage to find our place, matching it with the last thought we can remember, and, once having found it, reading on with connectedness. This inner awareness and the strategy of recovery are components of metacognition.

STRATEGIES FOR ENHANCING METACOGNITION

Following are a dozen suggestions that teachers of any grade level can use to enhance metacognition. Whether teaching vocational education, physical education, algebra, or reading skills, teachers can promote metacognition by using these and similar instructional techniques.

1. Strategy Planning

Prior to any learning activity, teachers will want to take time to develop and discuss strategies and steps for attacking problems, rules to remember, and directions to be followed. Time constraints, purposes, and ground rules under which students must operate should be developed and "interiorized." Thus, students can better keep these in mind during and evaluate their performance after the experience.

During the activity, teachers can invite students to share their progress, thought processes, and perceptions of their own behavior. Asking students to indicate where they are in their strategy, to describe the "trail" of thinking up to that point, and what alternative pathways they intend to pursue next in the solution of their problem, helps them become aware of their own behavior. (It also provides the teacher with a diagnostic "cognitive map" of the student's thinking which can be used to give more individualized assistance.)

Then, *after* the learning activity is completed, teachers can invite students to evaluate how well those rules were obeyed, how productive were the strategies, whether the instructions were followed correctly, and what would be some alternative, more efficient strategies to be used in the future.

I know a kindergarten teacher who begins and ends each day with a class meeting. During these times, children make plans for the day. They decide upon what learning tasks to accomplish and how to accomplish them. They allocate classroom space, assign roles, and develop criteria for appropriate conduct. Throughout the day the teacher calls attention to the plans and ground rules made that morning and invites students to compare what they are doing with what was agreed. Then, before dismissal, another class meeting is held to reflect on, evaluate, and plan further strategies and criteria.

2. Question Generating

Regardless of the subject area, it is useful for students to pose study questions for themselves prior to and during their reading of textual material. This self-generation of questions facilitates comprehension. It encourages the student to pause frequently and perform a "self-check" for understanding, to determine whether or not comprehension has occurred. If, for example: they know the main characters or events; they are grasping the concept; it "makes sense"; they can relate it to what they already know; they can give other examples or instances; they can use the main idea to explain other ideas; or they can use the information in the passage to predict what may come next. They then must decide what strategic action should be taken to remove obstacles that thereby increase comprehension. This helps students become more self-aware and to take conscious control of their own studying (Sanacore, 1984).

3. Conscious Choosing

Teachers can promote metacognition by helping students explore the consequences of their choices and decisions prior to and during the act of deciding. Students will then be able to perceive causal relationships between their choice, their actions, and the results they achieved. Providing nonjudgmental feedback about the effects of their behaviors and decisions on others and on their environment helps students become aware of their own behaviors. For example, a teacher's statement, "I want you to know that the noise you're making with your pencil is disturbing me," will better contribute to metacognitive development than the command, "John, stop tapping your pencil!"

4. Differentiated Evaluating

Teachers can enhance metacognition by causing students to reflect upon and categorize their actions according to two or more sets of evaluative criteria. An example would be inviting students to distinguish between what was done that day that was helpful and hindering, what they liked and didn't like, or what were plusses and minuses of the activity. Thus, students must keep the criteria in mind, apply them to multiple classification systems, and justify their reasons accordingly.

5. Taking Credit

Teachers may cause students to identify what they have done well and invite them to seek feedback from their peers. The teacher might ask, "What have you done that you're proud of?" "How would you like to be recognized for doing that?" (name on the board, hug, pat on the back, handshake, applause from the group, etc.). Thus students will become more conscious of their own behavior and apply a set of internal criteria for that behavior which they consider "good."

6. Outlawing "I Can't"

Teachers can inform students that their excuses of "I can't," "I don't know how to," or "I'm too slow to" are unacceptable behaviors in the classroom. Rather, having students identify what information is required, what materials are needed, or what skills are lacking in their ability to perform the desired behavior is an alternative and acceptable response. This helps students identify the boundaries between what they know and what they need to know. It develops a persevering attitude and enhances the student's ability to create strategies that will produce needed data.

7. Paraphrasing or Reflecting Back Student Ideas

Paraphrasing, building upon, extending, and using student ideas can make students conscious of their own thinking. Some examples might be by saying, "What you're telling me is . . . ," or "What I hear in your plan are the following steps . . . ," or "Let's work with Peter's strategy for a moment."

Inviting students to restate, translate, compare, and paraphrase each other's ideas causes them to become not only better listeners of other's thinking, but better listeners to their own thinking as well.

8. Labeling Student Behaviors

When the teacher places labels on students' cognitive processes, it can make them conscious of their own actions: "What I see you doing is making out a plan of action for . . ."; "What you are doing is called an experiment"; or "You're being very helpful to Mark by sharing your paints. That's an example of cooperation."

9. Clarifying Student Terminology

Students often use "hollow," vague, and nonspecific terminology. For example, in making value judgments students might be heard saying, "It's not fair . . ."; "He's too strict"; or "It's no good." Teachers need to get in the habit of clarifying these values: "What's *too* strict?" "What would be more fair?"

We sometimes hear students using nominalizations: "They're mean to me." (Who are they?) "We had to do that." (Who is we?) "Everybody has one." (Who is everybody?") Thus, clarifying causes students to operationally define their terminology and to examine the premise on which their thinking is based. It is desirable that, as a result of such clarifying, students would become more specific and qualifying in their terminology.

For older children, above age 11 or so, it appears helpful to invite them to clarify their problem-solving processes. Causing them to describe their thinking while they are thinking seems to beget more thinking. Some examples might be inviting students to talk aloud as they are solving a problem; discussing what is going on in their heads, for example, when they confront an unfamiliar word while reading; or what steps they are going through in deciding whether to buy some article at the store. After solving a problem, the teacher can invite a clarification of the processes used: "Sarah, you figured out that the answer was 44; Shawn says the answer is 33. Let's hear how you came up with 44; retrace your steps for us." Thus clarifying helps students to reexamine their own problem-solving processes, to identify their own errors, and to self-correct. The teacher might ask a question such as "How much is three plus four?" The student may reply, "12." Rather than merely correcting the student, the teacher may choose to clarify: "Gina, how did you arrive at that answer?" "Well, I multiplied four and three and got . . . oh, I see, I multiplied instead of added."

10. Role Playing and Simulations

Having students assume the roles of other persons causes them to consciously maintain in their head the attributes and characteristics of that person. Dramatization serves as an hypothesis or prediction of how that person would react in a certain situation. This also contributes to the reduction of ego-centered perceptions.

11. Journal Keeping

Writing and illustrating a personal log or a diary throughout an experience over a period of time causes the student to synthesize thoughts and actions and to translate them into symbolic form. The record also provides an opportunity to revisit initial perceptions, to compare the changes in those perceptions with the addition of more data, to chart the processes of strategic thinking and decision making, to identify the blind alleys and pathways taken, and to recall the successes and the "tragedies" of experimentation (a variation on writing journals would be making video and/or audiotape recordings of actions and performances over time).

12. Modeling

Of all the instructional techniques suggested, the one with the probability of greatest influence on students is that of teacher modeling. Since students learn best by imitating the significant adults around them, the teacher who publicly demonstrates metacognition will probably produce students who metacogitate. Some indicators of teacher's public metacognitive behavior might be

Sharing their planning by describing their goals and objectives and giving reasons for their actions;

Making human errors but then being seen to recover from those errors by getting "back on track";

Admitting they do not know an answer but designing ways to produce an answer;

Seeking feedback and evaluation of their actions from others;

Having a clearly stated value system and making decisions consistent with that value system;

Being able to self-disclose by using adjectives that describe their own strengths and weaknesses; and

Demonstrating understanding and empathy by listening to and accurately describing the ideas and feelings of others.

A form that teachers can use to rate themselves on their metacognitive behavior appears as Appendix 17.A at the end of this chapter.

EVALUATING GROWTH IN METACOGNITIVE ABILITIES

We can determine if students are becoming more aware of their own thinking as they are able to describe what goes on in their head when they are thinking. When asked, they can list the steps and tell where they are in the sequence of a problem-solving strategy. They can trace the pathways and dead ends they took on the road to a problem solution. They can describe what data are lacking and their plans for producing those data.

We should see students persevering more when the solution to a problem is not immediately apparent. This means that they have systematic methods of analyzing a problem, knowing ways to begin, knowing what steps must be performed and when they are accurate or are in error. We should see students taking more pride in their efforts, becoming self-correcting, striving for craftsmanship and accuracy in their products, and becoming more autonomous in their problem-solving abilities.

Teaching for thinking is becoming the great educational emphasis for the twenty-first century. Metacognition is an attribute of the "educated intellect." It must be included if thinking is to become a durable reality.

REFERENCES

Aspen Systems. (1982, April). *Topics in Learning and Learning Disabilities, 2*(1).

Bloom, B. S., & Broder, L. J. (1950). *Problem-solving processes of college students.* Chicago: University of Chicago Press.

Brown, A. L. (1978). Knowing when, where, and how to remember: A problem of metacognition. In W. Glaser (Ed.), *Advances in instructional psychology.* Hillsdale, NJ: Erlbaum.

Chiabetta, E. L. A. (1976). Review of Piagetian studies relevant to science instruction at the secondary and college level. *Science Education, 60,* 253–261.

Costa, A. L. (1991). The search for intelligent life. In *Developing minds: A resource book for teaching thinking* (pp. 100–106). Alexandria, VA: Association for Supervision and Curriculum Development.

Rigney, J. W. (1980). Cognitive learning strategies and qualities in information processing. In R. Snow, P. Federico, & W. Montague (Eds.), *Aptitudes, learning, and instruction,* Vol. 1. Hillsdale, NJ: Erlbaum.

Sanacore, J. (1984, May). Metacognition and the improvement of reading: Some important links. *Journal of Reading,* 706–712.

Sternberg, R., & Wagner, R. (1982). *Understanding intelligence: What's in it for education?* Paper submitted to the National Commission on Excellence in Education.

Whimbey, A. (1980, April). Students can learn to be better problem solvers. *Educational Leadership, 37*(7).

Appendix 17.A   Self-Reflection on Enhancing Metacognition

Please rate yourself according to the following scale on your use of Arthur L. Costa's strategies for enhancing metacognition.

	Very Often	Often	Some-times	Seldom	Not Yet
1. Strategy Planning (Planning, monitoring, and evaluating activities.)					
2. Question Generating (Asking students to generate their own questions about content.)					
3. Conscious Choosing (Considering the effects of choices prior to deciding.)					
4. Differentiated Evaluating (Establishing multiple criteria to reflect on one's own activities.)					
5. Taking Credit (Stating what students have done well and seeking feedback from peers.)					
6. Outlawing "I Can't" (Insisting on problem solving and possibility thinking.)					
7. Paraphrasing/Reflecting Back Students' Ideas (Inviting students to restate others' ideas.)					
8. Labeling Students' Behaviors (Stating what students are doing cognitively and giving these actions a name.)					
9. Clarifying Students' Terminology (Asking for definitions of nonspecific or vague words.)					
10. Role Playing and Simulations (Having students play the parts of other persons, characterizing their points of view.)					
11. Journal Keeping (Writing and illustrating one's personal thoughts.)					
12. Modeling (Teachers modeling their own thinking processes.)					

PART V

The Mindful School:
A Re-Vision

We are riding the crest of what may well be the greatest opportunity for educational reform in history; a growing dissatisfaction with the current quality of education; a realization of educational reform as a political platform; a heightened awareness of the demands of an uncertain future; a concern about our nation's global economic dependence upon an educated and highly skilled work force; and face-to-face encounters with our delicate ecological home. . . . Let us unite in common voice. If we desire our future world to be more compassionate, more cooperative, and more thoughtful, we must work together to make it happen. . . . Mind workers unite!

Arthur L. Costa

CHAPTER EIGHTEEN

Creating a Culture of Mindfulness

Studies by Karen Seashore Louis, H. Marks, and S. Kruse (1996) identified five norms that seem to characterize a professional learning culture in a school. If you were to adopt these five as powerful indicators of a learning community, the basic question is, To what degree are they present in your school community?

THE FIVE CHARACTERISTICS*

1. *Shared Norms and Values.* There is a sense of common values and expectations of and for each other. Members of a school community affirm, through language and action, common beliefs and values underlying assumptions about students, learning, teaching and teachers' roles; the nature of human needs, human activity and human relationships, the organization's extended societal role, and its relation with the surrounding environment.

Question: To what degree do members of your school community understand, value, model, celebrate, reward, communicate about, and use their combined resources cooperatively to achieve our school's stated mission, goals, and outcomes?

2. *A Collective Focus on Student Learning.* An undeviating concentration on student learning is a core characteristic of professional communities. Teachers' professional actions focus on choices that affect students' opportunities to learn and to provide substantial student benefit. Teachers discuss the ways in which instruction promotes students' intellectual growth

and development, as distinguished from simply focusing on activities or strategies that may engage student attention.

Question: To what degree do members of your school community focus on, collect, and share evidence of and discuss individual and collective students' continual learning and the instructional strategies they employ as students progress through the school?

3. *Collaboration.* Professional communities foster the sharing of expertise and faculty members call on each other to discuss the development of skills related to the implementation of practice. By collaborating they create shared understandings from complex and confusing data. Collaborative work increases teachers' sense of affiliation with each other and with the school and their sense of mutual support and responsibility for effective instruction.

Question: To what degree do members of your school community value human variability by drawing on staff members' unique expertise, seeking to understand and learn from others because of their differences in beliefs, levels of experience, learning preferences, and cognitive styles and in working cooperatively across grade levels and subject areas?

4. *Deprivatized Practice.* In professional communities, teachers move behind the classroom door of their colleagues to share and trade off the roles of mentor, advisor, or specialist. It is within these quasi-public relationships that teachers work to define and develop their own practice and control their own work. Peer coaching relationships, teamed teaching structures, and structured classroom observations are methods used to improve both classroom practice and collegial relationship. In this way, teachers also come to know each other's strengths and can therefore more easily obtain "expert advice" from colleagues.

Question: To what degree do members of your school community observe, discuss, coach, reflect on, and learn more about the craft of teaching from each other?

5. *Reflective Dialogue.* Reflective practice implies self-awareness about one's work as a teacher. By engaging in in-depth conversations about teaching and learning, teachers can examine the assumptions basic to quality practice. Public conversation concerning the school and instructional concerns of schooling as well as questions of student development and progress. Reflection on practice leads to deepened understanding of the process of instruction and of the products created with the teaching and learning process.

Question: To what degree are members of your school community striving to enhance their communicative competencies, by monitoring, reflecting on their own listening skills, practicing nonjudgmental and empathic dialogue, and making a commitment to enhance interpersonal communication?

Many out-of-conscious factors influence teachers' thinking as they make daily decisions about curriculum and instruction. Their own culture, knowledge of content, their cognitive style, knowledge about their students, and their professional values and beliefs about education influence their judgments about when to teach what to whom. Jack Frymier (1987, p. 10), however, states

> In the main, the bureaucratic structure of the workplace is more influential in determining what professionals do than are personal abilities, professional training or previous experience. Therefore, change efforts should focus on the structure of the workplace, not the teachers.

Frymier suggests that less obvious but vastly more persuasive influences on teacher thought are the norms, policies, and culture of the school setting in which teachers work. Hidden, but powerful cues emanate from the school environment. These subtle cues signal the institutional value system that governs the operation of the organization (Saphier & King, 1985).

Recent efforts to bring educational reform will prove futile unless the school environment signals the staff, the students, and the community that the development of the intellect and cooperative decision making are the school's basic values. While efforts to enhance the staff's instructional competencies, develop curriculum, revise instructional materials, and assessment procedures may be important components in the process of educational re-engineering, it is also crucial that the climate in which parents, teachers, and students make their decisions be aligned with these goals of development of intellectual potential. Teachers will more likely teach for thinking, creativity, and cooperation if they are in an intellectually stimulating, creative, and cooperative environment themselves.

EDUCATIONAL STRESSORS

Research by O. J. Harvey (1966) found that teaching is the second most stressful profession! Goodlad (1984), Fullan (1993), Rosenholtz (1989), Sarason (1991), and other authors have identified several sources of stress:

- Teachers may lack a sense of power and efficacy. They are often cast at the bottom of a hierarchy while the decisions about curriculum, staff development, assessment, instructional materials, and evaluation—decisions that affect them directly—are handed down from "above."

- Teachers feel isolated. Ours is probably the only profession that performs our most beautiful and creative craft behind closed doors. Contributing to this situation is the inadequate amount and inflexibility of time for teachers to reflect and meet, plan, observe, and talk with each other.

- The complex, creative, intelligent act of teaching is often reduced to a rubric, a simplistic formula, or a series of steps and competencies, the uniform performance of which naively connotes excellence and elegance in the art of teaching.

- The feedback of data about student achievement is for political, competitive, evaluative, or coercive purposes. It neither involves nor instructs the school staff members in reflecting on, evaluating, and improving their curriculum and instructional decisions.

- Educational innovations are often viewed as mere "tinkerings" with the instructional program. They are so frequent and limited in impact that frustrated teachers sometimes feel, "this, too, shall pass." Instead of institutionalizing the change, deeply entrenched traditional practices and policies in the educational bureaucracy such as assessment, reporting, securing parent understanding and support, teacher evaluation, scheduling, school organization, and discipline procedures are seldom revised to be in harmony with the overall innovation.

The effects of excessive stress on cognition, creativity, and social interaction are well documented (MacLean, 1978). In such barren, intellectually "polluted" school climate conditions, some teachers understandably grow depressed. Teachers' vivid imagination, altruism, creativity, and intellectual prowess soon succumb to the humdrum daily routines of unruly students, irrelevant curriculum, impersonal surroundings, and equally disillusioned coworkers. In such an environment, the likelihood that teachers would value the development of students' intellect and imagination would be marginal.

TOWARD AN ECOLOGY OF THE INTELLECT

> What is most needed in the public schools is not new personnel or new equipment but a new philosophy and a new structure for using what we have.
>
> William Glasser (1992)

The level of teachers' intellectual development has a direct relationship to student behavior and student performance. Higher-level intellectually functioning teachers produce higher-level intellectually functioning students (Sprinthall & Theis-Sprinthall, 1983). Characteristic of these teachers is their ability to empathize, to symbolize experience, and to act in accordance with a disciplined commitment to human values. They employ a greater range of instructional strategies, elicit more conceptual responses from students, and produce higher achieving students who are more cooperative and involved in their work. Glickman (1985) concluded that successful teachers are thoughtful teachers and they stimulate their students to be thoughtful as well.

To achieve our educational outcome of developing students' intellectual capacities, educational leaders must redefine their role as mediators of school and community-wide conditions for continual learning and intellectual development. A mediator is one who deliberately intervenes between the individual or group and the environment with the intention of creating conditions which will engage and promote intellectual growth (Feuerstein, Feuerstein, & Schur, 1997). They design strategies for achieving their vision of a learning organization; they generate data as a means of assessing progress toward that vision; they constantly monitor the intellectual ecology of the school community to determine its contribution to or hindrance of intellectual growth. Their role is analogous to an "Environmental Protection Agency"; monitoring and managing the environment to ensure that intellectual growth, creativity, and cooperation are continually sustained and regenerated.

Systems analysts believe in "leverage points." These are places within a complex system where a small shift in one condition can produce big changes in the rest of the system. As mediators of the school's "intellectual ecology," the following seven leverage points are interventions which are intended to enhance continual intellectual growth and sustain the professional zest of the stakeholders in the educational enterprise. The intent is not to alleviate stress entirely. It is, however, intended to shift from *DI*stress to *EU*stress. (*EU* is taken from the word *euphoria*.)

1. Shared Norms and Values

> If your vision statement sounds like motherhood, and apple pie and is somewhat embarrassing, you're on the right track. You bet the farm.
>
> Peter Block (1987)

Peter Senge (1990) states that leadership in a learning organization starts with the principle of "Creative Tension." He goes on to describe how creative tension emerges from seeing clearly where we want to be—the vision, and describing truthfully where we are now—our current reality. The gap between the two generates creative tension (see Figure 18.1).

This principle of creative tension has long been recognized by leaders such as Martin Luther King Jr., when he proclaimed, "I have a dream. . . ." King believed, just as Socrates did, that it was necessary to create a tension in the mind, so that individuals could rise from the bondage of myths and

Figure 18.1   Emergence of Creative Tension

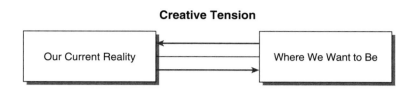

half truths . . . so must we create the kind of tension in society that will help men rise from the dark depths of prejudice and racism.

This tension, according to Senge, can be resolved by raising current reality toward the vision. Effective leaders, therefore, stimulate intellectual growth by causing creative organizational tension. Leaders create for themselves and facilitate staff, students', and the community's visions of what could be, images of desired states, valued aspirations, outcomes, and scenarios of more appropriate futures.

Mission and vision statements, however, are not just exercises. They are employed continually as criteria for making decisions, developing policies, and allocating resources, hiring staff, designing curriculum, disciplining, and lesson planning. A school's mission statement is given substance and value when it is systematically assessed. When our values are clear, the decisions we make are easy. What gives an organization integrity is how the staff members perceive the congruence between its policies, vision, and mission with its daily practices.

2. Reflective Dialogue

> Teamwork is the ability to work together toward a common vision. The ability to direct individual accomplishment toward organizational objectives. It is the fuel that allows common people to accomplish uncommon results.
>
> George Land and Beth Jarman (1992)

Trust is a vital element in enhancing cognition. We know that higher-level, complex, and creative thinking closes down when trust is lacking in the environment or in the relationship with others. Teachers will be encouraged to inquire, speculate, construct meanings, experiment, self-evaluate, and self-prescribe when the leader manages a trusting environment. Building an atmosphere of trust is the leader's most important task.

Humans, as social beings, mature intellectually in reciprocal relationships. Collaboratively, individuals generate and discuss ideas eliciting thinking that surpass individual effort. Together and privately, they express different perspectives, agree and disagree, point out and resolve discrepancies, and weigh alternatives. Because people grow their intellect through this process, collegial interaction is a crucial factor in the intellectual ecology of the school.

The essence of building trust and collegiality is when people work together to better understand how to work together. People are more likely to engage and grow in higher-level, creative, and experimental thought when they are in a trusting, risk-taking, and cooperative climate. Risk taking requires a nonjudgmental atmosphere where information can be shared without fear that it will be used for evaluative purposes.

Baker, Costa, and Shalit (1997) identify eight norms which may serve as standards that are understood, agreed upon, adopted, monitored, and assessed by each participant when working as a facilitating and contributing member of a group. They are the glue that enables school and community groups to engage in productive and satisfying discourse:

1. *Pausing:* Taking turns is the ultimate in impulse control (Kotulak, 1997). In a discourse, space is given for each person to talk. Time is allowed before responding to or asking a question. Such silent time allows for more complex thinking, enhances all forms of discourse, and produces better decision making. Pausing is the tool that facilitative group members use to respectfully listen to each other.

2. *Paraphrasing*: Covey (1989) suggests we seek to understand before being understood. Paraphrasing lets others know that you are listening, that you understand or are trying to understand, and that you care.

3. *Probing and Clarifying* is an effective inquiry skill to use when the speaker expresses vocabulary, uses a vague concept, or employs terminology which is not fully understood by the listener. The use of probing and clarifying is intended to help the listener better understand the speaker. In groups, probing and clarifying increases the clarity and precision of the group's thinking by clarifying understandings, terminology and interpretations.

4. *Putting Your Ideas On and Pulling Them Off the Table:* Groups are most productive when everyone shares their thoughts, dreams, mistakes, assumptions, and opinions. While they offer ideas, opinions, information, and positions they attempt to keep their suggestions relevant to the topic at hand. Because there are times when continuing to advocate a position might block the group's functioning, group members also volunteer to withdraw their ideas.

5. *Paying Attention to Self and Others:* Meaningful dialogue is facilitated when each group member is sensitive to and conscious of the subtle cues inside themselves and within the group. Paying attention to learning styles, modalities, and beliefs when planning for, facilitating of, and participating in group meetings enhances group members' understanding of each other as they converse, discuss, deliberate, dialogue, and make decisions.

6. *Presuming Positive Intentionality/Positive Presuppositions:* People operate on internal maps of their own reality and therefore we assume that they act with positive intentions. This assumption promotes and facilitates meaningful dialogue. Because our language contains overt and covert messages, deeper meanings may be misinterpreted. The subtle (and often not so subtle) way in which we embed presuppositions in our language can be hurtful or helpful to others. The deliberate use of positive presuppositions assumes and encourages positive actions (Costa & Garmston, 2005).

7. *Providing Data:* Groups exercising high levels of communicative competence act on information rather than hearsay, rumor, or speculation. Data serves as the energy sources for group action and learning. Seeking, generating, and gathering data from group members as well as a variety of other primary and secondary sources enhances individual and group decision making.

8. *Pursuing a Balance Between Advocacy and Inquiry:* Advocating a position as well as inquiring into another's position assists the group to continue learning. Senge, Ross, Smith, Roberts, and Kleiner (1994) suggests that balancing advocacy and inquiry is critical for an organization to perform in order to grow and learn.

Leaders encourage individuals and groups to monitor and assess their own use of these eight Norms of Collaboration. During and upon completion of meetings, group process observers provide feedback to the group about their performance of the norms. These data are discussed, the effects of their use on group effectiveness are illuminated, and strategies for individual and group improvement planned (Costa & Kallick, 1995).

3. Deprivatized Practice

> The current management culture, with its focus on controlling behavior, needs to be replaced by a management culture in which skillful coaching creates the climate, environment, and context that empowers employees and teams to generate results.
>
> Evered and Selman (1989)

Coaching is one of the most powerful means to overcome the extreme isolation and intellectual depression of teachers. Coaching produces intellectual growth for a variety of reasons:

Coaching enhances instructional thought. The act of teaching is, itself, an intellectual process. Jackson (1968) found that teachers make over 1,300 decisions a day. The behaviors observed in the classroom are artifacts of decisions that teachers make before, during, and after instruction (Shavelson, 1976). The purpose of coaching, therefore, is to enhance the teacher's capacity to plan, monitor, and reflect upon their instructional decision making, perceptions, and the intellectual functions. Costa and Garmston (2002) cite the intent of coaching is to modify teachers' capacities to modify themselves.

Humans who desire to continually improve their craft, seek and profit from being coached. Skillful artists, athletes, musicians, dancers—like Greg Louganis, Mikhail Baryshnikov, Kristi Yamaguchi, and Jackie Joyner-Kersey never lose their need for coaching. Likewise, in education, to continually perfect their craft, teachers profit from coaching as well.

To work effectively as a member of a team requires coaching. Welding together the individual efforts of team members into a well-organized and efficient unit requires the persistence and stamina of an expert coach. This concerted effort, however, does not "just happen." It takes someone—a conductor—who "knows the score" to provide the synergy. It takes time, persistence, practice and coaching to develop a winning athletic team, a celebrated symphony orchestra, or a learning organization.

Few educational innovations achieve their full impact without a coaching component. Joyce and Showers (1988) found that efforts to bring about changes in classroom practice are fruitless unless the teacher is coached in the use of the innovation. Only when the component of coaching was added was the innovation internalized, valued, and transferred to classroom use.

Coaching enhances the intellectual capacities of teachers which, in turn, produces greater intellectual achievements in students.

Every function in . . . cultural development appears twice: first, on the social level, and later on the individual level; first between people (inter-psychological), and then inside (intra-psychological). This applies equally to voluntary attention, to logical memory, and to the formation of concepts. *All the higher functions originate as actual relationships between individuals.*

Lev Vygotsky (1978)

Vygotsky's statement provides a strong theoretical support for coaching as a means of intellectual growth. It is through social interaction that new concepts and intellectual behaviors are formed and grown. And, as was cited earlier, the teacher's level of intellectual development influences the student's level of intellectual development.

4. Collaboration

> It is acceptance and trust that make it possible for each bird to sing its own song confident that it will be heard—even by those who sing with a different voice.
>
> Hateley and Schnidt (1995)

Human beings are made to be different. Diversity is the basis of biological survival. Each of us has a different genetic structure, unique facial features, a distinguishing thumbprint, a distinctive signature, diverse backgrounds of knowledge, experience and culture, and a preferred way of gathering, processing, and expressing information and knowledge. We even have a singular frequency in which we vibrate (Leonard, 1978). Leaders are sensitive to and capitalize on these differences to enhance intellectual growth.

Intellectually effective people seem able to "be at home" in multiple areas of functioning. They move flexibly from one style to another as the situation demands it. They have an uncanny ability to read contextual cues from the situation or the environment as to what is needed, then they draw forth from their vast repertoire those skills and capacities needed to function most effectively in any setting.

Organizational life might seem easier if all members of the learning community thought and acted in a similar fashion and remained in their own departments and grade levels. Limitations of time, isolation, and our obsession with the archaic compartmentalization of the disciplines and grades keep school staffs separated; thus opportunities for teachers' intellectual growth are limited. Leaders realize that humans grow intellectually through resolving differences, achieving consensus, and stretching to accommodate dissonance. They realize there is a greater possibility for making connections, stimulating creativity, and growing the capacity for complex problem solving when such differences are bridged. (In some businesses, this is referred to as "Skunkworks"—deliberately bringing together personnel from different departments, positions, and grade levels to make connections and find new and divergent ways to solve problems.)

Interdependent learning communities are built not by obscuring diversity but by valuing the friction those differences bring and resolving those differences in an atmosphere of trust and reciprocity. Therefore, leaders mediate appreciation for this diversity by deliberately bringing together people of different political and religious persuasions, cultures, gender, cognitive styles, belief systems, modality preferences, and intelligences. They structure groups composed of representatives from different schools, diverse departments, community groups, and grade levels to envision, describe learning outcomes, plan curriculum and staff development activities, and to allocate resources.

5. Focusing on Student Learning

> Curriculum is like a cemetery. It is etched in stone, visited only on special occasions, filled with dead subjects, aligned in straight rows, and is a monument to the past. Furthermore, we keep putting more in and take nothing out!

Senge (1990) emphasizes that a characteristic of the learning organization is that it challenges existing mental models. The leader, in an atmosphere of trust, challenges existing practices, assumptions, policies, and traditional ways of delivering curriculum. Intellectual growth is found in disequilibrium, not balance. It is out of chaos that order is built, that learning takes place, that new understandings are forged, that new connections are bridged, and that organizations function more consistently with its mission, vision, and goals.

We must finally admit that the process *is* the content. The core of our curriculum must focus on such processes as thinking, learning to learn, knowledge production, metacognition, transference of knowledge, decision making, creativity, and group problem solving and knowing how to behave when correct answers are not readily apparent. These *are* the subject matters of instruction. Content, selectively abandoned and judiciously selected because of its fecund contributions to the thinking/learning process, becomes merely the vehicle to carry the processes of learning. The focus is on learning *from* the objectives instead of learning *of* the objectives.

Since these process-oriented goals cannot be assessed using product-oriented assessment techniques, our existing evaluation paradigm must shift as well. Thus assessment of students' thinking will focus on students becoming more conscious, more reflective, more efficient, more flexible, and more transferable (Costa & Kallick, 1995; Costa & Liebmann, 1997).

The leader continually challenges the organization's mental models about what learning is of most worth as students face an uncertain, technological, and global future (Costa & Garmston, 1998).

LEARNING CONTINUALLY

> *Autopoesis:* (Greek) Self-production. The characteristic of living systems to continuously renew themselves and to regulate this process in such a way that the integrity of their structure is maintained. It is a natural process which supports the quest for structure, process renewal, and integrity.
>
> Wheatley (1992)

Experimentation implies that an atmosphere of choice, risk taking, and inquiry exists. Data are generated without fear that they will be used as a basis for evaluating success or failure. Creativity will more likely grow in a low-risk atmosphere. Frymier (1987) goes on to state,

> The solution is to empower teachers, to help them develop an internalized locus of control. Teachers and principals, supervisors and superintendents, boards of education and state legislators all must appreciate the possibilities of school improvement efforts that marshal the motivations and unleash the talents of those who work directly with children day after day. (p. 10)

For too long the process of assessment has been external to teachers' goal setting, curriculum, and instructional decision making. School effectiveness, student achievement, and teachers' competence have often been determined by a narrow range of standardized student achievement test scores in a limited number of content areas: reading, math, and language acquisition. Rank-order test results have been published in newspapers; awards of excellence have been granted to schools that show the highest gains in scores.

In the process, teachers have become disenfranchised. Educators have had little say about what the tests measured; what tests do measure is often irrelevant to the curriculum, and the results of testing disclose little about the adequacy of teachers' curriculum, and instructional decisions. In many ways the desire for measurable outcomes has signaled teachers that they are "incompetent" to assess student achievement. They, in effect, were told they could not be trusted to collect evidence of students' growth, that the observations they made daily in the classroom were suspect and of little worth.

The accountability movement caused educators to search for "hard data" by which to assess their efforts. What teachers observed, by inference, therefore, was "soft data." The "hardest," most objective data available may be that collected by an *enlightened* teaching team which systematically, and collectively, gathers data over time in the real-life, day-to-day interactions and problem solving of the classroom. Conversely, the "softest," most suspect data may be that which is designed and collected by testing "experts" external to the school setting and ignorant of the school's mission, values, and goals, the community's culture and socio-economics, the classroom's mix of learning styles, teaching strategies, and group dynamics in which their tests are administered!

Leaders assist the teaching staff to design strategies for collecting data and to use the assessment data as feedback and a guide to informed and reflective practice. Staff members will need help in learning how to design feedback spirals including multiple ways of gathering such data, establishing criteria for judgment, working together to develop their common understanding and reliability of observations, and reporting of results.

IN SUMMARY

> Some people think that it is holding on that makes one strong. Sometimes it is letting go.
>
> Sylvia Robinson

Because learning to think, to cooperate, and to respect human uniqueness is best learned through imitation and emulation of significant others, leaders strive to model in their own behaviors those same qualities and behaviors that are desired in students and staff.

The development of thinking, individuality, and collegiality as goals of education is not just kid stuff. Education will achieve an intellectual focus when the school becomes an intellectually stimulating environment—a home for the mind for all who dwell there; when all the school's inhabitants realize that freeing human intellectual potential is the goal of education; when staff members strive to get better at it themselves; and when they use their energies to enhance the intelligent behaviors of others. Educational leaders serve as an "environmental protection agency"—constantly monitoring the intellectual ecology of the school. Their chief purpose is to ensure that thinking, creativity, and collaboration will become neither endangered, nor worse, extinct.

REFERENCES

Baker, W., Costa, A., & Shalit, S. (1997). The norms of collaboration: Attaining communicative competence. In A. Costa & R. Liebmann (Eds.), *The process centered school: Sustaining a Renaissance community* (pp. 119–142). Thousand Oaks, CA: Corwin Press.

Block, P. (1987). *The empowered manager.* San Francisco: Jossey-Bass.

Costa, A., & Garmston, R. (1998, Spring). Maturing outcomes. *Encounter: Education for Meaning and Social Justice, 11*(1), 10–18.

Costa, A., & Garmston, R. (2002). *Cognitive Coaching: A foundation for Renaissance schools.* Norwood, MA: Christopher-Gordon.

Costa, A., & Garmston, R. (2005). *Cognitive Coaching: Foundation seminar learning guide.* Norwood, MA: Christopher-Gordon.

Costa, A., & Kallick, B. (1995). *Assessment in the learning organization: Shifting the paradigm.* Alexandria, VA: Association for Supervision and Curriculum Development.

Costa, A., & Liebmann, R. (1997). *Process as content: Envisioning a Renaissance curriculum.* Thousand Oaks, CA: Corwin Press.

Covey, S. (1989). *The seven habits of highly effective people.* New York: Simon & Schuster.

Evered, R., & Selman, J. (1989, Autumn). Coaching and the art of management. *Organizational Dynamics, 18*, 16–32.

Feuerstein, R., Feuerstein, R., & Schur, Y. (1997). Process as content in education particularly for retarded performers. In A. Costa & R. Liebmann (Eds.), *Supporting the spirit of learning: When process is content* (pp. 1–22). Thousand Oaks, CA: Corwin Press.

Frymier, J. (1987, September). Bureaucracy and the neutering of teachers. *Phi Delta Kappan, 69*(1), 10.

Fullan, M. (1993). *Change forces.* New York: Falmer.

Glasser, W. (1992). *The quality school.* New York: Harper Collins.

Glickman, C. (1985). *Supervision of instruction: A developmental approach.* Newton, MA: Allyn & Bacon.

Goodlad, J. I. (1984). *A place called school: Prospects for the future.* New York: McGraw Hill.

Harvey, O. J. (1966). System structure, flexibility, and creativity. In O. J. Harvey (Ed.), *Experience, structure, and adaptability* (pp. 39–65). New York: Springer.

Hateley, B., & Schnidt, W. (1995). *A peacock in the land of penguins.* San Francisco: Berrett-Koehler.

Jackson, P. (1968). *Life in classrooms.* New York: Holt Rinehart Winston.

Joyce, B., & Showers, B. (1988). *Student achievement through staff development.* New York: Longmans.

Kotulak, R. (1997). *Inside the brain: Revolutionary discoveries of how the mind works.* Kansas City, MO: Andrews McMeel.

Lambert, L. (1998). *Building leadership capacity in schools.* Alexandria, VA: Association for Supervision and Curriculum Development.

Land, G., & Jarman, B. (1992). *Break-point and beyond: Mastering the future today.* New York: Harper.

Leonard, G. (1978). *The silent pulse: A search for the perfect rhythm that exists in each of us.* New York: Bantam Books.

Louis, K., Marks, H., & Kruse, S. (1996). Teacher's professional community in restructuring schools. *American Educational Research Journal, 33*(4), 757–798.

MacLean, P. (1978). A mind of three minds. Educating the triune brain. In J. E. Chall & M. Mursky (Eds.), *Education and the brain.* Chicago: University of Chicago Press.

Rosenholtz, S. (1989). *Teacher's workplace: The social organization of schools.* New York: Longman.

Saphier, J., & King, M. (1985, March). Good seeds grow in strong cultures. *Educational Leadership,* 67–74.

Sarason, S. (1991). *The predictable failure of educational reform.* San Francisco: Jossey-Bass.

Senge, P. (1990). *The fifth discipline.* New York Doubleday.

Senge, P., Ross, R., Smith, B., Roberts, C., & Kleiner, A. (1994). *The fifth discipline fieldbook.* New York: Doubleday/Currency.

Shavelson, R. (1976). Teacher decision making. *The psychology of teaching methods. 1976 Yearbook of the National Society for the Study Education. Part I.* Chicago: University of Chicago Press.

Sprinthall, R., & Theis-Sprinthall, L. (1983). The teacher as an adult learner: A cognitive developmental view. In K. J. Rehage & G. A. Griffin (Eds.), *Staff Development: 82nd Yearbook of the National Society for the Study of Education Part II.* Chicago: University of Chicago Press.

Vygotsky, L. (1978). *Society of mind.* Cambridge, MA: Harvard University Press.

Wheatley, M. (1992). *Science and the new leadership.* San Francisco: Berrett-Koehler Publishers.

CHAPTER NINETEEN

Mind Workers Unite!

> When the forms of an old culture are dying, the new culture is created by a few people who are not afraid to be insecure.
>
> Rudolf Bahro

Within this first decade of the twenty-first century, we are at a sweet spot in time.[1] Forces are converging that signal the need for another renaissance in education.

• While well intentioned, the focus of No Child Left Behind has impressed the public and educators that holding schools accountable for making annual yearly progress as measured by test scores in math and reading is the supreme learning. This to the exclusion of arts, social sciences, sciences, vocational education, and athletics (at a time when youthful obesity is rampant).[2]

• Research on expertise suggests that superficial coverage of many topics in the domain may be a poor way to help students develop the competencies that will prepare them for future learning and work. Curricula that emphasize breadth of knowledge may prevent effective organization of knowledge because there is not enough time to learn anything in depth. Curricula that are "a mile wide and an inch deep" run the risk of developing disconnected rather than connected knowledge.[3]

• The United States is facing global crises in intellectual competition in entrepreneurship, social sensitivity, leadership, and creativity.[4]

- We need a new brand of employee, a new breed of enterprise, and a new social contract that will educate our young to break the rules and invent vivid new futures.[5]

> The first 30 years of technology were about paving cow paths. Now it is inventing at a fast pace. There will be 1000 times more change in the 21st century than the last one.
>
> Michael Hammer

From the futurists and corporate/social scholars and educators cited above, from the experiences of compiling several books, from visits to many "mindful schools," and from dialogues with school personnel, I have become keenly aware of some unfinished tasks for those interested in pursuing, sustaining, and expanding curriculum and instruction intended to develop students' intellectual powers.

The metaphor I choose to describe this task is *orchestration*. It is a fitting metaphor because it engenders a desired vision of precision, harmony, working diligently together toward a common goal, and, ultimately, producing beautiful music. I propose seven needed next steps in the orchestration process: definition, integration, application, articulation, individualization, politicization, and evaluation. Obviously, there are many schools that have taken these steps; others are not yet concerned with them. These are merely suggestions from one person's point of view.

Each member of a staff is an extremely talented professional. The third grade teacher may be similar to an outstanding "violinist." The high school history teacher is like a master "cellist." The middle school vocational arts teacher is comparable to a marvelous "flutist," and so on. Each, in their own right, is an expert. (The Italian word for teacher is *maestro*.)

In an orchestra, however, musicians play in the same key, and at the same tempo. They rehearse together and have a common vision of the entire score, each knowing well the part they play that contributes to the whole. They do not all play at the same time; there are rests, harmonies, fugues, and counterpoint. They support each other in a totally coordinated and concerted effort. In the same way, teachers can support each other in creating an overall curriculum. They neither teach the same thinking skills and strategies at the same time, nor do they approach them in the same way. Their cumulative effect, however, is beautiful, harmonious "music" in the mind and learning of the student.

1. *Definition.* Our first task of orchestration is to decide on and to be able to communicate our definitions and outcomes of instruction.

If you ask almost any individual school member to define "thinking," you'll get about as many definitions as there are staff members. The positive effects in those districts that have forged a common definition of thinking, however, are becoming increasingly apparent. Not that all schools have the same definition; rather, a school staff shares a common vision. They can describe the attributes of the efficacious thinking person; whether it be characteristics of the "critical thinker"; dispositions of intelligent human beings; qualities of the "thought-full" person; or performances of efficient, effective, and reasoned problem solvers; the name is not as important as the shared meaning and vision these terms convey.

2. *Integration.* The struggle to infuse thinking into curriculum content areas, instruction, and school climate continues.

Limitations of time and communication in school settings often prevent teachers from different departments, grade levels, and disciplines from meeting together. The mutual support, continuity, reinforcement, and transference of thinking skills throughout the grade levels and across the subject areas have yet to be accomplished. "Critical reading," the "scientific method," "problem solving" in mathematics, literacy, and numeracy, "modes of inquiry," study skills; the distinctions and connections are still vague when deciding which should be taught in science, which are most appropriate to math, which should be included in the social sciences, and how they all fit together.

Until we consider thinking as the core of the curriculum and that content is selectively abandoned and judiciously included because of its contributions to the thinking/learning process, we shall continue to endure this dilemma. The sooner we admit that the process *is* the content, the sooner we will find ways to infuse thinking across the curriculum. Our obsession with the distinct disciplines is what separates us.

Rather than including science or math or the arts in the curriculum as ends in themselves, we will ask, What are the unique nature, structure, and modes of inquiry that can be drawn from each of these disciplines to be learned and applied elsewhere? As we make this fundamental shift, our instruction will also be altered. We will change our view from learning *of* the content, to learning *from* the content. We will refocus from mastering content and concepts as an end, to the application of knowledge, the transference of cognitive strategies, and the tackling with confidence of new problems that command increasingly complex reasoning, more intricate logic, and more imaginative and creative solutions.

But thinking is not just for students. It must be infused into the total culture of the school. Teachers will more likely teach for thinking if they are in an intellectually stimulating environment themselves. Schools are increasingly employing practices that signal the school's real values: focusing on teaching as decision making; staff development intended to engage and enhance teacher's intellect; providing numerous opportunities for teachers to strengthen their collaborative problem-solving and decision-making abilities; and encouraging risk taking, creativity, and experimentation. To integrate thinking into the school culture may also require "purging" some school practices that detract from the central goal of thinking: discipline techniques or teacher evaluation practices, for example.

Such practices and policies send a powerful signal to the staff and the community that thinking is not just "kid stuff." Thinking will be integrated when it pervades all subject areas, is the central purpose of instruction, and is reflected in the policies and practices governing all the school's inhabitants.

3. *Application.* A consistent pattern of results of the National Assessment of Educational Progress indicate that while our students are improving in their basic skills, they still seem unable to apply reasoning and critical thinking skills in new and novel situations.

For transference of learning to become a reality, teachers will need to meet together to plan opportunities for bridging, revisiting, and generalizing concepts and processes. They will need to systematically collect evidence of transference across subject areas. Thematic, transdisciplinary instruction strategically designed to have students encounter similar problems and to apply analogous problem-solving strategies in increasingly more "distant" settings, and deliberately teaching for transfer by scaffolding and bridging can habituate the student's inclination to draw forth from previous experience and apply it to new and novel situations.[6]

4. *Articulation.* Over time, as students mature and progress, their problem solving will become more spontaneous, build toward more skillfulness, greater complexity , and increased creativity. This will necessitate a vertical coherence of the curriculum as well as the cross-disciplinary, horizontal integration described in point #2 above.

Many examples of repetitive curriculum can be cited. Ask a district faculty where, for example, fractions are taught. You may find they are introduced, practiced, reviewed, and retaught at almost every grade level through high school. Articulation further requires attention to student's developmental needs. Students will require less repetition when concepts and processes are taught at developmentally appropriate levels, employing all the senses, and in a manner that engages and transforms the mind.

5. *Individualization.* One of the great benefits of cognitive education is that it is so all-encompassing. Under this broad umbrella, there is room for creative and critical thinking, convergent and divergent thinking, precision and intuition, induction and deduction, metacognition and meditation, visualization, listening, and language production. There is no one way to think; rather, all of these intellectual capacities are valued and the broader the range we acquire, the more efficient problem solvers we become.

Human beings strive to be unique. We differ in our modality preferences, styles, culture, background of information, and early childhood rearing. We have different signatures and different fingerprints; we even emit unique vibration rates from the aura surrounding our bodies.

We place great value on athletes and recognize differences in their abilities. We appreciate the gracefulness of the lithe ballerina, the huskiness of the burly wrestler, the alertness of the swift quarterback, the speed of the lanky sprinter, the control of the diver, the stamina of the marathoner, and the agility of the ice skater. Seldom, however, do we find an athlete who excels in *all* sports. Individual disposition, skeletal structure, musculature, and perceptual abilities both place limits upon and enhance each athlete's performance.

Likewise, we know that each of us has an individual cognitive style that determines how we perceive and act upon our world. Like athletics, the teaching of thinking can help students celebrate their own unique "style" and genetic makeup, and to understand the effects of their individuality on their perceptions and thinking processes. We can assist them in respecting and preserving the uniqueness of others who possess and display different styles, and we can help them continue to add to their repertoire of styles and strategies.

6. *Politicization.* As a goal of education, the development of the intellect is not yet valued or understood by the majority of the public. While business and industry leaders are becoming increasingly supportive of the schools' endeavor to educate the future generation to become better individual and group problem solvers, to develop the creative capacities, to cope with uncertainty and ambiguity, to learn from our failures, to be open to new and continued learning, and to work cooperatively as a member of a team, there are still legislators, governors, school boards, and even an "Education President" who fail to include thinking in our national educational goals for the twenty-first century and beyond.

Educators, in conjunction with test makers, textbook publishers, business and industry leaders, and the media, need to mount a massive information and educational program intended to shift public policy and national values toward support of a more rational, cooperative, and compassionate mission statement for public education.

7. *Evaluation.* You cannot measure performance of process-oriented goals using product-oriented evaluations. How to organize a meaningful, systematic, rigorous assessment program and how to find ways of communicating results to parents, school boards, and the various publics still befuddles many educators. While we believe in authentic assessments—keeping portfolios, extended projects, interviews, journals, and the like—we must still transform the public's understanding of these procedures, all of which are quite contrary to their past experience and diet of college entrance exams, achievement tests, rank-ordered school ratings in the local newspapers based on gain scores, intelligence quotients, and qualification for gifted or special education programs.

My greatest worry about cognitive education, however, is that we will become complacent about our achievements. We have a history of being swept along by fads and bandwagons. I fear that groups will say, "Teaching skillful thinking? We tried that last year, and it didn't work." Any change takes time, energy, and devotion. We are deeply into the awareness stage of reform. Historical research on educational change effort indicates that many innovations were not fully realized because they were abandoned prematurely without institutionalizing the change.[7]

We are riding the crest of what may well be the greatest opportunity for educational reform in history: a growing dissatisfaction with the current quality of education; a realization of educational reform as a political platform; a heightened awareness of the demands of an uncertain future; a concern about our nation's global economic dependence upon an educated, creative, and highly skilled workforce, face-to-face encounters with our delicate ecological home, and coping with ethnic, cultural, religious, and language diversity.

Do not relent; don't give up in the face of adversity. One of the greatest of Habits of Mind is persistence. Let us unite into a common voice. If we desire our future world to be more compassionate, more cooperative, and more thoughtful, we must work together to make it happen.

NOTES

1. *Sweet spot:* The most effective place to hit the ball on a racket, bat, club, or other piece of sports equipment.

2. Basken, P. (2006). Early education key to scientific career choice. *Boston Globe*, May 29; Oxford Analytica. (2006). Bush's education reforms falter. *Oxford Analytica*, August 29; Commentary. (2006). Why present reform efforts will fail. *Education Week*, August 30.

3. McTighe, J., & Seif, E. A Summary of Underlying Theory and Research Base for Understanding by Design.

4. Florida, R. (2004, October). America's looming creativity crisis. *Harvard Business Review*, 82(10). Database: Business Source Premier, 00178012; Friedman, T. (2005). *The world is flat*. New York: Farrar, Straus and Giroux.

5. Peters, T. (2003). *Re-Imagine*. London: Dorling Kindersley.

6. Perkins, D. N., & Salomon, G. (2001). Teaching for transfer. In A. L. Costa (Ed.), *Developing minds* (pp. 370–378). Alexandria, VA: Association for Supervision and Curriculum Development.

7. Hall, G. E., & Hord, S. M. (1987). *Change in schools: Facilitating the process*. Albany: State University of New York Press.

Index

CORWIN PRESS

The Corwin Press logo—a raven striding across an open book—represents the union of courage and learning. Corwin Press is committed to improving education for all learners by publishing books and other professional development resources for those serving the field of PreK–12 education. By providing practical, hands-on materials, Corwin Press continues to carry out the promise of its motto: **"Helping Educators Do Their Work Better."**